DRAGON SLAYER

Jesus Christ

DRAGON SLAYER ✝ JESUS CHRIST

THE RISE OF THE NEW WORLD ORDER

MICHAEL J HARVEY

All Scripture references are taken from the *Authorized King James Version* of the Bible.

The duplication of this material by like-minded individuals without the expressed written consent of the publisher is encouraged. It has been said that if you steal from one person, it is called plagiarism, but if you steal from one hundred people, it is called research. Credit and thanks for the research in this book belongs to all the liberty-loving journalists, authors, pastors and friends whose research contributed to this book.

FOR THE KING

AND ALL WHO HAVE EARS TO HEAR

I do not think that it was by arms that our ancestors made the republic great from being small. Had that been the case, the republic of our day would have been by far more flourishing than that of their times, for the number of our allies and citizens is far greater; and, besides, we possess a far greater abundance of armour and horses than they did. But it was other things than these that made them great, and we have none of them: industry at home, just government without, a mind free in deliberation, addicted neither to crime nor to lust. Instead of these, we have luxury and avarice, poverty in the state, opulence among citizens; we laud riches, we follow laziness; there is no difference made between good and bad; all the rewards of virtue are got possession of by intrigue. And no wonder, when every individual consults only for his own good, when ye are the slaves of pleasure at home, and, in public affairs, of money and favour, no wonder that an onslaught is made upon the unprotected republic.

— Cato, Circa 63 BC

CONTENTS

If thou wouldst rule well, thou must rule for God, and to do that, thou must be ruled by him . . . Those who will not be governed by God will be ruled by tyrants.

— William Penn, Founder of Pennsylvania, 1644-1718

Many shall be purified, and made white, and tried; but the wicked shall do wickedly: and none of the wicked shall understand; but the wise shall understand.

The Book of Daniel 12:10

INTRODUCTION

As the sun was setting on twentieth century, the warnings from those with the foresight and courage to sound the alarm about the rise of the New World Order were, for the most part, ignored. They were mocked as alarmists, luddites, or isolationists. Meanwhile, globalization was being welcomed in all segments of society. Yet time has proven their warnings to be right. The outsourcing of jobs has destroyed the living wage of the American worker. Conceding the trade deficit to China and allowing them to take over manufacturing is literally choking the Chinese people to death. The international banking community has been found guilty of epic corruption and market manipulation, dwarfing the Enron scandal that surfaced after the turn of the century. Several other examples could be given, and will be.

I published *Where Did All the People GO?* in 2003. By that time the events of September 11, 2001 had cleared the way for the New World Order. One year before I published *Where Did All the People GO?*, David Rockefeller wrote the following:

"For more than a century ideological extremists at either end of the political spectrum have seized upon well-publicized incidents such as my encounter with Castro to attack the Rockefeller family for the inordinate influence they claim we wield over American political and economic institutions. Some even believe we are part of a secret cabal working against the best interests of the United States, characterizing my family and me as 'internationalists' and of conspiring with others around the world to build a more integrated global political and economic structure — one world, if you will. If that's the charge, I stand guilty, and I am proud of it."

— David Rockefeller, *Memoirs* (2002)

We will pick up where *Where Did All the People GO?* left off. Since 2003, events have continued to accelerate, quickening towards the inevitable *blessed hope* of the Christian. However, as with most things in life, it is prudent to hope for the best but prepare for the worst. Christians who believe in the pre-trib doctrine of the rapture are often accused of being escapists, dreamers, or more commonly of just having bad theology. I defended the pre-trib view of eschatology in *Where Did all the People GO?*, and it is not my intention to rehash the subject again. Rather, we will look at practical ways to navigate the territory of the emerging New World Order. Yet, our fellowservants who accuse us of being apathetic and indifferent have a point. Indeed many Christians who are pre-trib wrongly believe that their (orthodox) view of prophecy guarantees that they will escape persecution. The doctrine of the rapture makes no such guarantee. Those who count on the rapture to save them from persecution give themselves a dangerous false sense of security. This mistake was made by many Christians in China before the communists took over, and of course we know what followed was the reign of terror by Mao Tse-tung. Those who believed that the rapture guarded them from persecution soon found themselves faced with the same reality that Christians throughout history have had to face from time to time.

Since we have no way of knowing the day or the hour, we must fight for the freedom to practice our faith with the same vigilant tenacity of our forefathers, who had their blood shed and who braved assaults on all sides, that we may be a free and independent people, with the right to peaceably assemble and practice our faith, free of persecution or interference from the government. In our grandparents' day, the threat to our freedom came from overseas. In our day, the threat is within our own borders. To deny this is to deny the headlines of our day. To ignore this is to shirk our responsibility. We have a mandate called the Great Commission. We must guard our ability to carry it out at all costs. The prophet Jeremiah wrote, *Cursed be he that doeth the work of the LORD deceitfully, and cursed be he that keepeth back his sword from blood.* (Jer 48:10) Soldiers who refused to draw their weapons and engage the battle were actually cursed for it. We are in a battle today and I believe we are commanded to fight. What this means for you personally is a matter for you to settle with our Lord in the privacy of your prayer closet. Whatever your calling or ministry however, understanding the days we live in will help you navigate the waters more skillfully.

If you have not read *Where Did All the People GO?*, it is recommended you do so before reading this book. We will be building on its foundation, which was constructed using the materials of the holy apostles and prophets, which are being fulfilled in our day. If you have a good working knowledge of the Bible, and you understand the seventieth week of Daniel well enough to explain it to someone else, then you may not need not read *Where Did All the People GO?* But, it is also of the utmost importance that you have your armor on, ***and that you have a firm and resolute grasp on the importance of the belt of truth in particular***. In order to face the issues we will be discussing, one must understand the principles of spiritual warfare, and the importance of a close daily walk with his Redeemer. Once you see the importance of following the truth without prejudice, without fear of being mocked or persecuted, because Jesus *is* the Truth, then you are ready to face the enemy without fear as the soldier that you have been called to be. Whether you are an evangelist who works with inner-city youth, or a homemaker who teaches Sunday school in the suburbs, a chaplain in the Marine Corps, or a professor at a city college, whether you are a pastor, or a public servant who works for the government, to understand the days we live in with a full-spectrum, kingdom perspective is key in order for you to effectively survive and thrive until the coming of our Lord. These are the days the prophets wrote about and we have been called *for such a time as this*. Consider the following Scriptures:

> *Now therefore fear the LORD, and serve him in sincerity and in **truth**: and put away the gods which your fathers served on the other side of the flood, and in Egypt; and serve ye the LORD.*
>
> *Joshua 24:14*

> *Justice and judgment are the habitation of thy throne: mercy and **truth** shall go before thy face.*
>
> *Psalm 89:14*

> *None calleth for **justice**, nor any pleadeth for **truth**: **they trust in vanity, and speak lies**; they conceive mischief, and bring forth iniquity.*
>
> *Isaiah 59:4*

> *Then said Jesus to those Jews which believed on him, If ye continue in my word, then are ye my disciples indeed;*
> *And ye shall know the **truth**, and the **truth** shall make you free.*
>
> *John 8:31,32*

> *Pilate therefore said unto him, Art thou a king then? Jesus answered, Thou sayest that I am a king. To this end was I born, and for this cause came I into the world, that I should bear witness unto the **truth**. Every one that is of the **truth** heareth my voice.*
>
> *John 18:37*

*Am I therefore become your enemy, because I tell you
the **truth**?*

Galatians 4:16

*But speaking the **truth** in love, may grow up into him
in all things, which is the head, even Christ:*

Ephesians 4:15

As I was writing *Dragon Slayer Jesus Christ*, I labored in prayer,
seeking God's will as I considered the duty of a watchman, and how
to best present this material. It has been said, discretion is the better
part of valor. Yet, it was the cowardly Falstaff in Shakespeare's
Henry IV, who said this to rationalize his cowardice. I acknowledge
that the material in this book may not be appropriate for everyone.
I have done my best to temper the message and make it easy to
absorb. I encourage you to search the Scriptures and pray as you
continue to read. Seek God's will. Ask for wisdom. If you are a
pastor I believe you have a responsibility to review this material.
I understand these issues are 'heavy', but in Jeremiah 23:32, God
reproved certain of the prophets for *their lightness*, not to mention
their lies. In order to tell the truth, first we have to know what the
truth is. My purpose in writing *Dragon Slayer* is to dig in and find
out what we have not been told.

I have attempted not to use a lot of excessive footnotes. Most of
what I have to say can be easily verified on the Internet. Yet many
of the footnotes I *have* included are not mere references to source
material, but give important information that did not fit neatly into
the narrative. I have used footnotes instead of endnotes for ease of
reference and I encourage the reader to read them. The reader will
benefit from viewing the video references as well, as they will give a
broader perspective. Finally, I have been asked why I have capitalized
United when referring to the United States. While it is true that
this word is lowercase in the Declaration, it is uppercase in
the Constitution. What I think it is important to remember, is that
the beginning words of the Constitution, *We the People* are
written much larger than *United States*.

The theme of this picture is whether men are to be ruled by God's law, or whether they are to be ruled by the whims of a dictator like Ramesses. Are men the property of the State? Or are they free souls under God? This same battle continues throughout the world today.

— Cecil DeMille, *The Ten Commandments* (1956)

And ye shall hallow the fiftieth year, and proclaim liberty throughout all the land unto all the inhabitants thereof: it shall be a jubile unto you; and ye shall return every man unto his possession, and ye shall return every man unto his family.

The Book of Leviticus 25:10

PROLOGUE

Fritz Lang's *Metropolis* (1927), depicted a futuristic society where people could communicate with each other face-to-face on computer monitors, like we do now via Skype and FaceTime. The plot focused on a super-powerful elite corporate leader (Joh Fredersen), and the subjugation of his workers, who lived beneath the city. The privileged elite lived above them in a Utopian society, with amenities like the Club of the Sons, and the Eternal Gardens. Modern communication was not the only thing *Metropolis* predicted, however. Indeed, we are definitely witnessing a world-wide consolidation of power by a technocratic elite, who are systematically lowering the standard of living. In *Metropolis*, a group of the downtrodden workers began to organize, meeting together in secret. They were led by Maria, a beautiful Christian woman of virtue and purity. Maria taught the workers to be patient, to be men of peace and temperance, and that a mediator would come to help them. She gave them hope. When Fredersen learned about Maria, he used his technocrat science advisor, Rotwang, to create a counterfeit woman of their own design who they could use to trick the workers. The double looked like the real Maria, but her physical appearance was where the likeness ended. She was manipulative, crafty, and seductive. Whereas Maria told the truth and preached peace, the double acted as an agent provocateur, inflaming the passions of the more affluent members of society and pitting them against one another. She likewise whipped up the lower classes who trusted her as their spiritual leader, causing them to riot. This is what Fredersen wanted, to justify his use of excessive force against them. Fredersen's son, Freder, had fallen in love with Maria. Only he was able to tell that the counterfeit was not really Maria. Everyone else was fooled and manipulated by the fake Maria.

The Christians of the first century found themselves at odds with the Roman structure of cults and divination. They found the truth in Christ. They found his kingdom did not fit into the Roman system of subcultures. Just as in first century Rome, we are seeing a fragmenting of subcultures today. Most of Rome's subcultures were merely part of the larger culture of the empire. Then there were those that were in direct conflict with the empire, with Christianity posing the biggest threat. The two subcultures that the empire of today feels the most threatened by are arguably the church and the liberty movement. Yet many in the liberty movement see the church as an extension of the establishment. Many in the church see the liberty movement as a counterculture fringe group that advocates drug use. Both of these are very shortsighted characterizations. In reality, these two groups have a lot more in common than is typically acknowledged by those within them. To begin with, many in the liberty movement are, in fact, believers in Jesus Christ. Those who are not may find that people in the church are very receptive to their ideas. Freedom is at the heart of the gospel. Jesus said, *"Every one that is of the truth heareth my voice."* Therefore it is the prerogative of the Christian to search for the truth. The core values of peace and freedom that the liberty movement stands for will appeal to Christians when they are presented with the facts and philosophies underlying the movement. Contrariwise, the church will find that the liberty movement is a fertile mission ground, filled with people who are seeking the truth, who will oftentimes be receptive to the gospel. In short, these two subcultures have a lot they can learn from each other.

There are two dominant figures in the end-times prophecies of the Bible. There is *the bride, the Lamb's wife*, which is the true church, and there is the *great whore*, which is the false church of the New World Order. If the church is seduced by the siren's song of the New World Order, then it will no longer be the church. When the apostle John saw the whore in his vision, at first he was impressed by her (Rev 17). She was very attractive and polished, and he *wondered with great admiration*. But the angel who was walking John through his vision rebuked him, and showed him her true colors. The true church is called to be *the salt of the earth ... a city on a hill* and *the light of the world*. If she cannot stand for the truth; if she caves in to the pressure to go along with the New World Order; then it is clear which one of the two women in the biblical narrative she really is. Much like the fake Maria in Fritz Lang's *Metropolis*, the elite are engineering a pseudo church which will forsake the gospel and attempt to replace the bride of Christ. In *Metropolis*, the manipulation worked and the people were deceived into following the directives of the elite, through the whorish woman they scientifically engineered. Jesus, however, said, *My sheep hear my voice, and I know them, and they follow me: And I give unto them eternal life; and they shall never perish, neither shall any man pluck them out of my hand.* Jesus also said, *And a stranger will they not follow, but will flee from him: for they know not the voice of strangers.*

Like Freder, who loved Maria, anyone who loves Jesus will love the true church. Freder called out to the people and warned them that they were deceived. He pointed at the double and exposed her, charging "You are not Maria!" He forsook his family palace and stood with God's people. Freder followed the example of Moses, *who refused to be called the son of Pharaoh's daughter; Choosing rather to suffer affliction with the people of God, than to enjoy the pleasures of sin for a season; Esteeming the reproach of Christ greater riches than the treasures in Egypt: for he had respect unto the recompence of the reward.*

Never doubt that a small group of thoughtful, committed, citizens can change the world. Indeed, it is the only thing that ever has.

— Margaret Mead, American Cultural Anthropologist, 1901-1978

To all that be in Rome, beloved of God, called to be saints: Grace to you and peace from God our Father, and the Lord Jesus Christ.
The Epistle of the Apostle Paul to the Romans 1:7

Ⅰ

ΙΧΘΥΣ

nter Rufus Antony, the son of a cobbler in ancient Rome. The year is 64 AD, or to Rufus, DCCC XVIII AB URBE CONDITA.[1] As a citizen of Rome, Rufus leads a comfortable life. Although he is a plebeian, at least he is not a slave. And he keeps himself out of trouble. He has to, because the powers that be in Rome do not tolerate malefaction of any sort. Cæsar Nero makes sure that visitors to Rome understand this. For this reason, the roads leading into Rome are lined on either side with rotting corpses. Unfortunate offenders whom the State has chosen to make examples of — by crucifixion. This is *Pax Romana*,[2] the peace of Rome, strictly enforced and to be taken most seriously. The cross is feared throughout the empire, and the journey into the capital strikes fear into the hearts of all who come. Rufus does not find himself as impressed with these public spectacles as most of his fellow citizens do. They enjoy the public executions. But if they enjoy the executions, they relish the games. The Circus for example, with its deadly-fast chariot races.

[1] 818 years from the founding of the city.
[2] The *Pax Romana* was a period without civil war from 27 BC to 180 AD.

The arenas, where criminals are forced to defend themselves against wild beasts, or are sometimes tortured to death. And most popular of all, the gladiators — man against man, trained warriors, whose sole purpose in life is to entertain the populace by fighting for their lives against one another in the arenas. But lately even the popularity of the gladiators has been eclipsed by a new event — *the Christians.* A strange new cult has taken root in Rome. Ordinarily, Rome welcomes other gods. There are many temples and many gods in Rome. Religion is not just part of life in the Eternal City; it is the foundation of the culture, the cornerstone of the empire. Nothing is done without acknowledging the gods. For a citizen of Rome, each day begins and ends by bowing or offering something to a graven image of some god, any god — and there is certainly no shortage of them to choose from. But this new cult is different. Not only are they extreme in their views and dogmatic in their insistence that theirs is the one true God, but they are actually willing to *die* for him. Therefore they refuse to say "Cæsar is Lord," like every good Roman is accustomed to affirming. The Christians would often rather die than pay homage to the emperor and acknowledge him as Lord. Rufus was somewhat intrigued by this new cult. He heard that they follow a man who had been crucified under Roman law, whom they believe to be the Christus, hence their name — Christian, or literally, 'little Christ'. They follow him to the utmost degree, apparently attempting to emulate him in every way they can. Rufus had also heard they believe strange paradoxes, like their insistence that this Christus, this Iesus of Nazareth whom they worship, is indeed God Almighty himself, manifest in the flesh, and that he is the Son of the Father in heaven. Yet there is also a Holy Spirit, who is God as well. The Christians insist that these three are actually one — one true God. They believe him to be ubiquitous, yet also to live inside each of them, in their hearts. Rufus wondered what it was that gave them such peace when he had seen them being executed in the arenas. They sang beautiful songs together like he had never heard, even in the face of death.

What is it they have that is worth dying for? They seemed to be so happy with so little, having nothing but this faith of theirs. Rome had much to offer. There was culture, and luxuries imported from all over the world — pleasures of every kind for the flesh. The comforts available to those who could afford them were endless. There were the arts, philosophy, and the finest of everything that anyone could possibly want. Yet the Christians seemed to possess something else, something intangible.

What ever it was it was very strange, and very dangerous. There were rumors that they were cannibals, and as part of their religion they ate human flesh and drank human blood. Because of the persecution against them they hid themselves and met underneath the city in the catacombs, a maze of seemingly endless tunnels that connected together for miles and miles. After Nero began persecuting them, they had begun to bury their dead down there. Some even said they lived down there. Not only that, but they were probably terrorists as well. Cæsar Nero himself proclaimed that the recent fires which had destroyed much of the city were caused by them. Rufus did secretly wonder about this; it seemed too convenient to him that the fires had cleared the way for Nero's new building program, which included his new palatial complex.

To Rufus it all sounded spooky. But now he had more important things to be concerned about. There were a lot of orders to fill and he had to get his work done, because tonight was a special night. He was going to propose to Lady Vitellia. He had it all planned out. He had chosen the most romantic spot in Rome. After wine and a meal together at Mons Pincius, he would take her to Cæsar's Gardens, on the Tiberis just south of the Porta Portuencis. His friend Marcus was preparing a specially wrapped gift box which he would use to charm her before presenting the ring. It was filled with butterflies and when she opened it, they would encircle them both and flutter about as he proposed. And there was a full moon tonight. Everything was perfect. As he thought about it he worked faster than he ever had before.

"Rufus, I want you to meet somebody." His father entered from outside with a young man at his side. "This is Cadmus. He is going to be helping us out."

Rufus took one look and immediately he knew what his father meant. "A slave? What for? He's just going to be another mouth to feed," Rufus protested.

"Give him a chance Rufus. I thought you would be pleased. Besides, I don't have time to argue. I have to be going. I have business to attend to in the forum." And with that, his father was off, before Rufus could raise any more objections.

Rufus was *not* pleased about this. Not a very wise use of his inheritance, in his opinion. They had a small shop, like all of the shops in Rome. They were not patricians. They lived humble lives, and Rufus felt if they were ever going to get ahead in Roman society they were going to have to be frugal with their resources. That was how Rufus approached most things, pragmatically. His marriage to Lady Vitellia, for example. It was a golden opportunity. He had carefully planned everything. He had saved a large sum to obtain this marriage. He had it all worked it out with her father, who was of the equestrian order.[3] What luck! By marrying into his family he would be able to enjoy the benefits of being an equestrian now as well, all because of some bad business decisions her father had made. He was now desperate for cash — a perfect opportunity for Rufus. His thriftiness had paid off, finally now, after all the years of scrimping and saving. Now he would no longer be an ordinary plebeian, a second class citizen. Sure, he had spent his entire savings for this opportunity, but it was worth it. With his good work ethic and savvy business skills, he would be on his feet again and working his way up the ladder of society in no time. The proposal tonight was only a formality, but none the less, he wanted to start off on the right foot. Hence his plan to propose to her by moonlight. And besides, Lady Vitellia was not at all bad looking. He could see himself caring for her even if the opportunity for advancement was not there. But it was! So why

[3] The equestrians (Lat. *ordo equester*, or lit. order of the knights) were the third of the three orders of Roman aristocracy, after the patricians and the senatorial order. They served as the cavalry, and as commanders in the Roman army and the Praetorian Guard. For enough money one could buy his way into the order.

not take advantage of it? The cumulative weight of these things assuaged the resentment he ordinarily would have had about his father's impulsiveness, and since he did not have time to be troubled today, he decided to make the best of it. "So, Cadmus is your name?"

"Yes sir, Cadmus bar Damian," he replied.

"Where do you come to us from?" Rufus asked.

"I was born in Corinth sir, but for the last year I have been in Jerusalem."

Rufus did not have time for a lengthy introduction today. "Well Cadmus, we have a lot of work to do. Go out back and wash up. The first rule in shoe making is keep your hands clean."

As Cadmus unshouldered his pack, something embroidered on the side of it caught Rufus's eye: ἰχθύς, or *ichthus*. Because Rufus had painstakingly educated himself from the time he was a lad, he knew that *ichthus* was the Greek word for fish. You see, Rufus was not your ordinary pleb. He had always felt he was destined for something better. On another day he may have been curious enough to ask him about it, but today he had other things on his mind.

The next couple of hours seemed to go by as quickly as the first few hours of the day had. Although he had only known him for a couple of hours, Rufus found himself beginning to like Cadmus. He was a journeyman shoemaker, and seemed to be a good hard worker. But more than that, he was pleasant to be around. For a slave he seemed to be awfully happy. Rufus was even beginning to change his mind about his father's decision. Perhaps this was a wise acquisition after all. "I will be up in the loft if you need anything Cadmus," Rufus said as he exited the room up the ladder that extended onto the loft, to fetch a specially tanned hide he needed for his next order. Then he heard *that voice*, as Antonina entered below.

Oh, why today. He had all but put her out of his mind. Now his good spirits were not so good. *Why did she have to show up?* He had not seen her in over a year, and just as well. *Why today of all days?* For you see, Antonina was what Rufus really wanted. Wanted more than his status in society, wanted more than Lady

Vitellia to be sure. There was nothing he wanted more. Given the choice between love and money, Rufus would have surely chosen the former, namely Antonina. Yet it was not possible. To begin with she was a slave girl, and her master had no intention of either selling her or liberating her. To make matters worse, she did not return his affections. This had been the bane of his existence for almost as long as he could remember. If it had only not been for that dream. That cursed dream he had the night before he met her, when she arrived as a little slave girl from Hispania. For that reason his heart was not his own. Just what he had done to cause the gods to be so cruel to him he did not know. As he looked down now from the loft above, all thoughts of Lady Vitellia were gone. And as was always the case when he saw her again, whether it was after six months apart or six hours, he had forgotten how gorgeous she was. His eyes roamed over her beginning with the crown of her head, endowed with thick caramel locks that fell down upon her light brown shoulders, and then down about her peasant dress, which hugged her petite and perfect figure. *More gorgeous than Venus herself*, he thought to himself as his eyes climbed back up to her visage, and beheld her brilliant smile and small nose, fitly set below her dazzling brown eyes, both of which were accented with thick black eyelashes and perfectly curved brows. *That smile, what is she so happy about?*

Rufus listened as he watched her introduce herself to Cadmus. She needed a shoe latchet. Rather than call for Rufus he instructed her to hand him his pack, which sat on the floor where he left it upon his arrival. As she picked it up her eyes fell on the word that Rufus had noticed earlier — *ichthus*. She stood frozen as she looked over at Cadmus, then quickly regained her composure before he noticed. *What is this?* Rufus wondered. *She doesn't even know how to read Latin, let alone Greek.* Rufus watched intently as she strolled over to the workbench where Cadmus was and dropped the pack on the floor next to him. She then leaned over the workbench, and using the most nonchalant tone she could muster, she said, "So Cadmus, where are you from?"

"Israel huh? I've got some friends from back there..." As she spoke the words she drew an arc about the length of her span in the dust on top of the workbench, using the tip of her finger. As Cadmus's eyes fell on the figure, he almost dropped the hammer that was in his right hand. He shot a glance up at the loft, unable to discern that Rufus was well hidden behind a drape that afforded him a perfect vantage point to spy on them. Cadmus then reached over and completed the figure, drawing another arc, inverted beneath the one that Antonina drew, beginning first by touching the left side, then intersecting it on the opposite tail end, forming the shape of an *ichthus*, id est, a fish. What happened next flummoxed Rufus like an apparition of Jupiter himself. His mouth agape, he proceeded to watch as the two of them *embraced*. Then looking about to make sure no one was watching, they whispered quickly to each other.

"This is dangerous, my master is right up there in the Loft," Cadmus said.

"Rufus or his father?" Antonina asked.

"Master Rufus."

"Don't worry, we have known each other for years," Antonina said. "He would never turn me in. We are meeting tonight down in the catacombs. You must come."

"I do not know if I will be able to get away. This is my first day their service. Master Antony just purchased me, this morning at Palatine Hill," Cadmus said.

Antonina handed Cadmus her bracelet. "Tell Rufus I gave this to you to repair and I need it back this evening. See if he will agree to let you explore the city a bit after you have delivered it to me. He can draw a map to show you the way to my master's home."

Rufus could not discern what they were saying, but it looked like they were making some sort of plan. He then watched as they clasped hands and bowed their heads, still whispering with their eyes closed. *Are they . . . praying?* Then Antonina quickly parted from her new friend, and dashed away. On her way back home she realized she was so excited she had completely forgotten the shoe latchet she came for. *Well, no matter*, she decided. *I'm sure he will remember and bring it with him tonight.*

Well well well, Rufus thought to himself. *I'm going to get to the bottom of this.* Discretion had never been Rufus's strong suit. And he never did like the sight of Antonina talking to any man besides himself, let alone embracing him and holding hands with him. Climbing down the ladder he walked straight to Cadmus, who could tell by the look on his master's face that he was in trouble. Stopping to stand in the same spot where Antonina stood, Rufus turned and looked down at the dusty figure he and Antonina had inscribed together.

"What's this?" he asked in a sarcastic tone, pointing at the *ichthus*.

Knowing that he had been watched, Cadmus was paralyzed with fear, but he did his best to hide it. He did not say anything.

Picking up Cadmus's pack, he pointed to the Greek letters that were embroidered on the side. "Why don't you tell me what this is about?" The sarcasm was gone. His voice was now stern and serious. He could see that Cadmus was petrified, and who could blame him? He was far from home in a strange city, and he was at his master's mercy. If Rufus wanted to he could whip him, or even kill him, and it would be perfectly legal under Roman law. Rufus was beginning to get frustrated with his servant. He loosed the draw string and turned the pack upside down, emptying the contents of it onto the table. The last thing to fall out was what was at the bottom. When the leather canister fell out and rolled off the table and onto the floor, Cadmus closed his eyes and swallowed hard, which did not go unnoticed by Rufus. Picking up the canister, Rufus pulled out the contents, and unrolled it. As he read the Greek writing on the scroll, his eyes gradually grew bigger and his voice gradually grew softer. "*The beginning of the gospel of Iesous Christos, the Son of God; . . .*"

A nation of well-informed men who have been taught to know and prize the rights which God has given them cannot be enslaved. It is in the religion of ignorance that tyranny begins.

— Benjamin Franklin

Ye are the salt of the earth: but if the salt have lost his savour, wherewith shall it be salted? it is thenceforth good for nothing, but to be cast out, and to be trodden under foot of men.

Ye are the light of the world. A city that is set on an hill cannot be hid.

Neither do men light a candle, and put it under a bushel, but on a candlestick; and it giveth light unto all that are in the house.

Let your light so shine before men, that they may see your good works, and glorify your Father which is in heaven.

— Dragon Slayer Jesus Christ

II

THE SUBCULTURE OF CHRISTIANITY

Rufus's life, or the life of any citizen of Rome for that matter, was not all that far removed from our lives in modern times. He enjoyed rights and privileges as a Roman. He could read and write. He owned his own business. Much like us, Rufus dressed in the style of his day. He went to events with his friends — things like theater, events in the Circus and the arenas, and so on. He questioned his government, and he probably lamented that the old days of the Republic were gone — the days before the empire, the days before the treason trials, etc. Like us, he even questioned the religious system of his day. Like the people in the Bible (and us), he was raised to be proud of his heritage and he worked hard to make a good life for himself. The people of the ancient world were ordinary folks just like us.

What Rufus has already become cognizant of is the fact that the Christians are different from other people. He sensed that they had a peace about them. He seemed to also sense something else, something illusive, almost as if they had a secret; a secret that could lead to a revolution.

Christianity, like the Jewish people from whence it grew out of, is very diverse. It reaches the pinnacle of human potential and shows the depths of human depravity. In the latter case, it is only false Christianity masquerading as the real thing. The same could of course be said of Judaism. Carl Marx may have been Jewish by birth, but the idea that someone who invented an economic theory that posits that there is no God, is Jewish, is plainly spurious. All Christians are Jewish by adoption (Rom 11:17, Eph 2:12,13), but not everyone who claims the name of Christ is a Christian (Matt 7:22,23; 13:24-30). Likewise not everyone who claims to be Jewish, is, according to Romans 2:28,29.

The challenges that face the church today are daunting to say the least. However, since ignoring a problem will not make it go away, we need to find the inner strength to face the issues of our day head on. This is something God has equipped us for:

> *For God hath not given us the spirit of fear; **but of** **power**, and of love, and of a sound mind.*
> *II Timothy 1:7*

Yet some of the topics we will cover will be so unsettling that some will be tempted to stop reading. If that is the case, I recommend you first ask yourself what kind of Christian you want to be. Everyone likes to tell himself that if he had lived in Nazi Germany he would have been one of the good ones. He would not have been deceived by Hitler. If that is the kind of Christian you want to be, and it should be, then we are going to have to come to terms with what is happening in the world today, which first requires being educated about it. Major changes are taking place, every bit as radical as the changes that rocked the Roman Empire in the first century. Be courageous. Keep reading.

Rufus's friends, Cadmus and Antonina, engaged in dangerous covert activity in the first century. We have entered a time now in twenty-first century America where merely telling the truth is a revolutionary act. It is entirely possible that this book will be considered an illegal document in the near future if the Lord tarries.[1]

In the first century, taking the name of Christ and identifying with him was considered treason. It was something that could cost a man everything he had, including his life. This remained true throughout most of history in many areas of the world, until about 1800 AD. It is still true in many places today: Saudi Arabia, North Korea, and Burma just to name a few. One of my personal friends whom I met in Zimbabwe had to make that type of first-century decision when he became a Christian. He left his commitment to be a Muslim cleric and in the process he left his entire life behind — his possessions, everything. Besides all this, his wife was pregnant at the time. They started over from scratch with nothing except the clothes on their back. I should also mention that shortly before we met, he had one of the 'conversion dreams' that have become so famous throughout the Muslim world. God is still working miracles in the lives of those who are not too busy for him.

In the USA, However, being a Christian requires no risk or persecution. Why is this? The Bible says *all that will live godly in Christ Jesus will suffer persecution.* The pro-life groups have suffered persecution for decades. These Christians were persecuted because they took a stand. They chose a side. They got involved in the battle. If you are not suffering persecution, there is a problem according to II Timothy 3:12. We have recently seen that the Tea Party groups have suffered persecution. Now taking a political stand is getting dangerous as well.

Being a Christian in the USA, today in the twenty-first century, means something entirely different to most people than it did in first-century Rome. Of course, the true definition of a word is not predicated on popular opinion.

The term 'Christian' may bring to mind things like listening to nice music on the radio, or maybe watching a favorite pastor on television. Maybe getting dressed up and going to a nice building

---

[1] The lines between legal and illegal have begun to blur. Government personnel at all levels are making policy and calling it law. Judicial activism has become the norm. (Judges are only supposed to administer the law. It is the legislators that are supposed to make the laws.) In terms of law, the Constitution, which makes this book perfectly legal, is the highest law of the land. Yet the Constitution has been largely rendered null and void, either by unconstitutional laws, or by mere policy.

to socialize comes to mind. Nothing is wrong with any of these things, in and of themselves. However, the Christians of the early church could not have done any of these things. The only praise and worship music they could listen to was a song that they sang themselves. During the persecutions the only pastor they could watch, was one they found in an underground meeting, at the risk of their lives. Their idea of 'church' would have been the other believers they knew. There were no buildings called 'churches'.

In the middle ages they had church buildings, but the real Christians were still meeting in secret, or living in remote locations. The treason trials, once dreaded in pre-Christian Rome, had come back in another form. Anyone could be accused of heresy. They had to then appear before a tribunal of church officials. In pre-Christian Rome, no confession was considered reliable unless it was obtained by torture. During the Inquisition, torture was employed in much the same way. A great deal of intelligence was gathered by the 'Church' during these sessions. They learned of others who were guilty of 'heresy', which could mean something as innocent as secretly owning their own copy of the Bible. The Bible was a forbidden book, and for a layman to own a copy of it was a capital offence. Only civil and religious leaders had the privilege of reading it. Since the people could not read the word of God for themselves, they were inclined to believe whatever they were told by the 'Church'. If the Church told them that 'heretics' who were caught with their own Bibles were God's enemies, and good Catholics would reduce their time in purgatory by bringing faggots (bundles of sticks) to burn the heretics, they had no way of knowing any better. The Church was the gatekeeper of information. They were masters at controlling the thoughts and opinions of the people. The Christians were the enemies of the State. They refused to worship the pope. Millions were martyred by the Church. According to the Museum of Medieval Torture in Midona, Italy, it happened every week in every town in Europe, and people always came out to watch.

According to the Bible that same scenario will happen once again. Not just behind the bamboo curtain, not just behind the veil of Islam, but worldwide. Just as the Christians in the early church were martyred for refusing to worship Cæsar, the Bible says that once the church is removed from the earth (I Thess 4:17), those who become Christians and refuse to worship the coming world leader will likewise be martyred. This is what the stacks of FEMA coffins,[2][3] which can be seen on YouTube, will ultimately be used for. No, you say. Surely they are for contingency plans in case of a natural disaster or a nuclear exchange. I wish that were so, but it's not. There are guillotines in the FEMA camps. I am not talking about the bogus pictures of them on the Internet. For proof, I will cite the most trustworthy source of truth there is, the Holy Bible:

*And I saw thrones, and they sat upon them, and judgment was given unto them: and I saw the souls of them that were **beheaded** for the witness of Jesus, and for the word of God, and which had not worshipped the beast, neither his image, neither had received his mark upon their foreheads, or in their hands; and they lived and reigned with Christ a thousand years.*

The Revelation 20:4

It is inevitable. Revelation 20:4 shows that it is a future event that has been prophesied to occur and will occur. This is not merely a medieval form of execution. The Nazis used it, and the Muslims still use it today. The *good news* is that there is a way of escape:

Watch ye therefore, and pray always, that ye may be accounted worthy to escape all these things that shall come to pass, and to stand before the Son of man.

The Gospel According to St. Luke 21:36

However, since we have no way of knowing when the rapture will take place, we must obey the command to be salt and light,

---

[2] Patent # 5425163 — Multi-functional cremation container for a cadaver.
[3] http://www.youtube.com/watch?v=m3zSDdm-SHI

and to *occupy* (ie, keep busy, Lk 19:13) until Christ returns. While we pray for his kingdom to come, we must *work while it is day.*

Before the advent of Christianity, all cultures practiced slavery. Human sacrifice and infanticide were commonplace in every corner of the globe. In the Roman Empire, abortion and abandoning unwanted babies to die of exposure were both legal and common. It was Christianity, or more specifically Christians, that brought these pagan practices to an end. The war was fought by real people who were empowered by the Holy Spirit. Through the most difficult times, the Christians have fought the good fight and kept the faith: in the first century during Nero's reign of terror; during the middle ages when the Inquisition was terrorizing Europe; during the Reformation period, when the light was breaking through and God was transforming Western culture; and at the founding of America, when a new torch of liberty was lit in the world. It was the Christians who were engaged in the battle. When slavery was being conquered in the 19th century the Christians were leading the charge then too, just as they were during the civil-rights movement of the 1960s. But where are the Christians today, as the night is coming and tyranny is encroaching? While it is true that the two leading figures in the new liberty movement against tyranny are Christians, namely Ron Paul and Alex Jones, where is the rest of the church? Why the retreat? What happened to the pulpits that were once aflame with righteousness? It is the church's God given mandate to be salt and light and Jesus made it perfectly clear, that if Christians are not salty (salt was used as a preservative), they are good for nothing:

> *Ye are the salt of the earth: but if the salt have lost his savour, wherewith shall it be salted? it is thenceforth **good for nothing**, but to be cast out, and to be trodden under foot of men.*
>
> *The Gospel According to St. Matthew 5:13*

Although the Church has been very courageous in the

fight against abortion, new threats to humanity have crept in unawares, below the radar, presenting new dangers. It is up to the Christians to stand for truth and justice, and if the church does not rise to the occasion, we will be held accountable. *For the time is come that judgment must begin at the house of God.*

To give a little more historical context to how Christians have been the champions of liberty, America's historian, David Barton explains how Christians were instrumental in the abolitionist movement that was central to the American Revolution:

"In 1762, the king vetoed the charter for America's first missionary society; he also suppressed other religious freedoms and even prevented Americans from printing an English language Bible. How did Americans respond? They took action; and almost unknown today is the fact that Declaration signers such as Samuel Adams and Charles Carroll cited religious freedom as the reason they became involved in the American Revolution. And significantly, even though Thomas Jefferson and Ben Franklin (two of the least religious signers) are typically the only signers studied today, almost half of the signers of the Declaration (24 of 56) held what today would be considered seminary or Bible school degrees. Clearly, for many Founders, religious issues were an important motivation behind their separation from Great Britain; but that motivation is largely ignored today.

"Moral issues are accorded the same silence. The greatest moral issue of that day was slavery; and after several of the American colonies moved toward abolishing slavery in 1773, the King, in 1774, vetoed those anti-slavery laws and continued slavery in America. Soon-to-be signers of the Declaration Benjamin Franklin and Benjamin Rush promptly founded America's first abolition society as a direct response against the king's order. The desire to end slavery in America was a significant motivation not only for Franklin and Rush but also for a number of others; but the end of slavery in America could be achieved only if they separated from Great Britain - which they were willing to do, and six of the thirteen colonies abolished slavery immediately following the separation.

"There were many other significant issues that led to our original Fourth of July; so why aren't Americans familiar with the rest? Because in the 1920s, 30s, and 40s, a group of secular-minded writers (including Charles and Mary Beard, W. E. Woodward, Fairfax Downey, and others) began penning works on American history that introduced a new paradigm. For this group, economics was the only issue of importance, so they began to write texts accordingly (their approach is now described as "the economic view of American history" and since the 1960s has been widely embraced throughout the education community). Consequently, since "taxation without representation" was the economic grievance in the Declaration, it became the sole clause that Americans studied.

"As a result, God is no longer visible in American history; and His absence is now construed as a mandate for secularism. Texts now forcefully assert that the American founding produced the first intentionally secular government in history - even though the Declaration officially acknowledges God in four separate clauses. (But who still teaches the Declaration - or even reads it?) Similarly, leaders such as John Hancock and John Adams receive credit as being the source of our independence, even though John Adams himself declared that the Rev. Dr. Jonathan Mayhew and the Rev. Dr. Samuel Cooper were two of the individuals "most conspicuous, the most ardent, and influential" in the "awakening and revival of American principles and feelings" that led to American independence. Regrettably, God (and His servants) have largely disappeared from the presentation of American history in general and America's founding in particular."[4]

Nearly all of the founding fathers were Christians. Out of fifty-six founders who signed the Declaration, (1) was Catholic, (12) were Congregationalist, (30) were Episcopalian, (2) were Quaker, (11) were Presbyterian. (Two were Deists: Jefferson and Franklin.)

Out of the thirty-nine founders who signed the Constitution,

[4] David Barton, *wallbuilders.com*

(2) were Catholic, (5) were congregationalist, (17) were Episcopalian, (1) was Lutheran, (2) were Methodist, (8) were Presbyterian, (1) was Huguenot, and (3) were Quaker. (Only one was a Deist, Benjamin Franklin.)[5] Many made strong confessions of faith in the Lord Jesus Christ.[6]

Strong warnings were given to Israel for her backsliding. She did not heed the warning and paid dearly. Israel did not think that God would judge his chosen people, but they were wrong. We suffer from a similar problem in America. We have bought into the idea of American exceptionalism to the point where we have become 'holier than thou'. We feel we can do no wrong. We are so firm in this belief that we have quit examining the actions of our government closely. And even when they are caught red handed committing crimes, we explain it away and justify it. The old adage, 'right or wrong, it's my country', is not biblical and it's not Christian. Hosea Chapter IV gives a diagnosis that fits modern day America just as accurately as it fit ancient Israel. The prescription for this ailment is found in Isaiah 58. First the diagnosis:

*Hear the word of the LORD, ye children of Israel: for the LORD hath a controversy with the inhabitants of the land, because there is no **truth, nor mercy, nor knowledge of God** in the land.*[7]

By swearing, and lying, and killing, and stealing, and committing adultery, they break out, and blood toucheth blood.

*Therefore shall the land mourn, and every one that dwelleth therein shall languish, with the beasts of the field, and with the fowls of heaven; yea, the **fishes of the sea also shall be taken away**.*[8]

Yet let no man strive, nor reprove another: for thy people are as they that strive with the priest.

---

[5] *Adherents.com* http://www.adherents.com/gov/Founding_Fathers_Religion.html
[6] *Wallbuilders* http://www.wallbuilders.com/libissuesarticles.asp?id=8755
[7] The key words here are truth, mercy, and knowledge. God is calling us to worship in spirit and truth, and practice the 'one anothers' of the New Testament. See Appendix F.
[8] It appears that fish may be mutating and dying of radiation poisoning, from Fukushima. This is only a small foreshadowing of what will occur following the rapture (Rev 8:9).

Therefore shalt thou fall in the day, and the prophet also shall fall with thee in the night, and I will destroy thy mother.

My people are destroyed for lack of knowledge: because thou hast rejected knowledge, I will also reject thee, that thou shalt be no priest to me: seeing thou hast forgotten the law of thy God, I will also forget thy children.

As they were increased, so they sinned against me: **therefore will I change their glory into shame.**[9]

They eat up the sin of my people, and they set their heart on their iniquity.

And there shall be, like people, like priest: and I will punish them for their ways, and reward them their doings.

For they shall eat, and not have enough: they shall commit whoredom, and shall not increase: *because they have left off to take heed to the LORD.*[10]

Whoredom and wine and new wine take away the heart.

My people ask counsel at their stocks, and their staff declareth unto them: for the spirit of whoredoms hath caused them to err, and they have gone a whoring from under their God.

They sacrifice upon the tops of the mountains, and burn incense upon the hills, under oaks and poplars and elms, because the shadow thereof is good: therefore your daughters shall commit whoredom, and your spouses shall commit adultery.

I will not punish your daughters when they commit whoredom, nor your spouses when they commit adultery: for themselves are separated with whores, and they sacrifice with harlots: therefore the people that doth not understand shall fall.

Though thou, Israel, play the harlot, yet let not Judah offend;

---

[9] Vv. 6, 7 The *therefore* in vs 7 has happened to America. As a Christian nation we've turned to the health and wealth prosperity gospel. Our glory has become our shame in many other ways as well. As the entertainment capital of the world, we are exporting filth. As the world's superpower we have become bullies.

[10] Vv. 8–10 show the fruit of disobedience. Genetically Modified Organism (GMO) nutrient-depleted food is eaten, but is 'not enough'. With couples no longer getting married and having kids, we are not 'increasing'.

and come not ye unto Gilgal, neither go ye up to Beth-aven, nor swear, The LORD liveth.

For Israel slideth back as a backsliding heifer: now the LORD will feed them as a lamb in a large place.

Ephraim is joined to idols: let him alone.

Their drink is sour: they have committed whoredom continually: **her rulers with shame do love, Give ye.**[11]

The wind hath bound her up in her wings, and they shall be ashamed because of their sacrifices.

Hosea, Chapter IV

Isaiah, Hosea's contemporary, gives the prescription:

Cry aloud, spare not, lift up thy voice like a trumpet, and **shew my people their transgression,**[12] *and the house of Jacob their sins.*

Yet they seek me daily, and delight to know my ways, as a nation that did righteousness, and forsook not the ordinance of their God: they ask of me the ordinances of justice; they take delight in approaching to God.

Wherefore have we fasted, say they, and thou seest not? wherefore have we afflicted our soul, and thou takest no knowledge? Behold, in the day of your fast ye find pleasure, and exact all your labours.

Behold, ye fast for strife and debate, and **to smite with the fist of wickedness:**[13] *ye shall not fast as ye do this day, to make your voice to be heard on high.*

Is it such a fast that I have chosen? a day for a man to afflict his soul? is it to bow down his head as a bulrush, and to spread sackcloth and ashes under him? wilt thou call this a fast, and an acceptable day to the LORD?

---

[11] Ie, the rulers were telling the people they had to give more. Heavy taxes were a burden to the people in that day too, and God reproved them for it.

[12] We are on sound biblical ground here. We need to examine ourselves (I Cor 11:28, II Cor 13:5) and repent of our sins. Not only as individuals, but as a nation.

[13] We will look at the aggressive wars that have followed 9/11 in following chapters.

Is not this the fast that I have chosen? **to loose the bands of wickedness, to undo the heavy burdens, and to let the oppressed go free, and that ye break every yoke?**

Is it not to **deal thy bread to the hungry, and that thou bring the poor that are cast out to thy house?** **when thou seest the naked, that thou cover him; and that thou hide not thyself from thine own flesh?** [14]

Then shall thy light break forth as the morning, and thine health shall spring forth speedily: and thy righteousness shall go before thee; the glory of the LORD shall be thy rereward.

Then shalt thou call, and the LORD shall answer; thou shalt cry, and he shall say, Here I am. If thou take away from the midst of thee the yoke, the **putting forth of the finger, and speaking vanity;**

And if thou draw out thy soul to the hungry, and satisfy the afflicted soul; then shall thy light rise in obscurity, and thy darkness be as the noonday:

And the LORD shall guide thee continually, and satisfy thy soul in drought, and make fat thy bones: and thou shalt be like a watered garden, and like a spring of water, whose waters fail not.

And they that shall be of thee shall build the old waste places: thou shalt raise up the foundations of many generations; and thou shalt be called, The repairer of the breach, The restorer of paths to dwell in.

If thou turn away thy foot from the sabbath, from doing thy pleasure on my holy day; and call the sabbath a delight, the holy of the LORD, honourable; and shalt honour him, not doing thine own ways, nor finding thine own pleasure, **nor speaking thine own words:** [15]

Then shalt thou delight thyself in the LORD; and I will cause thee to ride upon the high places of the earth, and feed thee with the heritage of Jacob thy father: for the mouth of the LORD hath spoken it.

The Book of the Prophet Isaiah, Chapter LVIII

Some will inevitably say that it is not right to apply these passages from the Old Testament to our present day situation.

Such theology is hyper-dispensational at best, perhaps worse. It is true that these Scriptures were written to Israel, but *there is no new thing under the sun.* The church has been adopted into the commonwealth of Israel, so spiritually, these Scriptures speak to us as well (Eph 2:12,13; Rom 11:17).

All scripture is given by inspiration of God, and is profitable for doctrine, for reproof, for correction, for instruction in righteousness:
II Timothy 3:16

Now all these things happened unto them for ensamples: and they are written for our admonition, upon whom the ends of the world are come.
I Corinthians 10:11

God is no respecter of persons, and he is no respecter of nations either. The principles that guided people in Bible times are still in effect today. *Jesus Christ is the same yesterday, and to day, and for ever.* We must *earnestly contend for the faith that was once delivered to the saints.* Our faith is *much more precious than of gold that perisheth,* and that faith is under attack. It is so easy to forget that we must *work out [our] own salvation with fear and trembling,* or that we must *give diligence to make [our] calling and election sure.* Father, we have sinned against you. Forgive us Lord, and wake us out of our slumber. Transform us Father, that we may resist the temptation to be conformed to this world. Make us to see things as you see them, and give us the courage to stand in this evil day, in Jesus' name. Amen.

14 Vv. 6,7 God is telling us we are to do something about the wicked human trafficking that is the shame of our land, and the U.S. slave-labor penitentiary business that boasts the highest incarceration rate in the world. He is telling us to take care of our families and to care for the poor.
15 Today when you go to a 'Bible study' you are presented with a book by a popular author, written with 'biblical principles'. We are ignoring God's words and speaking our *own words*. God is telling us to get back to the Bible.

It is impossible to enslave, mentally or socially, a Bible reading people. The principles of the Bible are the groundwork of human freedom.

— Horace Greeley, American Newspaper Editor, 1811-1872

For all those things hath mine hand made, and all those things have been, saith the LORD: but to this man will I look, even to him that is poor and of a contrite spirit, and trembleth at my word.

The Book of the Prophet Isaiah, 66:2

III

THE
FORBIDDEN BOOK

There was a good reason Rufus's eyes grew bigger. What he was holding was an illegal document, and he was fully aware of the fact that it could land him in jail, or possibly even in the arena to wrestle with gladiators or wild animals. As to what happened next, although Rufus knew he should immediately destroy the contraband and punish his servant for bringing it into his shop, he couldn't. He was held captive by the mysterious words he was reading. So instead of shredding the document and scolding Cadmus, he simply said "Call me if we get any other customers," then slowly walked back over to the ladder, his eyes never leaving the parchment. After he was back up in the loft, Rufus continued, spellbound... *And it came to pass in those days, that Iesous came from Nazareth of Galilee, and was baptized of John in the Jordan. And coming up out of the water, he saw the heavens opened, and the Spirit like a dove descending upon him: And there was a voice from heaven, saying, Thou art my beloved Son, in whom I am well pleased...*

"Master Rufus, There is somebody here to see you," Cadmus called up from the workshop.

Rufus was just finishing the end of his scroll when Cadmus

called him. *...So then after the Lord had spoken unto them, he was received up into heaven, and sat on the right hand of God. And they went forth, and preached every where, the Lord working with them, and confirming the word with signs following. Ä·men.*

Rufus came back to himself. After he tucked the scroll inside a bag of fleece, he then peered over the edge of the loft. "Marcus! Gods below us, I lost track of time. . . What time of day is it? It must be getting close to sunset. Do you have my package ready?"

"You do not look much like somebody who is preparing to propose, Rufus," Marcus said.

"You do not miss a thing do you Marcus," Rufus said as he scampered down from the loft and then disappeared into the back room, then quickly appeared again with his best garment in hand. "I can still be on time if I hurry," he said as he plucked the gift box out of Marcus' hand. "All I have to do is run down to the Thermae Agrippæ,[1] wash up, then dash over to Viminalis to meet Lady Vitellia."

"You are most welcome, Rufus. Do not mention it," Marcus said sarcastically.

"You will have to afford me some latitude Marcus," Rufus said. "I will thank you later after I am engaged. I have to go now." As he headed out the door, Cadmus stopped him.

"Excuse me, sir, a customer named Antonina gave me this to repair, and asked me to return it to her this evening," Cadmus said, holding up her bracelet.

Rufus looked back at Cadmus, then left, then right, and then said, "Sure, all right. Take it to her."

"She said you would draw me a map," Cadmus replied.

"I do not have time. I have to go," Rufus said.

"I am going that way anyway," Marcus said. "I will take him there."

"Fine," Rufus muttered, as he made his way down the street.

"Sir will you be needing me for anything else today after I make the delivery?" Cadmus called out.

---

[1] Lit. The Baths of Agrippa.

"No, go ahead and take the rest of the day off," Rufus called back to him as he picked up his pace and started to jog. A dozen thoughts whirled about in his head. He was unable to make them stop so he could focus on them one at a time. It was like a tornado that just kept gathering dust and momentum: *Lady Vitellia . . . Antonina. . . It is better to enter into life maimed, than having two hands to go into hell, into the fire that never shall be quenched; Where their worm dieth not, and the fire is not quenched . . . ἰχθύς — what in the world was that all about? . . . Cadmus, why did I let him go meet with Antonina? . . . ἰχθύς? It was like they had known each other for years. . . And they that did eat of the loaves were about five thousand men. . . Lady Vitellia, will you marry me? . . . Antonina, I've never seen her so happy, she was radiant. . . For what shall it profit a man, if he shall gain the whole world, and lose his own soul?*

Rufus's shop was in Horti Luculiani, which was about two miles north of where Lady Vitellia lived with her family in Viminalis. He figured if he kept a good pace he could make it to Thermae Agrippæ in less than half an hour. After a hot bath he would be able meet Lady Vitellia before sundown.

An hour later, Rufus looked down at his reflection in the shallow pool outside the bath house, which served as a natural mirror as he adjusted his toga and combed his hair with his fingers. He looked like a new man. He felt like a new man. The jog and the bath had cleared his mind. After he was satisfied with his appearance, he practiced his lines as he strolled off to meet his soon-to-be fiancé. Lady Vitellia, you look wonderful tonight. Lady Vitellia, the moonlight is putting a sparkle in your eyes any one of the stars above would envy. . . Lady Vitellia, there is only one thing missing in my life. . . Here, before I say what I have to say, open this box. . . No, that's not it — Lady Vitellia, I have something I need to say to you, but first let us open this box together. . . Meanwhile, Marcus was exhausting every bit of charm he had on Antonina as she pretended to inspect the bracelet that Cadmus had supposedly fixed for her.

Cadmus only interrupted to say, "If that will be all miss I will leave you to your business." Antonina did not wear a slave tunic or tag and she could easily pass for a free-born Roman, but Marcus still gave Cadmus a look when he called Antonina 'miss'.

After he thanked Marcus for his help, Cadmus made his way up the street to a small market, which served as a good vantage point from which he watched and waited for Antonina to get rid of Marcus. A few moments later he made his way back and met her again, and they were on their way off to the meeting.

"You are not going to believe what happened after you left today," Cadmus said.

"There is not much that surprises me anymore," Antonina replied, as they walked the Porticus Liviae towards the center of Rome, where they would rendezvous with another brother, before descending beneath the surface of the city into the catacombs.

"Rufus — he saw us talking, and he knows," Cadmus said. He recounted the story back to Antonina, without leaving out any details. Not an easy task, since Antonina was wont to interrupt and ask questions.

"What? A new Gospel?? John Mark? I think I have heard about him. Brother Paul said he and Barnabas left for Cyprus years ago while they were on a missionary journey together."

By the time they reached their rendezvous point he had explained everything that had happened. "Well I'm glad he found it," Antonina said. "If reading that does not convince him then nothing will. Besides, at the meetings they have been teaching us that we need to trust God at all times, and that he uses all things and fits them together to work for good, for those who love God."

"Is that where you have been learning Greek?" Cadmus asked.

"I'm the one who's been teaching her that," came a voice from behind them.

"Lucius! How many times have I told you not to sneak up on me like that?" Antonina demanded.

"One thousand apologies, Domina" Lucius said. "It shall never happen again."

"Yeah right," Antonina shot back. A short time later, after making their way over to a small grove, near to where the Aqua Aepia passed over the Via Nova, they rolled back a covering that concealed an ingress, and entered.

"Is this your first sewer tour?" Lucius asked Cadmus as he hit flints together and lit a torch that illuminated the tunnel ahead of them.

"We had some underground places where we would meet sometimes in Jerusalem," Cadmus said. "But nothing like the catacombs."

"Well I hope you are not afraid of enclosed areas," Lucius said. Winding and twisting, they followed the tunnel, sometimes intersecting other tunnels, sometimes turning and going into a new tunnel, until they began to hear it.

"What a beautiful sound," Antonina said. "I can feel the Spirit welling up within me already." It started faintly and then grew louder the closer they came — the sound of the underground church lifting their voices together in praise to God. They joined together in praise, their voices in one accord with the other believers as they entered into the underground meeting hall. It was about twenty by thirty cubits, a hub of six different passageways that met together at portals on each side of the room. Most of the people were seated on the ground. A few who were around the perimeter stood next to the walls. The acoustics reverberated and echoed about the room creating a wonderful sound. The glow of the torches was dim but the warmth of the Holy Spirit was like a May sunrise reflecting off the Great Sea. Yet both Antonina and Cadmus heard a still small voice telling them to make their way around to the other side of the room and stand in the far entrance. They both looked at the portal opposite them, then at each other. Now the still small voice was no longer still or small, it was amplified and strongly reverberating inside them. They both made their way around the perimeter to the other side as the singing stopped and a man with a scroll in his hand rose to speak.

"Good evening, my name is brother Servius. Let us pray." Servius extended his forearms and prayed in the Roman fashion with his palms facing upward. "Father in Heaven, it is so good to be here among your people. We pray together in one accord, that you will bless this time we have to share together in fellowship with your Son, and to feast on his word together; the precious bread that came down from heaven, which is more than our necessary food. We pray these things in the name of our Lord Iesus Christus, the name above all names. Amen. Now, before we unroll the word of God and read together, we have to discuss some very troubling developments . . ."

The speaker of the evening continued, "I would like to welcome anyone who may be new to our fellowship. As you know, meeting this way is very dangerous. Cæsar Nero has declared all of us who worship the Lord Iesus Christus to be enemies of the State. For some time now, we have been communicating with each other through the secret *ichthus* symbol. For anyone here tonight who may be new to the faith, I will explain what it means: Using a stick, he drew the fish symbol in the earth on the floor of the meeting hall. Then below the fish, he scribed the word *ichthus* in Greek. He then scribed another word underneath each letter, revealing a hidden acronym. Here is what it looked like on the floor as Servius rendered it in the hard earth:

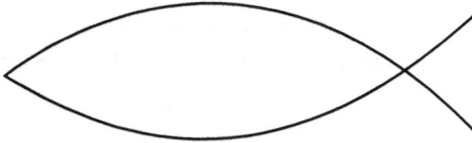

```
Ι   Χ  Θ  Υ  Σ
η   ρ  ε  ἰ  ω
σ   ι  ο  ό  τ
ο   σ  ῦ  ς  ή
ῦ   τ      ρ
ς   ό
    ς
```

"*Iesous Christos Theos Huios Soter*, this is what we know and believe: Iesus Christus, God's Son [and our] Saviour. My friends, it is no longer safe to rely on this method to communicate with one another, to identify ourselves as believers. We now know that Cæsar's men have learned the meaning of this symbol and can use it to identify us. They can pose as fellow believers. They can even use one of us to lead them to a meeting. Earlier today I learned that two brothers were identified and arrested by use of the *ichthus* code. Therefore we must be much more careful. I recommend you go to prayer before revealing your identity as a believer to anyone. Then to find out if they are likewise of the faith, recite part of a passage of Scripture. If they recognize it, and can complete it, you will know they are truly a fellow believer. False brethren sent by Cæsar to spy us out will not be able to complete the Scripture."

It was their custom to pass the scroll about and take turns reading from it. They had collected various letters written by the apostles, and they had acquired all thirty-nine books of the *Tanakh*.[2] As the scroll was passed, each would read a few lines, then pass the scroll to his neighbor, who would pick up where the other left off. Most did not know how to read until recently, but were learning.

And then, just as he was preparing to lead the congregation again in prayer before opening the scroll he held in his hand for to read, the peace was shattered by ten Roman soldiers who suddenly entered the room bearing spears, ropes and shackles. They entered together in pairs, two by two, from five different portals. Then there was a loud voice.

"In the name of Cæsar Nero, emperor of the great Roman Empire, you are all under arrest!" The only ones who stood a chance were Antonina and Cadmus, who before being noticed immediately each took two steps back into the shadows of the only portal the soldiers did not enter by, and clasped one another's hand as they held their breath. They continued to watch just long enough to see Lucius smile at one of the soldiers, then glance back to their side of the room to see they were gone.

---

[2] The Hebrew Bible, commonly referred to as the Old Testament.

"Quickly! Two of them got away through that portal!" they heard Lucius say, as they turned to run. As they ran away Cadmus reached and grabbed a torch from off the wall. They did not run far before the tunnel branched off in three different directions. They continued to run, taking turns into other passageways at each opportunity, and praying for their God to deliver them from the hand of their pursuers as they went. They ran until they were on the verge of collapsing, and then continued as soon as they recovered their breath.

VATICANUS

Circus Hadriani

Campus Vaticanus

Horti Caligulae

Circus Neronis

Mausoleum Hadriani

Via Triumphalis

Pons Aelius

Pons Neronis

Horti Agrippinae

Tarentum

XIV

JANICULUM

Theatrum Pompei

Porta Septimiana

Pons Aurelius (Valentiniani)

Via Aurelia

Via Aurelia

Porta Aurelia

Via Aurelia
Aqua Traiana

Horti Agrippinae

IX Thermae Agrippae

Circus Flaminius

Porticus Octaviae

CAPITOLINUS

Pons Cestius (Gratiani)

XIV

Pons Sublicius

Naumachia Augusti
Nemus Caesarum

XI

Pons Probi

Porta Portuensis

Tiberis

Emporium
Horrea

AVENTINUS

XIII

Horti Caesaris

Via Portuensis

M. Testaceus

Sepulcrum Cestii
Porta Ostiensis

Via Ostiensis

Curia Hostilia

Comitium

Cloaca

Macellum
(For Piscarium)

Basilica Fulvia et Aemilia

Lacus Curtius
T. Iani

Tabernae Novae

FORUM

Tabernae Veteres

Fornix Fabianus

Horti
Caesaris

Reg. Sac.

Aed. Vestae

Forum
zur Zeit der
Republik.

Maßstab 1:3600.

Meter

ROMA

Via Pinciana

Porta Salaria

Via Tremontana

Porta Chiusa

CASTRA PRAETORIA

LLIS HORTORUM

Horti Sallustiani

T. Veneris Erycinae

Via Salaria

Porta Collina

T. Fortunae

QUIRINALIS

Capitolium Vetus

T. Quirini

Sabaus

VI

Thermae Diocletiani

Porta Pinciana

Porta Tiburtina

VIMINALIS

Thermae Constantini

Aqua Marcia

Via Tiburtina

Porta Tiburtina

Horti Maecenatis

Porta

Porta Esquilina

CISPIUS

ESQUILINUS

III

Macellum Livium

Trofei di Mario

SUBURA

Porticus Livia

Horti Maecenatis

Horti Lamiani

Via Labicana

Horti Lamiani

Horti Nymphaeum

Horti Pallantiani

IV

T. Telluris

OPPIUS

V

Mon. Arruntiorum et Statiliorum

T. Syd. Veteris

Via Praenestina

Porta Praenestina

Via Praenestina nova

Via Labicana

VELIA

Amphitheatrum Flavium

T. Minervae Medicae

Horti Torquatiani

Aqua Claudia et Anio Nova

TINUS

X

T. Divi Claudii

CAELIOLUS

II

Amphitheatrum Castrense

Aqua Claudia

Aqua Appia

Porta Asinaria

CAELIUS

Castra Peregrina

Macellum Magnum

Porta Querqu. Setina

Porta Metrovia

I

Via Appia

Arcus Drusi

XII

Thermae Antoninianae

Via Latina

Porta Latina

Sepolcro Scipionum

Arcus Divi Trajani?

Porta Appia

Maßstab 1 : 23 000.

0   100   200   300   400   500   600
Passus Romani

0   1000   2000   3000
Pedes Romani

0   100   200   300   400   500
1000 Meter = 1 Kilometer.

Power corrupts; absolute power corrupts absolutely.

— Lord Acton, English Historian, 1834-1902

And upon a set day Herod, arrayed in royal apparel, sat upon his throne, and made an oration unto them.

And the people gave a shout, saying, It is the voice of a god, and not of a man.

And immediately the angel of the Lord smote him, because he gave not God the glory: and he was eaten of worms, and gave up the ghost.†

The Acts of the Apostles 12:21–23

---

† Flavius Josephus gives a matching account of Herod's death. He says that Herod Agrippa I appeared to accept the worship of the people. He was almost immediately struck by violent pains in his belly, and had to be carried back to his palace, where he expired five days later. Herod believed he was judged by God for allowing himself to be worshipped.

THE BEAST
CÆSAR NERO

The temple of Concordia was the home of the Roman Senate. It was the picture of Roman justice, reason and government. At least that is what it was supposed to represent, and perhaps at one time it may have. In the early days of the Republic, long before Julius Cæsar or Cicero addressed the council, the goddess of peace and harmony may have been pleased with the unity and justice that prevailed on the floor of the Senate. The Roman Senate was a place of representative government, based on a separation of powers. Roman law would become the basis of good government for ages to come. No Roman citizen could be convicted of a crime without a trial that allowed the accused a chance to answer for himself.[1] If nothing else, the Romans had brought a sense of justice to the world.

Early in the first century BC, General Sulla broke Roman law by marching across the Rubicon River, and bringing his army within the borders of Italy. He then marched on Rome, and made himself king. The illustrious Julius Cæsar came to power in the same way

---

[1] This concept existed before Rome made it a precedent that was widely known throughout the world. The Code of Hammurabi, circa 1772 BC included it, as well as the concept of presumed innocence.

that General Sulla did, by marching on Rome with his army. Cæsar then made himself dictator over the Senate. Cæsar's great-nephew, Octavian, likewise took control of the Senate by force. Octavian deified his great-uncle, making himself a son of god as Cæsar's adopted son. He rejected the titles of dictator, king, and emperor, before settling on Augustus (Luke 2:1). The title implied he was to be worshiped, and thus began the cult of the deified emperor. Next came Tiberius, and the beginning of a downward spiral for the Julio-Claudian dynasty. Tiberius had an island he resorted to where he indulged his perverse appetites with sex slaves, which included children. After Tiberius came the most deranged and depraved of all the Roman emperors — Caligula. Caligula was popular at the beginning of his reign. He brought an end to treason trials. During the reign of Tiberius treason trials had become commonplace. Anyone could accuse anyone of treason. If convicted, a portion of their estate was awarded to the accuser. No one of means was safe; those of the patrician class suffered much persecution. Caligula showed benevolence in many other ways. He was a gifted speaker and acted as a genuine statesman who had the public interests at heart. Then at one point in his short four year reign, following a serious illness, Caligula went insane. He transformed from a rising star who was loved by the people into a despot who levied heavy taxes on everything from marriage to prostitution. He declared himself to be a living deity and demanded to be worshiped. Under Augustus, the imperial cult was by and large symbolic. He was not formally deified until after his death. Tiberius had little interest in the cult. Caligula, however, had the temple of Castor And Pollux (twin sons of Jupiter) converted into his own personal temple. He had the heads removed on the statues of Roman gods and goddesses throughout the empire, and replaced with those of his own likeness. He made his horse a senator, and had a house built for him, complete with a golden stable. Caligula took the wives of the senators at will, and demanded to be catered to in the most perverse and extravagant ways imaginable. He enjoyed humiliating people and boasting about it afterwards. He was also a cannibal and ate some of those closest to him when they displeased him. In the end he was murdered by his own servants. Most of the emperors in the Julio-Claudian dynasty were assassinated, as were many of the later emperors. There was rarely a peaceful exchange of power. After the seat of power was secured, then came the death warrants to dispose of any rivals who may have posed a threat. After Caligula's death, his nephew Claudius (Acts 18:2) became emperor. Like Caligula before him, he had many enemies and there were many attempts on his life. Consequently he had many members of the Senate killed to maintain his power. He was finally poisoned by his doctor on orders from his fourth wife in AD 54, in the 14th year of his reign. This made her son the emperor.

Enter the most wicked and infamous emperor of the Julio-Claudian dynasty, Cæsar Nero. His name appears in Scripture only once as a postscript at the end of II Timothy, but he is referred to in Acts 26 when Paul appeals his case to Cæsar. Nero was a great-great-grandson of Cæsar Augustus through his mother. Through his father he was a grandson of Mark Antony and Octavia Thurina Minor, Cæsar Augustus' sister. Therefore, he was the grandnephew of Cæsar Augustus as well as his great-great-grandson. He was nephew to Emperor Caligula. Like his uncle, Nero eventually went insane. It may have been the lead pipes the Romans used in their aqueducts. Or maybe it was the inbreeding that had trickled down through the Julio-Claudian dynasty. Or maybe it was Nero's rejection of the gospel of Jesus Christ and his persecution of the church that drove him mad. Maybe it was a combination of all of these, but there is yet another possibility; it is quite probable that he was in fact demon possessed. Eg, Nero had a game he invented and liked to play which involved him dressing up like a tiger, then attacking and eating people. His term in office did not start out like this though. Like Caligula, he started well, but there was something that caused a sudden change in Nero. It has been theorized that it was Paul's witness to Nero, and Nero's subsequent rejection of the gospel that caused Nero to become demon possessed.

In 62 AD Nero heard Paul's appeal, after he was accused by the Jews of insurrection. At every juncture in Paul's trials he used his testimony in court to preach the gospel. First he was apprehended in Jerusalem for preaching the gospel. Then during his trial he preached to Governor Felix, and again later to Porcius Festus, along with Agrippa II and Bernice. The Bible seems to indicate that he followed the same pattern when Nero heard his appeal (Acts 23:11). When Nero rejected Paul's testimony, it was then that he opened himself up to possession. His lascivious lifestyle, his pagan idol worship, and his family's history of satanic occult involvement, all made Nero a lightning rod for demonic activity.

There have been Neros in every age. They may not wear togas but they are still just as ruthless, just as disturbed, and just as evil. The Neros of our day have employed strategies and techniques far more sophisticated than anything Nero ever dreamed of. They trade *souls of men* (Rev 18:13, read human trafficking),[2] just as Nero did. They wear suits that are tailor made, every bit as fine as Nero's togas. Their influence and power is truly god-like compared to Nero's. Any one of them would be the envy of Nero, yet there is no one person with absolute power. Today's Cæsars share their power through contracts, international treaties and tacit agreements.

The Bible says that one day there will be another Nero, who will not just be emperor of a vast empire, but indeed the entire world. My challenge to you, dear reader, is to avoid being his victim. Not physically, but spiritually. Jesus teaches us that there are things worse than death:

> *And fear not them which kill the body, but are not able to kill the soul: but rather fear him which is able to destroy both soul and body in hell.*
>
> *Matthew 10:28*

Revelation 13 says that one day, perhaps in the not-too-distant future, the entire planet is going to worship the devil. Those who resist are going to be beheaded. But how much better to die with

---

[2] https://www.youtube.com/watch?v=Px1t1-a9uxk

honor than to spend the rest of eternity separated from God? The real battle here will not be fought with guns. It will not be the militia against goose-stepping NWO soldiers, although that may happen too. The real battle will take place in your mind.

Cæsar Nero serves as a biblical model for the Antichrist. He took mind control very seriously. In the first century, mind control was done through religion. In Rome everything was validated by the priests, who supposedly received their oracles directly from the gods. By worshiping false gods, and accepting the priest's version of reality, the Romans were subjected to one of the most powerful forms of mind control, religion. The head of the college of the priests was called the *Pontifex Maximus* (lit. Greatest Pontiff). With his support, the people would accept the dictates of the Senate. Hence, the strange relationship between politics and religion. Mind control is still done this way in almost every religion to some degree, even American Christianity. In 12 AD, Cæsar Augustus assumed the title of *Pontifex Maximus*. This gave him absolute power, being the head of both politics and religion (as well as being a god himself). The imperial cult of the deified emperor grew in practice until Nero demanded the absolute religious devotion of his Roman subjects. Under Nero, anyone who refused to affirm Cæsar as 'Lord' suffered the consequences. The only ones who resisted this strange order were the Christians. They endured horrible persecutions for their disobedience. Christians were broiled, burnt, stoned, hung, and worried (torn by dogs). Some were slain with the sword, some were scourged with whips. Some were crucified, some had their tongues cut out. Some were frozen in the cold. Some were starved. Some had their hands cut off, or were dismembered in other ways. Fox, citing ancient sources like Augustine and Hierome (Jerome), puts the number of early Christian martyrs in the first three centuries in the millions.

Ultimately it will only be the Christians who refuse to worship the leader of the New World Order (Rev 13:8), or to take the mark of the beast. They will likewise be martyred for it.

In all of the epic struggles that have happened throughout

history, there have been over-arching spiritual battles taking place behind the scenes. These battles, both material and immaterial, are all part of an extended war that began in the garden of Eden and will end with the battle of Armageddon. Empires rise and fall. God weighs them in the balances and when they are found wanting (Dan 5), God brings them to an end. The Greeks had a proverb, "Those who the gods destroy they first make drunk with power." Solomon wrote that *there is no new thing under the sun*, and history has proven his statement to be accurate. We are witnessing the end of a cycle that has played itself out many times in history. We are witnessing the decline and fall of the American empire.

Constant wars and heavy spending were two of the main reasons that the Roman Empire fell. Debasing the currency led to inflation.[3] This, along with heavy military spending, led to increased taxes. The resulting economic problems were arguably the main reasons for the fall of the Republic.[4] We are seeing all these same trends in the United States. Just like Rome, we were founded as a republic, with a separation of powers. Just as Rome devolved from a consul (Pompey Magnus), to a dictator (Julius Cæsar) to an emperor (Cæsar Augustus), America is going down the same path. There used to be an understanding that it was the law that was king in America, a law that explicitly protected the citizens and gave them rights and protections that superseded the authority of the state. In the same way that these ideas were popularized in the colonies, and became the zeitgeist of the age, they can be revived again. As Americans we not only have a birthright of freedom and liberty as guaranteed by the Constitution; we also have a moral obligation to check our government when they engage in immoral and bad behavior. For example, engaging in unjust wars for the benefit of the military industrial complex. If we do not repent as a nation, our sovereignty will continue to erode until our republic ceases to exist. Nineveh repented at the preaching of Jonah, and was given another 250 years. We must repent as well.

[3] Bruce Bartlet, *Cato Journal*, Vol. 14, No, 2 (Fall 1994).
[4] Ibid.

After our involvement in Iraq, it was admitted that Iraq had nothing to do with September 11, nor were there any WMDs in Iraq.[5] Instead of liberation, our involvement only badly destabilized the area, forcing the Christians to flee the country. They sought refuge in Syria, where it was granted. Then we aided in the destabilization of Syria by supporting the Syrian rebels. The Christian refugees and the local Christians were badly persecuted by the very rebel forces the United States was supporting. The Christians were raped, killed, forced to convert to Islam, or beheaded in many cases. Many fled for their lives back to Iraq again.

Before the Iraq war, Christians were not persecuted in Iraq. They even had a Christian representative in the regime of Saddam Hussein. Iraq was one of the few secular governments left in the Middle East. With the exceptions of Israel, Lebanon, and the current military regime in Egypt, Syria is the last secular government in the Middle East that is not hostile to Christianity. Just as Syria was no longer safe for Christian refugees after the uprising against the al-Assad regime, Egypt became a nightmare for Christians as well. After the ouster of Hosni Mubarak, Christians were exposed to forced conversions, rapes, and state-sanctioned torture chambers. The U.S. supported the Muslim Brotherhood and the ouster of Mubarak, despite the fact that the Mubarak regime had been an ally of not only the U.S., but Israel as well. In July of 2013 the Egyptian military ousted Muslim Brotherhood President, Mohamed Morsi, ending the state-sanctioned persecution of Christians, but causing more civil unrest. As of this writing 85 churches have been destroyed or forcibly converted to mosques by the Muslim Brotherhood. Yet, after the Military Regime (our previous allies from Mubarak's regime) deposed Morsi and began restoring order, the U.S. promptly cut off aid to Egypt. The U.S. also aided in destabilizing Libya, by providing air support to the al-Qaeda rebels. The new government is far worse than the al-Gaddafi regime was. Whereas Gaddafi was using Libya's natural resources to build Africa, and was regarded by many as

---

[5] George W. Bush, press conference, 8/21/06, et al.

a great pan-African leader, the new regime promptly engaged in ethnic cleansing, murdering black Africans, and wreaking havoc as far south as Timbuktu.

While it is true that each of the leaders that were recently ousted or rebelled against with the support of the U.S. are or were indeed dictators (Hussein, Mubarak, al-Gaddafi, and al-Assad), their countries were by and large stable. We are complicit in the killing and destabilization that has taken place in these countries, in many cases affecting Christians who lived peaceably for centuries in these regions, until the overthrow of their governments and the installation of Muslim authoritarian governments.

These wars have cost American lives, lives of people in foreign lands, trillions in taxpayer dollars, and destroyed our good name in the eyes of the world. All this, combined with the systematic dissolution of morals here at home, is leading America to the same inevitable fate as Rome. It may be too late for America, *but the point is that America has sinned, and we need to repent*. Only then can we expect God to hear from heaven, forgive our sin, and heal our land (II Chron 7:14).

If the church returns to its place as the moral compass of the nation, we can turn the minds of the people back to the early teachings of the founders. It is our willingness to depart from these foundational American values that has led us to where we are today. The founders were:

• Against aggression in foreign wars.
• Against partisanship.
• Against a central bank (by law of the U.S. Constitution).
• Against tyranny that infringed on the Bill of Rights.
• For Christian education in public schools.
• For freedom of religion in general and Christianity in particular.

Non-Christians may be reluctant to agree to the last two bullet points, but history is clear and undeniable. It was this American spirit that made our nation great. We have forsaken the God of our forefathers; *my people have changed their glory for that which doth not profit*.

Freedom is not so much a gift as a responsibility. Of the people, by the people, and for the people means that we have a responsibility to govern ourselves, which requires work. It does not necessarily mean that you fight city hall, maybe it means you become city hall. Unlike a monarchy where people are ruled over by a king, America was intended to be a nation of citizens who were involved in the process of government, ie they would govern themselves. If history proves nothing else it proves that being ruled over is not a good position to be in. Yet it is already happening. We no longer have a president so much as a monarch. A president does not spend billions of dollars on his personal vacations. That is what a king does. Just as Rome spiraled downward from nation of laws with a Senate and a consul, to an empire that glorified its leaders, America's leadership is becoming an aristocratic, technocratic, nobility with absolute power.

George Bush: Passed the Patriot Act. Allows government to spy on citizens without court orders, nullifies almost the entire Bill of Rights, and sets up secret Star Chamber style courts.

Barack Obama: Campaigned to reform the Patriot Act, but instead approved extending it without reform.

Barack Obama: Passed the 2012 National Defence Authorization Act, which allowed government to indefinitely detain citizens without a trial, suspending due process and habeas corpus.

Barack Obama: Authorized a secretive panel (that operates above the law, as no laws were cited for its existence or operation) which creates kill lists[6] that can target and indeed have[7] targeted and killed American citizens. No judge, no jury; bang — you're dead.

Consider that President Barack Obama has spent well over a billion dollars so far on vacations, and has broken the record set

---

[6] "Secret panel can put Americans on "kill list"", *Reuters*, October 5, 2011.
[7] "Attorney General Holder defends execution without charges", *Salon*, March 6, 2012.

by Bill Clinton for a single vacation, by racking up $100 Million[8] for a single vacation to Africa. How are we any different from the country we fought a war against for independence, that annually pays the royal family a combined total of around £175 Million? Some will say, who cares? What's the big deal? Things change, why fight it? If it were only a matter of lavish lifestyles for the new political elite, and making some exceptions to the Bill of Rights to fight terrorism, I may agree with that, but it goes much deeper than that. That is how it is sold to the American public, but by reviewing what has been going on, it's clear it is much worse than almost anyone supposes.

Our police departments are purposely hiring cadets with low IQs, ostensibly so they will follow orders and not think for themselves. Applicants with IQs above the threshold have been rejected, and this asinine policy has been upheld by the courts.[9] In other words, they will protect and serve their masters, instead of upholding the law, and protecting and serving the people. (Recent abuses include things like roadside anal cavity searches, and forced catheters resulting from routine traffic stops.)[10][11][12] It is important to note here that the way to fight tyranny is not to mouth off to cops and refuse to show ID. If you take that stance, you very well may end up being cavity searched, or worse. For example, on May 29 of 2013, 22 year old Alexis Alpha was walking by the scene of a routine traffic stop in San Marcos, Texas. A Texas police officer asked her why she was walking by his traffic stop. (While nobody likes to be harassed, the wise thing to do in a situation

---

8 "Document: Major resources needed for Obama Africa trip", *Washington Post*, June 13, 2013. The Africa vacation was reported to cost between $60 Million and $100 million. Yet later in October of that same year, the president saw fit to shut down the WWII veterans' open air memorial to supposedly save money because of the government shut down.

9 http://abcnews.go.com/US/court-oks-barring-high-iqs-cops/story?id=95836

10 http://www.dailymail.co.uk/news/article-2356618/Pictured-The-women-suing-police-unconstitutional-roadside-cavity-search.html

11 http://crooksandliars.com/diane-sweet/women-given-body-cavity-searches-publi

12 http://www.abajournal.com/news/article/forced_catheterization_alleged_suit_says_cops_wanted_quicker_urine_sample_a/

like this is go the extra mile.)[13] Alpha sassed back, and the next thing she knew, she was beaten, her teeth were knocked out, and she was charged with obstruction, a third degree felony, resisting arrest, a Class A misdemeanor, and public intoxication, a Class C misdemeanor. It has since come out that Ms. Alpha had only ingested 1/2 of one beer at the time of this incident. *It was only after widespread media coverage using the video footage from her friend's phone, that the charges against her were dropped.* Corporal Palermo has been arrested and charged with aggravated assault by a public servant. Police Commander Penny Dunn said Alpha was not guilty of any of those crimes. Adding "Cpl. Palermo had no reason to detain Ms. Alpha nor did he ever develop probable cause to arrest her for any offense." Cmdr. Dunn said, "Ms. Alpha made no contact with either the driver or Cpl. Palermo. She did not look at them as she walked by and made no suspicious movements, gestures or comments that would indicate she was anything more than a passerby [and] appeared unaware of the actions of either the driver or Cpl. Palermo." Once Cpl. Palermo's supervisors reviewed the case, Ms. Alpha was released.[14] This story is important for two reasons: First of all, Alexis Alpha could have been anyone's daughter, or sister, wife, or mother. Second, the only thing that vindicated her was a friend with a cell phone. It has been upheld by the courts over and over that we have the right to film officers, and oftentimes that is all that can save someone from false charges and police brutality.

The problem is not just a few bad apples who cannot control their temper. It is more of a trend towards policies that harass and intimidate instead of protect and serve. "When I first heard about the quotas I was appalled," says former Auburn police officer Justin Hanners, who claims he and other cops were given

---

[13] In Matthew 5:41, *Jesus said, And whosoever shall compel thee to go a mile, go with him twain.* The reason Jesus made this statement is because of a law that stated a Roman soldier could command anyone in one of their colonies to carry his pack for up to one mile.
[14] Julie Wilson, *Infowars.com*, July 17, 2013.

directives to hassle, ticket, or arrest specific numbers of residents per shift. "I got into law enforcement to serve and protect, not be a bully."[15] Justin Hanners was fired for refusing to comply with the new guidelines and quota policies that his department was given. He says that the problem goes way beyond the Auburn police department, and as more good cops leave the force because of these policies it leaves only the ones who like to bully.

In Texas women are being given roadside 'cavity searches' for crimes as arbitrary as 'flicking a cigarette out the window' and the cop 'smelling marijuana'. As horrific as that is however, the tyranny goes much deeper, in more subtle and sinister ways.

Dr Maurice Hilleman, the world's foremost vaccine scientist, admitted during an interview that his vaccines contained SV40 as well as AIDS and cancer viruses.[16] This was actually admitted even on the CDC website, but was removed. The page was cached on Google, but shortly after Mike Adams of *Natural News* published it, the cached page was taken down as well. What the redacted information revealed was that as many as 96 million people were given the cancer causing virus SV40 through polio vaccines between 1955 and 1963. It is estimated this adversely affected as many as 30 million people.

There are a whole host of testimonies on YouTube exposing how Gardasil and other vaccines have killed hundreds of young women and infants, respectively.[17]

In India, in 2011, the Oral Polio Vaccine (OPV) paralyzed 47,500 children. The OPV was banned in the U.S. in 2000, but that did not stop the Bill and Melinda Gates Foundation from using the vaccine in India, with catastrophic results.

I cannot think of anything more inhuman than not being willing to address a problem that affects children and causes cancer and autism. The word **inhuman** is defined as follows:

[15] "Cop Fired for Speaking Out Against Ticket and Arrest Quotas", Tracy Oppenheime, *Reason.com*, July 24, 2013.
[16] http://www.youtube.com/watch?v=Rr15ikUS1vI
[17] e.g. youtube.com/ Type in searchwords: 'shocking testimony about vaccines!'

Adjective
1. Lacking human qualities of compassion and mercy; cruel and barbaric.
2. Not human in nature or character.

The pharmaceutical companies have their shills everywhere, but when a celebrity like Jenny McCarthy becomes a thorn in their side, it makes for an interesting debate as the shill is forced to defend what is an indefensible position. This is what happened when McCarthy and her friend J.B. Handley, co-founder of Generation Rescue, appeared on "The Doctors."

Dr. James Sears: Here's the, here's one thing Jenny, and you know I've got an open mind, um, but, you know back in 1983, back in the 90s, we did have child, children dying ... every week of meningitis, and, and uh ... you know I remember doing rounds with my dad and almost, almost everyday he needed to go to the hospital and take care of a child that had some sort of vaccine preventable illness, and you know with the increase of vaccines, we've seen a huge decline in some of the really nasty things, that I don't -- that I am so glad I don't have to deal with. Epiglottitis, meningitis, you know a lot of pneumonias; your kids just aren't dying of that sort of stuff anymore and as a pediatrician, that's the last thing I want to say is for people to stop vaccinating because we'll start seeing kids die of polio again.

Jenny: Okay, let me tell you this. We do not need that many vaccines that ... we need -- the chicken pox I think can be a parent's choice, the Rhoda-virus. The flu shot that still contains mercury. J.B., Hepatitis B go ahead, wait let--

J.B. Handley: The devil is always in the details, and one of the problems with vaccines is they have been so great that people overly generalize about them as if they're only great. We looked at other first world countries. We're 34th in Under-5 Mortality, behind such luminaries as Cuba and Slovenia. However, we have 36 vaccines. The top five which include countries like Finland, Norway, Iceland average 11 and 13 vaccines. From 1994, we added 8 vaccines to our schedule. There are vaccines like Flu, Rhoda-virus, Varicella that have only been picked up by 2 or 3 of the other 30 countries. So what do they know that we don't? Why are they picking up vaccines that have been around for 15 years, and why are their Autism rates 1 in 1000, 1 in 1500, 1 in 2000? It doesn't take a brain surgeon or an ER doctor to figure out there might be a correlation.

Dr. James Sears: We don't want a narrow - be too narrow minded and say, it's only the vaccines and not -- and ignore other potential problems.

Dr. Travis Stork: In my opinion, and this is just me wanting to have an open debate about this, vaccines are really the one thing we have looked at, as causing autism...

Dr. James Sears: Yeah I agree with you.

J.B. Handley: That is completely bogus. That is such a bogus statement. How many vaccines have they looked at in their studies. How many? What's the answer? It's 2. How many ingredients have the studies out of 35? What's the answer? It's 1. You've looked at 2 of 36 shots and 1 of 35 vaccines and you're going to stand on the stage and say that vaccines and autism are unrelated? It is the most bogus tobacco science. It's a smoke screen and anybody who takes the time to read it would agree. I am so sick of doctors who don't read the studies, who don't know the details, sitting here, telling parents and reassuring them that vaccines don't cause autism. It is irresponsible.

Dr. Travis Stork: And this is the biggest problem, and the reason that doctors in this country are frustrated! Because...

J.B. Handley: Read the science.

Dr. Travis Stork: Listen, all you are doing is your antagonizing the medical community that wants to help these kids!

J.B. Handley: You haven't read done the research.

Dr. Travis Stork: Okay, you are antagonizing me, you're antagonizing doctor Sears! Why would you do that, this show is all about -- Okay, everyone wants to blame someone right? Yes, this is what we are trying to figure out here is how to help kids, but all you do when you yell at me on my stage, all you do is anger me.

J.B. Handley: I am sorry you have to feel like this, you don't know the details.

Dr. Travis Stork: I have asked to defend your stance and all you did was attack me. As an individual, why would I want to listen to you when you do that to me? Instead I want to listen Dr. Jerry here who rationally walk through, why they are removing certain things from foods they could be causing problems. Why we are removing the environmental toxins that could be causing autism. You know, I, I want to help these kids live better lives, just like everyone else. I don't understand why we all have to argue so much with one another, because when you attack, all you do is create frustration....

J.B. Handley: We are so frustrated by not being heard. We are so tired of not being heard. And we're so tired of hearing uh, doctors like the second doctor there, who says, "It's been proven that vaccines and autism are unrelated." It's simply untrue and it's maddening as a parent to know the truth. It's maddening as a doctor, to take these phone calls. It's maddening to take all the calls.

Dr. Travis Stork: But you don't know the truth. The point of this whole debate and to talk about autism ... we don't know all the things that, that are going on ... in our environment, there are environmental toxins out there. There are things in our food, and there's so ... many ... possible ... things in our universe that could be making autism ... symptoms worse. And, and to say that that you have the truth and, and ... 99.9% of pediatricians don't is just .. lets, let's find a common ground here where we can all work towards solutions. Vaccines have been studied, and you know what? Lets continue to study vaccines. Lets, study....

Dr. James Sears: Exactly yeah, they've been so looked at, scrutinized, I mean that's the one thing ... of all the things out there that could, it could be ...

J.B. Handley: Two of 36 shots.

Dr. James Sears: They've been looked at so carefully over the last few years though.

Jenny: Two of 36 shots have been looked at.

What was clear from that interview, was that 'The Doctors' could not answer the embarrassing data presented to them but instead chose to ignore it, and whine about how they were being 'antagonized' and 'attacked'. Then they doubled back and kept repeating the same lies that Mr. Handley and Ms. McCarthy had already pointed out to them. The debate can be seen on YouTube: http://www.youtube.com/watch?v=6oEtF8FdqpA

Our food is being poisoned with genetically modified

organisms (GMO) that have been proven to cause cancer.[18] Our children are being injected with autism-causing vaccines.[19] Our water is being poisoned with fluoride that has been shown in Harvard studies to lower IQ scores by 7 points on average in children. And non-organic food has been found to contain 150% more fluoride than fluoridated water in many cases.[20]

Our life savings are being stolen from us by way of the inflationary currency of the unconstitutional Federal Reserve. Our sons are being trained to fire on us and load us into FEMA camps if we refuse to comply with the New World Order.[21] [22] Armed drones were rolled out as a new way to fight terror, but now the drones are here in the U.S., to be used on Americans. Meanwhile the media keeps us distracted with the story of the day. It should be apparent by now that the illness is systemic; *the whole head is sick, and the whole heart is faint. From the sole of the foot even unto the head there is no soundness in it; but wounds, and bruises, and putrifying sores:* Isaiah's prophecy is an old one, but his advice is still the same: *Come now, and let us reason together, saith the Lord* (Isa 1). The problems we are facing require a reasoned examination. Let us set our mind to the task.

Scientific investigation has shown vaccinations to be a causative factor in: sudden infant death syndrome; developmental disorders

---

[18] A French study, published in the peer-reviewed journal *Food and Chemical Toxicology*, found that rats fed a diet of 33 per cent NK603 corn, and others exposed to Roundup, the weed killer used with it, developed tumors, liver damage and digestive problems.

[19] A January 10, 2011 *Mail Online* (UK) article entitled "Scientists fear MMR link to autism" reported a Wake Forest University (USA) medical study that found measles virus in 70 out of 82 autistic children tested. None of them were wild measles strains. They were all vaccine strains, common to MMR shots. http://www.naturalnews.com/031056_autism_vaccines.html#ixzz2ZvgSIKX8

[20] Ethan A. Huff, *Natural News*, Monday, July 22, 2013 http://www.naturalnews. com/041311_fluoride_exposure_foods_consumption.html#ixzz2azsnwHyg

[21] The DHS is now using "no hesitation" targets that look like ordinary Americans with guns, including grandpas, children, pregnant women, and young mothers with children.

[22] A leaked Army document called "Internment and Resettlement Operations" outlines the procedures for "reeducation camps," which will include U.S. citizen inmates.

such as autism, seizures, mental retardation, and hyperactivity; immune deficiency, including Epstein and Barre syndrome; and degenerative disease such as muscular dystrophy, multiple sclerosis, arthritis, leukemia, lupus, and fibromyalgia.[23] [24]

Prevalence of autism in the U.S.:[25]

2013 - **1 in 50 children** (*1 in 29 boys in New Jersey*)
1 in 6 children have a developmental delay
2008 - 1 in 88
1990 - 1 in 200
1980 - 1 in 1000
1960 - 1 in 10,000

In 1986, the U.S. Congress passed the National Childhood Vaccine Injury Act and has awarded over $2 billion in compensation for deaths and injuries caused by vaccines. (For further research see: *National Vaccine Injury Compensation Program. National Vaccine Information Center.*) The February 1981 issue of the *Journal of the American Medical Association* found that 90% of obstetricians and 66% pediatricians refused to take the rubella vaccine.

Vaccines contain toxic ingredients such as thimerosal, aluminum,[26] and monosodium glutamate. Thimerosal is a methyl mercury compound that is highly toxic to the brain.[27]

---

[23] Dr. Sheri Tenpenny, NMA Media Press. *www.sayingnotovaccines.com*

[24] "Our children face the possibility of death or serious long-term adverse effects from mandated vaccines that are not necessary or that have very limited benefits." — Dr Jane Orient, MD, AAPS Executive Director, American Association of Pharmaceutical Scientists.

[25] *Prevalence of Autism Spectrum Disorders - Autism and Developmental Disabilities Monitoring Network.* Centers for Disease Contorl and Prevention (CDC).

[26] "Aluminum (Al), the most commonly used vaccine adjuvant, is a demonstrated neurotoxin and strong immune stimulator. Hence, adjuvant Al has the potential to induce neuroimmune disorders." *Journal of Inorganic Biochemistry,* Volume 105, Issue 11, November 2011, pp. 1489-1499.

[27] "Our best estimates are that thimerosal has contributed to about 75% of these cases [of speech disorders] of neurodevelopmental disorders while the MMR contributed to about 15%." *Journal of American Physicians and Surgeons.* Vol 8, no. 1 Spring 2003.

The state claims the right to force vaccinations on children, and interfere in families in many other ways. It is big business. One practical step to take authority over your own family is to not enter into a contract between your family and the government in the first place. If you are considering marriage, you should watch this video: http://m.youtube.com/?#/watch?v=4tTs5-WtGEI

Apollonius of Tyana called Cæsar Nero a "beast," and clearly he was a beast, metaphorically speaking. But when one stops to closely examine modern America, it becomes plainly obvious that we are living under a tyranny that is in some ways worse than that of Nero's Rome. True, our churches are not being raided by soldiers who demand we say the bishop of Rome is Lord on threat of death, but our lives are threatened in several other ways that Nero never dreamed of. We are being destroyed as a species. 1 in 50 children are now autistic. I don't say that they are born with autism, because I do not believe they are born with it. The leading cause of death in the United States today is modern medicine. Our doctors have been completely brainwashed by the Big-Pharma-controlled medical schools to treat absolutely everything with drugs. This is translated as witchcraft in the Bible (Gk. *pharmakia*, Lat. *pharmacology*) and it is a horrible sin. The human body is able to heal itself if it receives the proper nutrients. Dr. Joel Wallach conducted research conclusively proving that the human body needs to take in 91 different essential nutrients and minerals every day. Yet only a small percentage of what the body needs can be obtained by the ordinary American diet. I highly recommend Dr. Wallach's Youngevity products, which are available at *Infowars.com*. While there is no such thing as a cure-all or fountain of youth, using the Youngevity products and eating only organic foods will greatly improve your health, and considerably reduce your chances of getting cancer.

One inexpensive and very important mineral your body needs is called selenium. ***200 mcg per day reduces your chances of getting breast cancer by more than 80%.*** This was published in 1982 by Dr. Gerhard Schauzer. In 1998, Dr. Larry Clark from the University of Arizona found that 200 mcg of selenium per day reduced prostate cancer by 69%, and colorectal cancer by 64%.

The sad truth is that there is big money in sick people, which is why this kind of information is suppressed. Using *nutrition,* the animal industry has eliminated muscular dystrophy since 1957. Dr. Joel Wallach has been eliminating muscular dystrophy in humans using these same methods. In 2011 he shared his findings with Jerry Lewis, who subsequently shared the findings with the medical committee of the Muscular Dystrophy Association. Lewis was summarily fired, along with all of his supporters. He was not even allowed to make a final farewell appearance at the next 2011 Telethon — the Telethon he himself started in the 1950s.

If you eat meat, you can *reduce your chances of breast cancer by 462%* by simply not overcooking your food. Ie, by eating your steak medium or medium rare, instead of well done. This finding is from a study by the University of South Carolina in 1998, which examined a Harvard health study involving 90,000 nurses, and reexamined how the women in the study cooked their food. Most of the good alternative cancer-treatment clinics have been driven out of business by Big Pharma. There are still some, however. Dr. Michael Danielson of Thousand Oaks, CA, is using among other methods, concentrated vitamin C, a method that won Dr. Linus Pauling a Nobel Prize in 1954.

If we are to have the abundant life that God wants for us (John 10:10) we need to carefully consider these things. If we allow ourselves to be weakened our enemy will easily subjugate and control us. We began this chapter with the devolution of the Julio-Claudian dynasty, which ended with the persecutor of the church, Nero. We are seeing the same downward spiral today. Barack Obama has committed every one of the crimes that Nixon was impeached for.[28] Nixon was caught committing his crimes secretly, but a good argument could be made that Obama has committed his publicly. If we do not hold our leaders accountable they will only become more brazen and dictatorial. This story always ends the same way.

---

[28] http://academic.brooklyn.cuny.edu/history/johnson/rnimparticles.htm

And I turned to see the voice that spake with me, And being turned, I saw seven golden candlesticks;

And in the midst of the seven candlesticks one like unto the Son of man, clothed with a garment down to the foot, and girt about the paps with a golden girdle.

His head and his hairs were white like wool, as white as snow; and his eyes were as a flame of fire;

And his feet like unto fine brass, as if they burned in a furnace; and his voice as the sound of many waters.

And he had in his right hand seven stars: and out of his mouth went a sharp two edged sword: and his countenance was as the sun shineth in his strength.

And when I saw him, I fell at his feet as dead. And he laid his right hand upon me, saying unto me, Fear not: I am the first and the last:

I am he that liveth, and was dead; and behold, I am alive for evermore, Ä•měn; and have the keys of hell and of death.

The Revelation of St John the Divine 1:12–18

In that day the LORD with his sore and great and strong sword shall punish leviathan the piercing serpent, even leviathan that crooked serpent; and he shall slay the dragon that is in the sea.

The Book of the Prophet Isaiah 27:1

DRAGON SLAYER
JESUS CHRIST

The perfect Utopian society. It was within their grasp. Jesus fed the multitudes. He preached with power and cast out devils. He took on the religious machine of that day and confounded them. He made the deaf hear and the blind see. He made the lame leap for joy. He walked on water, and calmed the storm. He raised the dead. It was the hope of the ages, now fulfilled. But alas, it was over. They crucified him and now he was gone. The Roman government still reigned. But then three days later, he rose again, and ascended into heaven. And he promised to return.

Jesus gave us three years to see the power available to us through the Holy Spirit. He gave us his word to show us what we can expect from him and what our future holds. (We win.) He gave his life to redeem us. He showed that in order to rebuild we have to die to ourselves. The cross shows us that circumstances that look like defeats can be tuned into victories. Rome was not built in a day, and neither is God's kingdom. Jesus laid the cornerstone. It is up to us to continue to build, and patiently continue his work.

Jesus has a sword. The sword that goes out of his mouth is his word (Eph 6:17). When Jesus served the last supper, John leaned on his bosom as they ate. But at the end of his life, when John was allowed to behold his King in all his glory, just being in his presence was more than he could withstand. John fell at his feet as dead. While exiled to the isle of Patmos, John was instructed to write what he saw and seal up the canon of Scripture. So what exactly did Jesus mean when he said, *"I am the first and the last: I am he that liveth, and was dead; and behold, I am alive for evermore, Ä•měn; and have the keys of hell and of death."*? Let us meditate on that a little more before we continue; read it at least three more times:

> *. . . I am the first and the last:*
> *I am he that liveth, and was dead; and behold, I am alive for evermore, Ä•měn; and have the keys of hell and of death.*
>
> *The Revelation 1:17b–18*

If this means anything at all, it means that Jesus is somebody who is to be taken seriously. By now a new picture should be forming. The vague images of a defeated and bleeding martyr should be giving way to the clear concept of a victorious, living King. I pray the effigy of the weak and docile pacifist who went about sprinkling rose water is fading, giving way to the living form of a mighty warrior, who is riding triumphantly in his chariot. Jesus has power over the enemy to liberate, and he holds a glorious future in store for all who will trust in, and submit to him.

In order to strip away the layers of glitz and tinsel that have clouded our vision, and break down the images that have distorted his historicity and defaced his beauty, we will first highlight some of his traits and characteristics that are often overlooked. Then we will examine his continuing ministry, and its impact on our world. Let's begin by recognizing the plain truth that he is Jewish:

> *And one of the elders saith unto me, Weep not: behold, the **Lion of the tribe of Juda**, the Root of David, hath prevailed to open the book, and to loose the seven seals thereof.*
>
> *The Revelation 4:5*

He is a member of perhaps the most persecuted people group that has ever existed. Added to this is the fact that he did not come from a wealthy family. It is true that he was from a noble blood line, but the home he was born into was from an area that was not well reputed in Israel. Nazareth was known for its bad element, and little else. Furthermore, he chose to come at a time when Israel was not doing well among the nations. He chose not to come in a time of their glory, like that of Solomon's reign, but a time of their sorrow, when they were under the yoke of the Roman Empire. The time and manner in which he chose to make his appearance demonstrate key foundational Christian principles, among them:

> *Not by might, nor by power, but by my spirit, saith the LORD of hosts.*
>
> *Zechariah 4:6b*

Most of the world's religions teach good moral precepts, but only Christianity provides the means to live them out. That means is the Holy Spirit, which is freely given to all who ask (Luke 11:13). The Christian is not to reform his flesh, but to crucify it. Romans 12:2 says, *And be not conformed to this* [new] *world* [order]*: but be ye transformed* [Gk. *metamorphoō*] *by the renewing of your mind...* When you allow the Holy Spirit to work, you can find true freedom. I personally believe that *freedom* is the most beautiful word in the English language. On the surface it sounds so simple, yet actually attaining freedom is one of the most complex and challenging pursuits there is. To be free you need liberty, which is freedom from oppressive government. You also need personal freedom, which is perhaps even more difficult to attain. Everyone is born a slave to some degree. To sin, if nothing else. Only through faith in the death and resurrection of Jesus Christ can one be liberated from the power of sin and find true freedom.

At its peak, the Roman Empire was home to 120 million people. According to Edward Gibbon, about half of them were slaves.[1]

---

[1] As cited in Sheehan, *The Mind of James Madison*, p 128.

Rome needed tens of thousands of new slaves each year just to operate, to replenish the thousands that died each year through attrition from hard labor. Jesus clearly stated at the beginning of his ministry that he had come to set the captives free (Luke 4:18). Once a person receives Christ as his personal Saviour, he naturally loathes slavery in all of its forms. As Christianity took root in the Roman Empire, attitudes about slavery changed. Eventually the practice ended in Europe. Just as Christianity ended slavery in the ancient world, it was also Christianity that ended slavery in the modern era. Whether they were radicals like John Brown, who used violent methods, or peaceful activists like Frederick Douglas, what almost all abolitionists had in common was some form of Christianity. Truth be told, it was actually the Muslims who first brought the slave trade to Africa. There were three major leaders on three different continents who each made vital contributions to finally ending the African slave trade, and all three were Christians; David Livingstone in Africa, William Wilberforce in England, and Abraham Lincoln in the U.S. But there are many other forms of slavery, besides what immediately comes to mind when one hears the word. There is the slavery of inequality that imprisons people unjustly. There is the slavery of cults and isims that entraps people in spiritual bondage. There is the soft slavery of social injustice where people have no upward mobility, and are trapped in a cycle of poverty that leaves them in a virtual prison. Human trafficking traps people in a vicious cycle of exploitation and slavery.

All this is eclipsed by the over arching issue of the slavery that Jesus sets us free from when we first believe. Somebody can be in bondage to any or all of the things mentioned above, yet if he knows Jesus Christ as his personal Saviour, he is free in is soul. You may not be secure in your person, your house, your papers and effects, but if you are secure in Christ you are free indeed. Early on in his ministry, Jesus explained why he came by quoting Scripture:

The Spirit of the Lord GOD is upon me; because the LORD hath anointed me to preach good tidings unto the meek; he hath sent me to bind up the brokenhearted, to proclaim liberty to the captives, and the opening of the prison to them that are bound;

— Dragon Slayer Jesus Christ, quoting *Isaiah 61:1*

In Chapter V of Mark's Gospel, Jesus encounters a man who was in the worst form of bondage. He was demonically possessed. He no longer had any control over his faculties and he was living in a graveyard. There was nothing the physicians could do to help him. There are many today like this man, who are complete slaves to the god of this world. They are in constraints and have no freedom to move, because the physicians can not help them. But Jesus can! We know of a girl who was strapped to a table in the basement of a mental hospital, whom the doctors had given up on, until a group of Christians asked to be allowed to come in and minister to the patients. After a few weeks, when they had gained the trust of the staff, they were allowed to go down to where the really bad cases were. After only a few brief encounters between the Christians and the demon possessed girl, she was completely delivered and set free.

Jesus is a liberator, but he does not use an army in the traditional sense. His army uses spiritual weapons. He gave us ideas, and his ideas are truth. Jesus said, *If ye continue in my word, then are ye my disciples indeed; And ye shall know the truth, and the truth shall make you free.* (John 8:31, 32)

Once you are free in Christ you are free from the need to sin. You are free from crippling behaviors and thought patterns. You are free from the bondage of false belief systems that make it impossible to make good decisions. You are free to worship and believe on the God who created you in his own image, who suffered and died for you, who is building a mansion for you in heaven, and who is coming back again to rule in glory from the throne of David in Jerusalem. You are free to reach your God-given potential as a servant in his kingdom. (Provided you have the liberty to thrive without harassment and oppression from an unjust government.) This is one of the many problems facing the world today — tyranny.

All the constraints are in place now. It is only a matter of time before the clamp-down. We fought a war to be free from tyranny in the late 18th century, but somewhere along the way we became complacent. We forgot what Jefferson said: The price of liberty is eternal vigilance. See, Jefferson understood the complex nature of freedom. Freedom is not the absence of tyranny. That is how it is often viewed, like cleaning up a room. If you remove the dirt, the room is clean. But freedom requires more than just removing the tyrant. When slavery was ended in the South, some people did not want to leave the plantation. When a lifelong convict is released from prison, oftentimes he does not want to leave. Freedom is something that needs to be created in the minds of people. It is something they need to treasure and be willing to fight for. After it is achieved it needs to be cultivated and maintained.

> My God! How little do my countrymen know what precious blessings they are in possession of, and of which no other people on earth enjoy!
>
> — Thomas Jefferson

Jesus came to this earth during the reign of one of the most brutal and oppressive empires in the history of the world. Although he never attempted to reform the Roman government, his followers changed the world, one individual at a time. His best friend held his local government accountable and Jesus commended him for it.[2] Jesus showed us that true freedom does not mean amassing a lot of wealth so you can do whatever you please.[3] He taught us that true freedom is achieved by breaking out of the mold that this world has forced us into, and serving our Creator, *to will and to do of his good pleasure.*

The Christians changed history. They did it by following simple Christian precepts like telling the truth, submitting to God, and resisting the devil. They did it by preserving and distributing the word of God. This required an army of dedicated believers. During

---

[2] Matthew 11:11.
[3] Luke 12:15–21.

the dark days of the Roman persecutions, copies of the word of God were being burnt, right along with the owners. During the first four hundred years following the death and resurrection of Jesus Christ, the Bible was translated into 500 languages.[4] By the sixth century it had been reduced to one, Latin. Yet there was always a faithful remnant who protected and preserved the word of God, in all of its splendor: Greek, Hebrew, Old Latin (a version which preceded the corrupt Vulgate of Jerome), Syriac, Armenian, Gothic, etc. Then came the Reformation period, when the word of God was finally distributed throughout Europe and became available to the common man. It was at this time that the revolution caught fire again. The dark ages, which were a result of removing the word of God from the hands and hearts of the people, gave way to the Reformation. One of Jesus' names is the Word (Gk. *Logos*). Faithful martyrs such as Huss and Tyndale translated the word of God into the language of the common man. Once new translations were widely circulated, following the invention of movable type by Johannes Gutenberg, the death-grip that the papacy had on Europe was eventually broken. Tyndale's English translation became available in the early 1500s. Around this time Bibles in other languages were also appearing: Luther's German Bible, Olivétan's French Bible, followed by the Reina-Valera Bible in Spanish, the Italian Diodati Bible, etc. By 1806 the Inquisition had ended, at least in its crude medieval form of dungeons and Dominican tribunals. (The Holocaust in Germany was a 20th century Inquisition, as was the bloody massacre in Rwanda. So the persecution continues today in other forms, yet the gospel still prospers.)

> *For he hath looked down from the height of his sanctuary;*
> *from heaven did the LORD behold the earth;*
> *To hear the groaning of the prisoner; to loose those*
> *that are appointed unto death;*
>
> *Psalms 102:19, 20*

---

[4] Brian Barkley, 1997, *The Forbidden Book*, Exploration Films.

While it is true we are all responsible for our own actions, it is equally true that there is a puppet master who is manipulating people behind the scenes. His most effective method in deceiving the world was convincing people that he and his minions do not exist. If Hitler could have convinced the world he did not exist, the Allies would have all stayed home as he steamrolled over Europe, with nobody to oppose him. See, that is the key to stopping any enemy — resistance. In the case of the devil, you will never be able to resist him on your own. You are going to need divine aid. *Submit yourselves therefore to God. Resist the devil, and he will flee from you.* This can be something as simple as resisting the temptation to raid the refrigerator at 2:00 AM. The Bible says, *He that hath no rule over his own spirit is like a city that is broken down, and without walls.* In the ancient world a city's defense was its walls. Without walls an invading army could easily rush in and conquer the city. Likewise there is an army of fallen angels who are at war with every man, woman, and child on this planet. A demon's desire is to possess a human vessel. Without defenses, the enemy can manipulate and control an individual's desires, place thoughts in his head, and lead him to make bad decisions, which in turn lead to bad habits, which in turn lead to bad consequences. The less a person resists, the more susceptible he becomes to this manipulation. In the most extreme cases, we see examples like Adolf Hitler, who was initiated into the secret doctrine of Mme. Blavatsky and practiced occult techniques. He became an extreme paranoid who could not be reasoned with. To those with eyes to see, it is clear that Hitler was not the real enemy. *We wrestle not with flesh and blood.* There was a spirit behind him. Hitler was simply a puppet; he had become a tool in the hand of the devil. It can happen to anyone. How many people espouse anti-Semitism without even knowing why? Not everyone who is deceived by Satan is in a position of power as Hitler was, but the results can be just as devastating to one's personal life as they were for Hitler and those affected by his madness.

Sometimes I wonder if perhaps it would not be such a bad thing if persecution came to America. History proves that persecution makes the church grow. Making something illegal just increases its allure. Second of all, persecution removes one of the biggest barriers to evangelism, hypocrisy. When persecution comes, the gospel is no longer a club. It's rebellion, or more specifically, a revolution. That is exactly what the gospel is — a revolution. A revolution is not a war, but an idea that changes things. Take for example the American Revolutionary War. It is more accurate to call it the American War of Independence. The real revolution took place in the marketplace of ideas, when the idea was popularized that an individual is a free and independent being. He has a God-given autonomy. Those who rule over him derive their just powers from the consent of the governed. These were radical ideas that were new to the world. The colonists understood this philosophy and they liked it. They liked it so much they were willing to fight and die for it. But had it not been for the revolution that changed the thinking of the colonists, the War of Independence would have yielded very different results. America would have only exchanged one dictator for another. Instead of the king of England being their sovereign it would have been the king of America. The colonists had many real-life illustrations and object lessons to show them how the dichotomy between individual freedom and authoritarian rule worked. They had been denied their basic rights and freedoms. Yet, in some ways we are under a much worse form of tyranny than they were. They had been fired on by the king's troops, but so have we. Ruby Ridge and Waco[5] are only a couple of examples. They had suffered the injustice of foreign mercenaries being used against them, but that may happen again too.[6] The idea of the monarchy

---

[5] Much of the American public was convinced through propaganda like the film *In The Line Of Duty* that it was okay to burn the children in the Branch Dividian compound alive, because David Koresh was supposedly a child molester. Well one thing is for sure, nobody will molest them anymore.

[6] http://en.mchs.ru/news/item/434203/ The Russia Emergency Situations Ministry and FEMA have agreed to exchange personnel for "disaster response operations" and to "provide security at mass events" in the U.S. FEMA has denied that the wording of the press release meant what it implied. (They wouldn't lie right?)

was in question now, especially the idea that the king was divinely selected; that his authority was absolute and could not be questioned. This subject will be explored further in Chapter XIII.

Ultimately a King will rule on planet earth; a good King, a just King, a King who will crush his enemies and reign in righteousness. Christianity is a radical idea, every bit as radical as the American Revolution — much more so in fact. One day there will be a great battle, commonly referred to as Armageddon, that will seal the fate of Christ's enemies. This will usher in the millennial reign of Jesus Christ, but the battle itself will only be one small piece of the revolution. The real revolution is taking place right now, as Christ gathers those out of the world who want to be part of his kingdom. It will not go well for those who rebel. We are living in an age of grace, when all are welcome to come to Christ and receive the free gift of everlasting life. When Christ returns for his church however, the grace will be over. There will still be a small seven-year window of opportunity to receive him before his second coming, but that will be a time of hell on earth. Although people will still be able to receive Christ as their personal Saviour after the rapture during the tribulation period, they will be martyred for it. Then after Christ returns it will be time for judgment. At that time Jesus will say,

> But those mine enemies, which would not that I should reign over them, bring hither, and slay them before me.

> *The Gospel According to St. Luke 19:27*

Jesus said, *Whosoever will come after me, let him deny himself, and take up his cross, and follow me.* Jesus' ideas were radical. Here are a few more of the radical statements Jesus made:

> But I say unto you, Love your enemies, bless them that curse you, do good to them that hate you, and pray for them which despitefully use you, and persecute you;

> *The Gospel According to St. Matthew 5:44*

Under the old covenant, the kingdom was taken violently by force (Matt 11:12). But Jesus changed that:

> *But I say unto you, That ye resist not evil: but whosoever shall smite thee on thy right cheek, turn to him the other also.*
>
> *The Gospel According to St. Matthew 5:39*

To become a follower of Jesus is to take a radical path. To take up the cross is to die to self, and deny one's flesh. This is contrary to what the world tells us to do, but this is true Christianity. This does not mean that Christians are to be pacifists, per se. There is a time to fight, and Jesus told his followers that they should arm themselves (Luke 22:36).

The American Revolution would have never worked without Christianity. Consider that France had a revolution about the same time that America did. Their revolution however, was much different than ours, inasmuch as they tried to do it without God. During the reign of terror from 1793–1794, upwards of 40,000 people were accused of counter-revolutionary activities and killed by guillotine. They changed the calendar from a seven-day week to ten days, since the seven-day week came from the Bible. They attempted to divest the culture of any form of Christianity, and the results were disastrous. While the American Revolution was a great success, the French Revolution was a complete failure. The French Revolution changed regimes and drafted new constitutions several times before coming back full circle to complete tyranny when Napoleon was declared emperor in 1804. The American philosophy of good government and religion was summed up like this:

> Men, in a word, must necessarily be controlled either by a power within them or by a power without them; either by the Word of God or by the strong arm of man; either by the Bible or by the bayonet.
>
> — Robert Winthrop, Speaker of the U.S. House of Congress

What Robert Winthrop was pointing out here is that Christians make good citizens. This embodies the American philosophy of good government. When people have Christ in their hearts, they are well behaved. Napoleon expressed his philosophy of good government and religion like this:

> You don't govern men who don't have religion, you
> shoot them.
>
> — Napoleon Bonaparte

Righteousness exalteth a nation: but sin is a reproach to any people (Pr 14:34). When we were a nation that feared God, the United States out produced every other nation in the history of the world, and became a model of freedom and excellence. (I say *became*, because this was a long process, and it had to be fought for.) A God-sent revival can bring back our good name and our moral high-ground, not to mention our prosperity — according to the *NY Times* the U.S. no longer has the richest middle class — but only if we repent as a nation. The problems with our economy and our government are problems that are going to require courage and integrity to tackle. Only hearts and minds that have embraced the truths of the gospel will have the courage and the foresight to take these issues on. From cover to cover, the Bible teaches us to be courageous and to have integrity. Besides, a healthy American system of free individuals is only a means to an end, which is to spread the gospel. The whole reason that our forbearers came to America in the first place was to spread the gospel. This is clearly recorded in the first document that they wrote, the Mayflower Compact:

> Having undertaken *for the Glory of God, and Advancement of the Christian Faith*, and the Honour of our King and Country, a Voyage to plant the first Colony in the northern Parts of Virginia; Do by these Presents, solemnly and mutually, in the Presence of God and one another, covenant and combine ourselves together into a civil Body Politick . . . [Emphasis added.]

They clearly stated in their first public document that their reason for coming to America was for the glory of God and the advancement of the Christian faith. Furthermore, following the Revolution, several states incorporated into their constitutions requirements that those who hold office be Christians, and in most cases Protestant Christians. The only two states not to include the Christian requirement were Virginia and New York. It has been noted by some atheists that Article VI of the Constitution makes these requirements null and void, but this claim is false, as Article VI of the Constitution only applies to those who hold federal office. Some find the Christian underpinnings of our Republic distasteful, but why should we expect those who hold public office to behave in an honorable manner if they do not believe in an afterlife that involves punishments and rewards? Why would we expect such people to act in any way other than in their own self interest, and for their own advancement? Some state's constitutions still have requirements that those who hold public office do at least believe in God, and for good reason. The simple truth is that atheists do not make good public servants. There may be a few exceptions to this but generally that has held to be true.

In days gone by God spoke through prophets, by giving them life experiences that related to future events and God's relationship with them. For example, the prophet Hosea was told to marry a harlot, who continued to be unfaithful to him. It was typical of God's relationship with Israel (and perhaps the church), who had been unfaithful and worshiped idols. Hosea's experience showed him what God experienced. It allowed him to experience the hurt that God felt, being betrayed by his wife, Israel. Israel was an unfaithful wife to God and eventually he issued her a bill of divorce. Just as Hosea took Gomer back and forgave her, eventually God will restore Israel and forgive her (Rom 11:26).

In the New Testament, the church is called the bride of Christ. The same way a man is madly in love with a beautiful bride, Jesus is in love with his church, only much more so.

In the book of Revelation there are letters to seven churches that were in Asia Minor. Besides being seven literal churches, they also represent seven ages in church history. The letter to the last church, Laodicea, represents the last time period in the church age. This period ends with the rapture of the church. This is the period of history in which we are now living, and we did not receive a good report (Rev 3:14-22).

Anyone who has ever been in love with someone who does not return their affection knows how painful it is. If said person refuses to speak to you, it is the loneliest, most painful feeling there is. Almost — there is something even worse, far worse. It is when you are in love with a beautiful woman, and she leaves you for someone who is bad, who has made themselves your enemy. And that is what the church, Christ's beloved, is doing today. Not only is she ignoring the Lord Jesus, effectively giving him the silent treatment by watching filth on the Internet instead of reading the Bible, and sleeping in on Sunday instead of going to church, but she is giving her affection to the very one who tortured and killed him, Satan. (Although Jesus willingly went to the cross, it was Satan who entered Judas and betrayed Jesus to his enemies.) The church follows doctrines of devils and worships idols. Because iniquity abounds, the love of many has waxed cold. The church has become *wretched, and miserable, and poor, and blind, and naked*. (If you cannot see that, follow Jesus' command in Rev 3:18 and anoint your yes with eyesalve, that you may see.) The church is embracing the culture of death, where human life is cheap. The church is worshiping the almighty dollar. Jesus said *Ye cannot serve God and mammon*. (See also I Tim 6:5-11.) The church, Jesus' bride, is running into the arms of Satan, Jesus' arch enemy, and she is completely oblivious to the tremendous amount of pain, heartache, and sorrow it causes Jesus to have to watch it. It is as if a woman was rescued from a violent murder by a courageous husband, who negotiated her release and then took the torture that was intended for her. The husband is tortured before her, and she is set free. But then, instead of running back to her husband, she decides the bad guy is pretty cool, and embraces him instead of her husband! I can only imagine how painful that would be. Perhaps it feels like not being able to breathe, and slowly suffocating, as if the one you love is strangling you to death. That is how I think I would feel anyway. Yet when a man truly loves a woman, he will forgive anything, whatever she has done, if she will only come back. How much more will Jesus forgive his bride if she will only repent?

Thus saith the Lord:

> *I counsel thee to buy of me gold tried in the fire, that thou mayest be rich; and white raiment, that thou mayest be clothed, and that the shame of thy nakedness do not appear; and anoint thine eyes with eyesalve, that thou mayest see.*
>
> ***As many as I love, I rebuke and chasten: be zealous therefore, and repent.***
>
> *Behold, I stand at the door, and knock: if any man hear my voice, and open the door, I will come in to him, and will sup with him, and he with me.*
>
> *To him that overcometh will I grant to sit with me in my throne, even as I also overcame, and am set down with my Father in his throne.*
>
> *He that hath an ear, let him hear what the Spirit saith unto the churches.*
>
> — Dragon Slayer Jesus Christ

Eye hath not seen, nor ear heard, neither have entered into the heart of man, the things which God hath prepared for them that love him. Jesus has given absolutely everything for us. He continues to patiently intercede for us, and freely gives us all things. How can we possibly deny him, when he calls us to repentance?

I believe that above all else, what the Spirit is saying to the church at this time is to prepare, and make ourselves ready to meet the Lord.[7] All of the philosophy and doctrine and good work is meaningless, unless we apply it to ourselves and allow the word of God to transform us.

---

[7] See Rev 19:7.

They came first for the Communists... but I didn't speak up because I wasn't a Communist. Then they came for the Jews... but I didn't speak up because I wasn't a Jew. Then they came for the Unionists... but I didn't speak up because I wasn't a Unionist. Then they came for the Catholics... but I didn't speak up because I was a Protestant. Then they came for me...and by that time... there was no-one left to speak up for me.

— Rev. Martin Niemoller, commenting
on events in Germany 1933-1939

Fear none of those things which thou shalt suffer: behold, the devil shall cast some of you into prison, that ye may be tried; and ye shall have tribulation ten days: be thou faithful unto death, and I will give thee a crown of life.
— Dragon Slayer Jesus Christ

THE BLOOD
OF THE MARTYRS

Since neither Rufus nor Lady Vitellia were drinkers, the wine had them both feeling a little light-headed. The full moon helped torches and lanterns light the streets of the city as they made their way toward Cæsar's Gardens. The warm evening air was perfectly still.

"Rufus you have not been at all yourself this evening. Why are you so distracted?" Lady Vitellia asked. The truth was Rufus did not know. He was not sure if he was just nervous about the question he was preparing to ask, or whether he was distracted by the thoughts of what he had read earlier that day, still dancing around in the back of his head. Or was it . . . *her*.

"You must excuse me for my poor company Lady Vitellia. I promise to make it up to you soon," Rufus replied.

Lady Vitellia stopped, and Rufus followed her lead as they turned to face each other. She took his hand and looking directly into his eyes said, "Perhaps it is time for you to start calling me Sexta, is it not Rufus?" He had indeed been right about her eyes and the effect the full moon had on them. In fact, the effect was so powerful he forgot to use his line. He just stared back into her twinkling eyes, speechless, as he involuntarily took her other hand in his, then kissed her, all the while completely under her spell.

Romans do not normally refer to each other by their first names. Only family members and very close friends do so. Although Sexta had not known Rufus for very long, they both knew what their future held in store for them, and therefore she saw no reason not to speed things up a little. Her forwardness afforded her a little more than she had bargained for. Rufus was no longer distracted. The thoughts of Antonina, the thoughts of the words he had read that burned deep down into his soul, they were all gone now as he savored the taste of Sexta's soft lips. This was what he wanted; there was no longer any confusion about that.

When they finally pulled their lips apart, hands still clasped together, for a moment they just looked into each others eyes, mischievous smiles on their faces. Then Sexta said, "I believe this is a breech of our Roman virtues, Mister Antony."

"Let's not revert back to formalities now Domina," Rufus said, still grinning. "Come, I have a surprise for you." He then let go of her right hand but kept hold of her left as they resumed their course towards the gardens. The box would be right where he left it, hidden in the bushes behind the bench on the side of the walkway, in the center of the gardens. The moonlight highlighted not only her eyes, but her silver necklace as well, showcasing her light complexion. Her fair skin reflected a soft glow from her countenance, slender neck, and shapely shoulders. Rufus felt warm inside. Her hand was warm in his. He liked the refined manner in which Sexta conducted herself. He did not feel like an ordinary pleb when he was with her. For a fleeting moment everything seemed right with the world, but as they neared the gardens, the sounds of a commotion could be heard. The closer they drew the louder it grew. *What was it? Some sort of event? There was nothing on the calendar in the Forum.* Rufus had checked and made sure of that. Then alas, as they made their way into the gardens Rufus could not believe his eyes.

The faces in the crowd did not seem to be in agreement either. As they watched some were enjoying it, but others seemed troubled. "Gods below us — what is going on here?" Rufus said. Sexta turned and asked a fellow Roman, who stood watching with the rest of the crowd.

"They found a group of them meeting under the city. That one there is the ring leader," He replied. He explained it all to Sexta but Rufus did not need any explanation. He knew exactly what was going on. Sexta's hand was still in his but his heart was now departed. As he beheld the burning figures nailed to the crosses, all he could think about was whether one of them might be Antonina. Most were motionless, but fresh ones were still being lit. They writhed and twisted, screaming in pain as the flames leapt into the night air. The crosses formed a line along the side of the Via Portuensis, the Roman road that wound through the gardens. Human torches, covered with pitch and lit while the victim was freshly crucified and still alive. From down the street the sound of horse hooves and chariot wheels on granite could be heard drawing closer. Many cheered as the emperor's chariot came speeding up the road. The emperor was screaming, but what was this? Was he also, *naked?* Now Rufus was beginning to understand. Things were finally making sense to him. It was not the ones who were being crucified who were the criminals. They were not the ones who were insane. This man who Rufus once looked up to as the level-headed leader of the empire, the same one who had charmed Rome with his public performances on the harp; *he* was mad. He halted his chariot in front of the platform where brother Servius knelt with his arms bound behind his back. Nero stepped down from his chariot and strode up onto the platform, then addressed brother Servius.

"Well well well, the light of the world," the emperor said as he looked down at Servius. "Do you wish to recant?" he asked. Servius shook his head. "The cross is going to be uncomfortable to say the least. You need not feel it very long though. The flames will take care of that." Roman soldiers applied pitch to brother Servius's naked body. The emperor then turned to the crowd and screamed, "This is Servius, a ringleader of the rebel Christians caught this evening by Cæsar's Imperial Praetorian Guard! What say ye we do with such an one?"

Some shouted one thing and others another, but it was what Sexta said in almost a whisper that sent a chill down Rufus's spine. "He deserves whatever he gets, cursed rebel." Her hand was still in his but now he wanted to let go. He did not dare though. His heart was melting inside him like hot wax. He knew the chances were good that Antonina was dead. *Antonina*, Rufus thought within himself, *I will find out exactly what you believed that brought you such joy. I will follow it to wherever it is it took you.*

Nero knelt down next to brother Servius and looking into his eyes he said, "I am not without compassion. Indeed, am I not a god? My friend, there is an easy way to avoid this, all you have to do is bow to me, and acknowledge me as Lord. I will release you. It will all be over."

One of the soldiers unsheathed his blade and held it to brother Servius's neck. "Say it man," the soldier said. "Say Cæsar is Lord!"

Looking up at his captor, brother Servius said a silent prayer, then with the loudest preacher's voice he could muster he shouted, "I love Iesus Christus with all my heart, soul and body! *He* is my Lord!" A hush fell over the audience, and all that could be heard was the sound of the soldiers hammering the nails through his wrists and feet. After nailing him to the cross, they then raised it up with ropes until it stood fully erect, then fell into the post hole. Servius let out a gasp of agony as it made a thud. He would not suffer for long though. The last thing that could be heard as the soldier lifted his torch and lit the pitch that was smeared over Servius's body, was brother Servius echoing the words of his Lord, "Father, dear precious Father, please forgive them. They know not what they do."

How many more like Servius would follow after him? Over the next few centuries there would be millions, which would only continue to multiply in the two millennia following the death and resurrection of Jesus Christ. The blood of the martyrs would water the church and keep it alive — keep it alive as it went underground through the years of the Dominican tribunals, being watered by the blood of the martyrs of the Inquisition. The blood of the martyrs would water the church and keep it alive through the years of the Reformation, then later as the blood of missionaries was shed in the furthest corners of the world. The blood of the martyrs would water the church and make it grow behind the Iron Curtain through the years of the Gulags, and behind the Bamboo Curtain of Red China. It would water it during the later rain, behind the veil of the crescent moon, as the sword of Allah devoured God's faithful. How much longer before it happens here in the U.S.? At a recent protest at the Texas State Capitol, as the Christians stood against infanticide the children of Belial chanted, "Hail Satan."[1] Only a God-sent revival and an obedient body of believers can change things and delay the inevitable, prophesied in the book of Revelation.

As for Nero, he climbed back into his chariot, even more crazed than before. "Light of the world are you?! Well you can light Cæsar's Garden!!" And he rode off shrieking into the night.

[1] http://www.youtube.com/watch?v=joFzuM9eiJY

Freedom is still the bonus we receive for knowing the truth. Ye shall know the truth, says Jesus, and the truth shall set you free.

— Dr. Martin Luther King, Jr.

In times of universal deceit, telling the truth is a revolutionary act.

— George Orwell

To this end was I born, and for this cause came I into the world, that I should bear witness unto the truth. Every one that is of the truth heareth my voice.

— Dragon Slayer Jesus Christ

VII

QUID EST VERITAS?

Truth.

Quid est veritas? That is the question that Pontius Pilate asked Jesus Christ before he washed his hands and sentenced him to be crucified. Pilate's insolent question to Jesus revealed a serious flaw in his thinking. Pilate was struggling with his worldview. Your worldview is how you view the world. Ie, how you view the people that live on the earth, and the way they relate to each other as individuals, as communities, as nations, etc. In short, the way you believe the world works. It is very much like your personal philosophy. If you do not formulate these ideas on your own, it will be done for you, perhaps without you even knowing.

Christianity is a faith that is founded on the principle of truth. Definitive, unchanging, unalterable truth. The truth that Christianity is based on is a truth that is independent from human definitions or denials. This was well understood in the first century when Christianity was taking root and throughout most of history. It is still understood by many believers today, especially in the parts of the world where the gospel has been deemed illegal by the powers that be. When being a believer is a matter of life and death, the truth of it is a lot more important. When confessing Christ as Lord could have meant crucifixion, or being thrown to the lions, or being burned alive, it was important to know that what you were dying for was really the truth. Today however, in twenty-first century America, there are no life threatening consequences for confessing Christ publicly. Hence, many people do so without ever giving much thought to whether or not it is really the truth or not. Consequently they never become real Christians. They are Christians in name only, and their faith is shallow at best and meaningless at worst. If you are offended by that statement, you may be one of the people I am referring to.

The world operates on the principle of "show me and I will believe," while Christianity operates on the principle of "believe and I will show you." It may surprise you to know that there actually is definitive verifiable proof that the Bible is God's word, and uniquely different from any other book ever written. Yet, I have found that it does little good to show said proof to someone who has not already decided to accept Christ as his Saviour. It tends to only upset him, as he is confronted with the reality that his convenient excuses for rejecting Christ are no longer valid.

Accepting Christ is not an intellectual exercise. It is a matter of the heart. However, once one makes the heart decision to accept Christ and follow him, he will find an endless supply of evidence testifying to the veracity of the Scriptures. Not only so, but once you begin to understand the truths of Scripture, it eventually becomes apparent that most of what you believed before — i.e. most of what the world believes; believes about the origin of life, the value of life, the history of the world, the foundations of our government, the reasons for our institutions, and in general the way the world works — was a lie. You will probably find that most of what you believed about the church and its history was also a lie. You will find that Christianity has been the cause of everything good that has ever happened in the world since the time of Christ. You will find that the 'Church' operating in the name of Christ, has been the cause of most of the bad in the world ever since it took the mantle of power from pagan Rome. See,

Rome never died, it only changed its naming conventions. They renamed the statues of Venus to Mary. They renamed the statues of Jupiter to Peter. They kept the same pagan traditions and festivals but called them by Christian names.

The Roman goddess of sex and fertility was Venus. Her Mesopotamian counterpart was Ishtar (or Astarte); in Greece they called her Aphrodite. The Romans had two celebrations in April related to Venus: Veneralia, and Vinalia. Hislop records that,

> According to Hyginus, the Egyptian, the learned keeper of the Palantine library at Rome, in the time of Augustus, who was skilled in all the wisdom of his native country: "An egg of wondrous size is said to have fallen from heaven into the river Euphrates. The fish rolled it to the bank, where the doves having settled upon it, and hatched it, out came Venus, who afterwards was called the Syrian Goddess" — that is Astarte. Hence the egg became one of the symbols of Astarte or Easter.[1]

During the winter solstice, the Romans celebrated Saturnalia, and paid homage to Saturn by giving gifts to one another. Going back a little further, the Babylonians celebrated the birth of the son of the queen of heaven on December 25.[2] The people of ancient Israel were reproved by God for worshiping the pagan 'queen of heaven' (Jer 7; 44). When Rome merged Christianity with their pagan traditions in the fourth century AD, Mary became the new 'queen of heaven'. To keep the office of Pontifex Maximus intact, they invented the pope. No where in the Bible do you find a 'pope' or Mary being referred to as a queen. The worship of idols and the glorification of the Pontifex Maximus are still intact to this day. These are just a few of the ways our traditions are influenced by ancient pagan ideas. It goes much deeper than that though. These things are by and large only ceremonial and do not generally affect most Protestants in any significant way. Let's

[1] Hislop, *The Two Babylons* (Neptune, NJ: Loizeaux Brothers, 1959), p. 109.
[2] Ibid, p. 93.

examine some history and science that is a bit more relevant to us and our daily lives.

At one time homeopathic doctors were just as prevalent in the United States as doctors who favored synthetic drugs. Then the AMA, funded by the Rockefeller and Carnegie institutes, succeeded in shutting down all of the homeopathic schools of Medicine. Financiers who saw the profit potential in synthetic drugs and surgery heavily funded medical universities, and the money came with strings attached. Doctors were trained to use prescription drugs instead of proven homeopathic medicine. Drugs are now taught as the answer to everything, when in fact the real key to good health lies in nutrition. Like almost every other important issue facing us today, the founding fathers saw this coming:

> Unless we put medical freedom into the Constitution, the time will come when medicine will organize into an undercover dictatorship and force people, who wish doctors and treatments of their own choice, to submit to only what the dictating outfit offers.
>
> — Dr. Benjamin Rush

Recent studies show that today your odds of getting cancer are more than 38% for women, more than 44% for men. If you want to be on the right side of that statistic you are going to have to take control and make some simple yet highly significant life changes. Consider the following research by the makers of *The World According to Monsanto*:

A recent European Commission report stated, "Avoidance of rBGH dairy products in favor of natural products would be the most practical & immediate dietary intervention to ... (achieve) the goal of preventing cancer." What that means is you are going to have to read the label on your milk. The easiest and safest thing to do is buy organic milk, or raw (unpasteurized) milk if you can find it. The IGF-1 hormone is caused by milk with rBGH (also called rBST), and increases the chance of breast cancer 7X in women. Men are who drink milk containing rBGH are 4X more likely to get prostate cancer. This is how it is produced: Scientists take genes from cows and insert them into ecoli bacteria; the new genetically engineered ecoli then produces the cow's hormone.

Many schools and hospitals in the U.S. have banned milk with rBGH. Countries that have banned rBGH include Canada, Australia, New Zealand, Japan, Israel and all European Union countries. So why is it not banned in the U.S.? Probably because of the fact that a former attorney for big agriculture was in charge of policy at the FDA. Other reasons include the fact that the research on rBGH was rigged, and news coverage was suppressed.[3]

Now that you have been warned about the skyrocketing cancer rates, and the cause of them, what are you going to do about it? Are you going to get a reverse osmosis or good gravity-fed filter to remove the fluoride from your drinking water? (Fluoridated water decreases bone density and increases the risk of bone cancer.)

The wisdom of the day is telling you to cut your breasts off to avoid getting cancer, but would it not it be smarter to just drink organic milk, eat organic food, cut out sugar, take your vitamin C and selenium, magnesium and calcium, along with a good multi-vitamin, and get plenty of sunshine and exercise?

Are you going to stop eating GMO? Will you start eating organic food instead? The inevitable complaint is, 'it's too expensive', but cancer is more expensive. As Christians we need to start taking as good of care of our temples as we do our cars or our lawns. *Know ye not that ye are the temple of God, and that the Spirit of God dwelleth in you?* All of us own (1) human machine. It was issued to us upon our conception. It is valuable — one of our most valuable possessions. We ought to maintain it properly.

It is not enough to just believe these things. You have to act. In order to stay healthy you have to act on your knowledge and eat and behave appropriately. Such is the case with the gospel. It is not enough to just believe. *[T]he devils also believe, and tremble.* Belief

[3] *The World According to Monsanto*, Dir. Marie-Monque Robin, 2008. DVD. For more information go to: http://www.responsibletechnology.org/

must lead to repentance. *For godly sorrow worketh repentance to salvation not to be repented of.* That does not mean you will not make mistakes. Of course you will, but you will not give up.

If we confess our sins, he is faithful and just to forgive us our sins, and to cleanse us from all unrighteousness.

I John 1:9

In John's writings in the Bible (John's Gospel, I John, II John, III John, and the Revelation) the word truth appears in one form or another well over 100 times. John records that Jesus said,

*Howbeit when he, the Spirit of **truth**, is come, he will guide you into all **truth**: for he shall not speak of himself; but whatsoever he shall hear, that shall he speak: and he will shew you things to come.*

John 16:13

The truth is also part of the Christian's armor:

*Stand therefore, having your loins girt about with **truth**, and having on the breastplate of righteousness;*

Ephesians 6:14

The truth is the Christian's top priority. The Christian has no part in lies. My prayer is that all who love the truth will begin their own in-depth research as they read this book, as we will only be scratching the surface of the topics presented. A lover of truth is diligent to verify what she believes. She is not satisfied with mere footnotes. She does not trust *Snopes* to be the arbiter of truth. She questions and confirms everything. The more research one does, the more familiar one becomes with the truth, and the more readily one recognizes the truth when she sees it. Once one realizes just how far-reaching the deception really is, she is confronted with the choice of whether to stay in the matrix, or whether to reject it and embrace reality. When one begins his journey, everything is theoretical, but through carefully studying and obeying God's word, *a posteriori* research builds on *a priori* foundations, forming a strong philosophical fortification. When you come to the realization that the Bible is itself, an *a priori*, you are then a true soldier.

I recall my initial research after first committing my life to Christ in the mid-nineties. I started spending a lot of time at the library and in book stores. I was obsessed with investigating the veracity of the Bible. I quickly learned that there is a wealth of manuscript evidence for the Bible, outstripping the textual evidence for all other ancient writings, by far. Consider for example, everything we know about Socrates is known chiefly through the writings of other philosophers, such as Plato. The oldest manuscripts we have from Plato, which are used to reconstruct Socrates, are written about 1300 years or more after Plato lived. There are only seven copies from this time period, circa 900 AD.

By contrast, we have fragments from the same time period of the New Testament writers. At least one of them may even be from the original document. We have more than 90 papyri. 35 papyri date within about 200 years of the original writings. We have several other manuscripts — cursives, uncials, and lectionaries — that were written anywhere from 300 to 1600 years after the original texts were written by the New Testament authors in the first century. When you add up all the Greek manuscripts you have more than 5200 ancient manuscripts from diverse locations such as Greece, Asia Minor, England, Ireland, Constantinople, Syria, Africa, Gaul, and Southern Italy. The vast majority of these manuscripts agree with one another in their texts, proving their authenticity. (The few that do not agree with the vast majority of manuscripts do not even agree with each other, and only come from one geographic location, Alexandria, proving them to be spurious.) Therefore, the manuscript evidence for the New Testament of the Bible far outweighs the evidence for any other ancient writing.

Then there is the vast amount of archaeological evidence for the Bible. This has been thoroughly examined by several different scholars. Among the most prominent was Nelson Glueck, who uncovered 1500 ancient sites in the Holy Land. He stated, "No archaeological discovery has ever controverted a biblical reference." Another of the world's foremost archeologists, William F Albright, said, "There can be no doubt that archaeology has confirmed the substantial historicity of Old Testament tradition." I recommend that every student of the Bible obtain a copy of *Halley's Bible Handbook* (original blue-cover edition). It is packed with relevant history, archaeological discoveries, and commentary of the Bible. One last scholar I will mention is Sir William Mitchell Ramsay of Oxford University in England. He set out to disprove the historicity of the Book of Acts, but he instead ended up concluding that it was indeed written by Luke himself in the first century, and that Luke was a first-class historian of the highest caliber. In the course of his research, Ramsay became the foremost authority on the history of Asia Minor and a leading New Testament scholar. After Ramsay woke up and realized the Bible was reliable, having proved the authenticity of the Book of Acts, he turned his attention to Paul's epistles. In Ramsay's day, the epistles of Paul were by and large dismissed by the critics as forgeries. After his careful study of the matter, Ramsay decided that all thirteen New Testament letters bearing Paul's name, were indeed written by him. Hebrews is also most likely written by Paul, which would make fourteen. There are several other great scholars whose testimonies we could examine. I will leave it to the reader to conduct his own further study in this area.

Then there is the greatest proof of all, Bible prophecy. Unlike many other holy books, the Bible was not written by just one author. It was written by forty authors over hundreds, perhaps thousands of years. It is very likely that the book of Job was written circa 1900 BC, which would make the authorship of the Bible span about 2000 years. Unlike other religious figures, who showed up unannounced and became self proclaimed prophets or deities, Jesus was foretold from the beginning of time, with several details that would mark not only his birth, but his life, as well as his death and resurrection. The first place in the Bible that foretold the birth of Messiah is in the book of Genesis. It is called the Protoevangelium:

[God said to Satan,] And I will put enmity between thee and the woman, and between thy seed and her seed; it shall bruise thy head, and thou shall bruise his heel.

Genesis 3:15

This verse revealed that mankind would be given a Saviour, and also that he would be born of a virgin. The text says "her" seed, yet the woman possesses the ovum which is fertilized by the seed from the man (*cf* Isa 7:14). It has been calculated by one mathematician that the odds of Jesus fulfilling just eight Messianic prophecies by chance would be 1 in 10^{17}, based on the law of compound probability. Yet there are hundreds of prophecies that foretold the coming of Christ. For instance, he had to come from the tribe of Judah.[4] He had to be born in Bethlehem.[5] He had to come at a specifically appointed time.[6] He had to suffer and die for our sins.[7] These are just a few of the many specific details given in Scripture concerning Messiah.

There is one final area we will look at which authenticates the Bible as God's word. In 2003 I published a book about Bible prophecy called *Where Did all the People GO?* The following is a brief excerpt from Chapter IX.

Is there a divine watermark which sets Scripture apart from every other piece of literature? There are in fact several. We have already mentioned manuscript evidence, prophecy evidence, and touched on archeological evidence, but what about the controversial Bible codes?

Two of the first scholars to investigate the various mathematical phenomena unique to the Hebrew text of the Old Testament, as well as the Greek New Testament were Russian mathematician Ivan Panin, and Czechoslovakian Rabbi, Michael Dov Weissmandl. One such phenomenon is hidden codes known as equidistant letter sequences (ELS's). By counting for example,

---

[4] Genesis 49:10.
[5] Micah 5:2.
[6] Daniel 9:25.
[7] Isaiah 53.

every seventh letter, in the original text, certain words and sentences appear to have been encoded into the Bible. Consider for example this very scholarly and well-documented study on ELS's, published in *Statistical Science*:

The eminent *Statistical Science* journal (August 1994, Volume 9, number 3), published by the Institute of Mathematical Statistics, documented the work of three Israeli professors: Eliyahu Rips of Hebrew University in Jerusalem, along with Doron Witzum and Yoav Rosenberg of Jerusalem College of Technology. They took sixty-six of the most prominent men in Jewish history from the *Encyclopedia of Great Men in Israel*, and then they looked for their names in the book of Genesis. What they found is absolutely amazing — not only their names, but next to their names were the dates they were born, and the dates they died — all encoded in the book of Genesis in ELS's! The probability of these codes occurring by chance is less than 1 in 2,500,000,000. The editor of *Statistical Science* stated, "Our referees were baffled: their prior beliefs made them think that the book of Genesis could not possibly contain references to modern day individuals, yet when the authors carried out additional analyses and checks the effects persisted." Thus, objective scientists who lack the emotional bias that other writers and researchers in this area perhaps may have do not repudiate the presence of supernatural codes in the Bible's text. The study was also published in the respected *Journal of the Royal Statistical Society* in 1988.

Perhaps even more fascinating, if not more applicable to English speaking people, is the fact that the codes only appeared when using the traditional Masoretic Text used to translate the King James Version of the Bible. When the professors looked for the codes using the Samaritan Pentateuch, which new versions rely on, the codes were "completely absent." Besides using the Samaritan Pentateuch, the researchers said they also looked for the codes in a Hebrew translation of Tolstoy's *War and Peace*, and found none.[8]

I would like to express my sincere gratitude to Gail Riplinger and AV Publications for publicizing this information and supplying me with facsimiles of the *Statistical Science* journal and related articles.

That brings us to the subject of the different English versions of the Bible. I highly recommend you study the *Authorized King James Version* of the Bible, especially for memorization of Bible verses. The most common objection to this suggestion is that it is too hard to understand. Even if that were true, and I have serious doubts about that, it is not a Christian attitude to take, especially about something as important as God's word. A Christian should never 'take the easy way out', just because it is easy. I am a big fan of working smarter and not harder, but there are a lot of situations where that philosophy simply does not apply. In many areas of life, the right way is the hard way. The KJV is the only English version that rightly says in Revelation 13 that the mark of the beast will be *in* the right hand and *in* the forehead. All of the new versions say "on" the right hand or "on" the forehead, which opens the door to a deceptive invitation to take the mark but refuse the tattoo, or some other possible scenario. In Chapter XIV, where the Bible says the tribulation saints will be marked with the Father's name written in their foreheads, the new versions add another name in that verse, to make it appear as if they should have two different names in their foreheads. Again, this appears to be an attempt by the enemy to deceive people into taking the mark of the beast in a moment of weakness. Undoubtably some will accuse me of splitting hairs and making a big deal out of nothing by pointing this out. I would ask them to heed the final warning of Jesus in Revelation 22:

---

8 [California] *Modesto Bee*, Saturday, November 4, 1995, p. G-1. The unique nature of the Masoretic Text is even more fascinating considering the fact that the Masoretic Text contains vowels and spaces which were not in the original text. The original text contained no spaces and the vowels were implied. It appears that the word of God is literally *"purified seven times"* (Ps 12:6), and that God's hand is upon it to preserve it, just as He promised (Ps 12:7). The study published in *Statistical Science* also gained the attention of Jeffrey Satinover of *Bible Review* (October, 1995), and David Briggs of the Associated Press (Baton Rouge, LA, November 4, 1995).

> *For I testify unto every man that heareth the words of the prophecy of this book,* **If any man shall add unto these things, God shall add unto him the plagues that are written in this book:**
> **And if any man shall take away from the words of the book of this prophecy, God shall take away his part out of the book of life,** *and out of the holy city, and from the things which are written in this book.*
>
> The Revelation 22:18, 19

Incidentally, there are similar numeric phenomena, just as fascinating as the ELS's of the Old Testament Hebrew text, that validate the Greek *Textus Receptus* (Received Text), or Majority Text, that the New Testament of the KJV is translated from. Likewise, these phenomena are absent in the Minority Text manuscripts that the new versions are translated from. The phenomena are based on patterns of seven that can be seen in the Greek text.[9] For a little information on this subject, go to: www.khouse.org/articles/2000/201/ or see *Cosmic Codes*, by Chuck Missler (Koinania House, 1999).

Volumes have been written on the superiority of the *Textus Receptus* and the KVJ. I refer the reader to AV Publications, where scores of volumes by scholars who thoroughly investigated this subject can be found.

Ivan Panin said, "I used to doubt certain parts of the Bible, now I just doubt my understanding of the Bible." That is the right way to look at Scripture. It's like an algebra problem. When you do not get it right the first time, you do not say there is an error in the text book. You keep working on it until you figure it

---

[9] Seven is the number of completion (Gen 2:2). Eg, there are seven days in a week, seven colors in a rainbow, and seven notes in a musical scale. God often uses *seven* as his signet. This unlocks the mystery behind Psalm 90:4 and II Peter 3:8. In context, these verses refer to the second coming; just as God rested on the seventh day, the earth is scheduled for a seventh millennium of rest. God created the sun on the fourth day, a type of Christ (Ps 19:5), prefiguring his advent in the 4000th year (*cf* Mal 4:2).

out. We have only scratched the surface of all the verifiable proof there is for the accuracy of Scripture. God promised he would preserve his word in Psalm 12. It does not say God crossed his fingers and hoped that men would do a good job in preserving his word. God said he himself would preserve it. Jesus reiterated this promise in Luke 21:33 and John 10:35. Of course there is also the evidence of the countless lives that have been changed by the promises of the Bible. Each of these changed lives is a testimony to the reliability of Scripture.

We live in a day and age when many have become convinced that there is no such thing as truth. People like to say "everybody has an opinion," to excuse themselves from taking responsibility and finding out the truth. It is basically discrediting the witness. It is an old trick that every trial lawyer knows, but it also posits a false premise, namely that there is no such thing as truth. If that is true, that there is really no such thing as truth, then we should get rid of our court system and erase all our laws. We should let people do whatever they feel is right for them. Try to imagine what kind of a society that would be. Somebody you know is murdered. You see the crime committed. But you cannot prove it, because the perpetrator denies it. His truth is different than yours. Your truth does not work for him. Our legal system is based on the principle that there is such a thing as truth, and if we diligently search for the truth, we can find it. What if we were to truly operate as if there was no truth? We could all do whatever we wanted, according to our own truth. One could say, I do not want to obey the traffic signals because I do not believe in them. You can imagine the results. Therefore, there is such a thing as truth, and to diligently search for that truth is arguably the most important pursuit there is. Whatever it is you are trying to achieve, whether you are a carpenter or a postman, a musician or a welder, the truth is essential to your success. If you are an engineer for example, you need true data to build your bridge, your automobile or rocket, whatever the case may be. If you have bad data the results can be catastrophic. If you are a financial advisor, the truth is all that you can use. False data is of no use to anyone (except the enemy — deceit is his weapon).

Therefore to be informed you are going to have to stop relying on the mainstream media (MSM). The MSM is dying and becoming more irrelevant each day. For example, *The New York Times* bought the *Boston Globe* in 1993 for $1.1 billion, then sold it in 2013 for a mere $70 million. That is a 93% loss, not counting inflation. The historic *Washington Post* sold days later for a mere $250 million. That's **$65 million less** than the **Huffinton Post**, the cheap *Washington Post* knock-off, sold for in 2011. When journalists caved into political correctness and started selling opinion as investigative journalism, they reaped what they sowed.

There is still some good reporting going on in the MSM but it is much wiser to glean from news services that post stories from a variety of different sources, like *Drudgereport.com*, *Infowars.com*, *WND.com*, or *Newsmax.com*. If you have a left leaning political preference, go to *larouchepac.com* and *paulcraigroberts.org*. When you truly understand freedom you know that the left-right paradigm is no longer a valid mechanism; it now serves only to divide and conquer. The mainstream media would more accurately be called the state-run ministry of propaganda. Eg, MSNBC receives state subsidies. Drew Johnson, a page editor for *The Chattanooga Times Free Press,* was axed after he published an article titled, "Take your jobs plan and shove it, Mr. President: Your policies have harmed Chattanooga enough." Commenting on his dismissal Johnson tweeted, "I just became the first person in the history of newspapers to be fired for writing a paper's most-read article."

And then there is the fact that when you rely only on the MSM you are always late in getting the story, if you get it at all. One week after the Benghazi incident where four Americans including a U.S. ambassador were killed, *Infowars* reported that Benghazi was a cover up of a black operation which was transferring weapons to al-Qaeda Syrian rebels. A year later the truth started coming out in the MSM. On August 1, 2013, CNN's Jake Tapper reported that there were 'dozens' of CIA operatives on the ground near the consulate in Benghazi at the time of the incident, and they have been subjected to threats and monthly polygraph tests to keep them from leaking information about what really happened. Tapper also reported on 'speculation' in Washington that the CIA was involved in transferring surface to air missiles from Libya through Turkey to the rebels in Syria. The report stated that the CIA refused to comment. Then Greta Van Susteren of Fox News interviewed Rep. Trey Gowdy (R-SC), who disclosed that the Obama Administration has been busy relocating and changing the names of the Benghazi survivors, ie the firsthand material witnesses. The same day, August 1, as these stories were being reported, the Obama Administration issued a terror alert, and announced it would be closing all of the foreign embassies throughout the Muslim world the following Sunday — a blatant red herring to distract people from the media coverage emerging around Benghazi. (The White House has gone on to call Benghazi a "phoney scandal.") On Aug 2, the *London Telegraph* published the headline, CIA 'running arms smuggling team in Benghazi when consulate was attacked'.[10] Yet the top story in the 'reliable' American MSM was the closing of the embassies in Muslim countries on Sunday; not a clandestine gun-running operation to militant al-Qaeda rebels in Syria, which circumvented Congress (which has the exclusive power over war under Article I, Section 8 of the U.S. Constitution); not how the White House tried to cover up the operation by blaming it on a hack B-movie trailer on the Internet; not how Fox News had reported on October 25, 2012 that Russian-made anti-aircraft weapons called MANPADS were received in the Turkish port of Iskenderun just 35 miles from the Syrian border, 5 days prior to the Benghazi attack. The nearer we get to the return of Jesus Christ, the more the news will cease to exist and be nothing more than state-run propaganda.

I believe it is the duty of the church to tell the truth, however controversial said truth is. When the church marries the state, as is happening in America today, the pulpit is compromised and the

---

[10] http://www.telegraph.co.uk/news/worldnews/africaandindianocean/libya/10218288/CIA-running-arms-smuggling-team-in-Benghazi-when-consulate-was-attacked.html

truth is the first casualty. It happened in Europe, which was why the Pilgrims came to America. They wanted to be free to worship God without any government intervention or entanglements. This has always been the way religion has operated in America, and is clearly spelled out in the **First** Amendment to the Constitution:

AMENDMENT I

Congress shall make no law respecting an establishment of religion, or prohibiting the free exercise thereof; or abridging the freedom of speech, or of the press; or the right of the people peaceably to assemble, and to petition the Government for a redress of grievances.

The 501 C3 system of tax exemption was a way to remove this freedom given to the church. There are specific rules in the contract that prohibit the church from speaking on certain subjects forbidden by the government. Then George W Bush enacted his Faith-Based Initiative, which further solidified the new relationship between church and state, by funneling federal funds into the churches that wanted government contracts. Step one was taking away the churches' tax exempt status if they breached their contracts. Step two was offering the churches federal funding. But even before Bush took office in 2001, plans had been made to deal with churches who refused to cooperate with the emerging New World Order. In 1998, under the Clinton Administration and the Janet Reno Justice Department, a plan classified as Top Secret, called Operation D, was devised to control all the uncooperative churches in the United States. To rein in these churches the state would use:

1. The financial power of the IRS.
2. International powers using the treaties of the UN.
3. The investigative and intelligence forces of the FBI, CIA and NSA.
4. The judicial and prosecuturial assets of the of the Justice Department and federal courts.
5. Congressional legislation.

The Biblical Law Center (BLC) was started by Baptist pastor Greg Dixon, to educate and equip churches on how to resist government overreach. Pastor Dixon, who worked closely with Jerry Falwell in founding the Moral Majority, started the BLC because after he decided he wanted to get out of his 501 C3 contract, and stopped collecting taxes from the ministers in his church, his church was seized by the federal government in 2001. Seizing Illinois Temple Baptist was one of the first acts of the Bush Administration. It was the first time in the history of the United States that a church was seized by the federal government.

In short, the government is using the power of the purse to remove the free speech of the church. If the church does not resist, what will stop us from becoming like China, where the church is monitored by the state and dissent against state policy is punishable by prison sentences? What will stop us from becoming like Hitler's Germany, where the church was silent as the Third Reich was running roughshod over Europe and throwing millions of people into concentration camps? We **must not** let money control us. The Bible says, *Resist the devil, and he will flee from you.* And again, *Ye have not yet resisted unto blood, striving against sin.* The Bible says *the time is come that Judgement must begin at the house of God.* We must speak the truth and not fear man. The roll of the church in speaking truth on the issues of the day will be further developed in Chapter XIII.

We began this chapter with Pilate's question to Jesus, *What is truth?* According to the church historian, Pilate committed suicide and died in his sins. He missed the most important truth there is; the essence of truth itself, that *the truth* is a person:

> *I am the way, the **truth**, and the life: no man cometh unto the Father, but by me.*
> — Dragon Slayer Jesus Christ

The only thing necessary for evil to triumph is for good men to do nothing.

— Edmond Burke, Irish Statesman, 1729-1797

And the light shineth in darkness; and the darkness comprehended it not.

The Gospel According to St. John 1:5

VIII

A LIGHT
IN THE DARKNESS

ife, like death, is as untamable and unpredictable as it
is unmerciful. Although he had never considered himself
a poet, Rufus now found himself waxing eloquent in his
thoughts as he wallowed in his self pity. He wondered
about this and decided it must be the wine. *Alas, the play is over,
and now the curtain is drawn across the stage of those players
who dared to have their own minds. What profit is there in a life
lived with purpose? What reward have those who want something
more than vanity from this wicked world? Oh Antonina, are you
now just another martyr who has gone and left me alone in this
Babylon we call Rome?*

Rufus had kept his guard up as he walked Sexta back to her
parents' house, but now on his way home he had no reason to act
any other way than how he felt. Rufus walked back to the gardens
to retrieve his box, and saw that the crosses were still burning. He
had never felt so low. Now the world he once saw as his oyster
was his master, and a cruel master it was. He no longer wanted to
marry Sexta, but what choice did he have? He had already given
his fortune to her father for her hand in marriage.

Everything in his shop looked the same as he left it. Ordinarily he would have cleaned up but tonight he felt too low to do any more labor. He was exhausted. All he wanted to do was crawl into bed and sleep, but there was something else that was pulling him in another direction. Although he was drained, instead of heading for his bedroom he climbed up into the loft and pulled out the scroll he had hidden in the fleece. He felt a warm virtue surge through him as he unrolled it. He knew in his heart that he was no longer the same. The words had somehow changed him. Then the sound of the back door startled him and woke him out of his daze. He was holding an illegal document. He was an enemy of the State. What if Cadmus had confessed he had an illegal document under duress? What if Cadmus had implicated him as having it in his possession? His blood ran cold as he slipped the roll back into the sack and quietly peered over the edge of the loft.

"CADMUS! ANTONINA!!! I thought you were both dead!" Rufus ran back to the sack to retrieve his precious contraband and then raced down the ladder to embrace them both at once. He had never been so happy to see anyone in his entire life. He was so overjoyed he kissed them both, then quickly peered outside to see if anyone may be following them.

"We made sure we were not followed," Cadmus said.

"We have gone in circles and made our way down every road in Rome just to be safe," Antonina added. "Is that the scroll that Cadmus was telling me about you have there?" Antonina asked Rufus.

"Yes it is. I've read it and, well, I think I . . . " Rufus did not quite know how to say what he wanted to say.

"You think you want to be a Christian?" Antonina asked.

"I think I already am one," Rufus said. "I've never read anything like this before in my life. Then when I saw the Christians being burned tonight in the gardens everything changed. I knew I had changed. I thought maybe you had gotten caught and were burning on one of those crosses. I was spying on you and Cadmus earlier today and I figured you two were going to some illegal meeting together tonight."

"You were right," Antonina said. "We were the only ones who escaped."

As the three continued to discuss the evening's events, Cadmus began to ask Rufus some probing questions about his newfound faith. Rufus soon became aware that his new servant was every bit as educated as he was, and he possessed a high degree of spiritual maturity as well. Rufus found himself looking at Cadmus as a counselor and not a servant. He told Cadmus and Antonina about Sexta and his dilemma. Cadmus told him that it would be a big mistake to marry someone who did not believe in Iesus Christus. He explained that to believers marriage was much more than the civil union that most Romans viewed it as. He explained to Rufus that if he was going to follow Christus he would have to accept his will in every aspect of his life, not just when it was convenient. When Rufus asked, "Well what about all the money I am going to lose?" Cadmus responded by telling him a story about a king who had hired mercenaries to help him fight the army of Seir.

"There was a king in Judah, named Amaziah, who had hired an hundred thousand mighty men of valor out of the northern kingdom of Israel, to help him to go to battle against the kingdom of Seir. But a man of God came to him, and told him that God was not with the mercenaries he hired. Amaziah had already given the mercenaries an hundred talents of silver. The man of God told Amaziah that God was able to give him much more than this, if he faithfully obeyed and sent the mercenaries back home. As a result, Amaziah won the battle without them, it was an overwhelming victory."

"Did he get his money back?" Rufus asked.

"Well no, actually he backslid and worshiped the pagan gods of Seir, which he took from them after the battle. Then he got cocky and picked a fight with the same army he had previously fired. They crushed him and stole all the treasure he had looted from the Edomites."

"Oh," Rufus replied.

"The point, Master Rufus, is that if you want to follow Christus it is going to be on his terms; this is not a game," Cadmus said.

Rufus did not have to think about it. He knew in his heart that what he had found was worth far more than what he had given Sexta's father. "I am willing to follow Iesus wherever he leads," he said. "Is there any reason I cannot be baptized?"

"If you believe with all your heart, no reason at all. I can baptize you now," Cadmus said.

"I believe Iesus Christus is the Son of God," Rufus replied. And with that the three rose in one accord, and made their way out behind the workshop where there was a bath of water, large enough to submerge Rufus in the name of the Father, and of the Son, and of the Holy Spirit.

"Buried with Iesus in his death, and raised with him in newness of life," Cadmus said, as he lifted Rufus up out of the water.

The water still beading from his beaming countenance, Rufus could feel the Spirit welling up inside him. He knew something had been changed inside of him. He felt different. He felt free. He felt alive like never before.

Then was Cadmus moved in the Spirit, and he found words flowing out of his mouth, before he even thought to speak them. "Rufus, you have been bought with a price and you are no longer your own. You belong to Christus. This life will buffet you but you must stand strong in the evil day, and be faithful unto death. Always remember, that Christus is your Master, not Paul, not Apollos, but the Lord Iesus Christus. He will never leave you or forsake you. To die to self and become servant of all, is where your journey begins and ends."

Rufus felt so overcome that he began to pray, but to his surprise it was not Latin that came out his mouth, but some dialect unknown to him. It startled him and he stopped.

"Don't stop," Antonina said. "It looks like Iesus gave you a birthday gift. I've been praying to speak in tongues ever since I became a Christian."

Rufus continued and the unknown tongue came easier for him. It seemed to flow out without any effort at all.

"Why does Rufus receive the gift of tongues just like that and after all my prayers and faithful service I still don't have it?" Antonina asked Cadmus.

"I don't know," Cadmus said. "But this I do know; when I was in Corinth, in his first letter to us, Paul gave us detailed instructions concerning the operation of the gifts, and he made it clear that we all receive different gifts, but not all speak in tongues. I would not feel bad about it Antonina. According to Paul there are better gifts to have than an unknown tongue."

"Like what?" Antonina asked.

"Paul listed several gifts in his letter: the word of wisdom; the word of knowledge; faith, he said, was a spiritual gift; miracles; prophecy; discerning of spirits; besides tongues, there is also the interpretation of tongues; there are people like Paul who are gifted to be apostles; there are those who are gifted to be prophets; after that, there are those who are teachers of the word; then those who can work miracles; then others who have been gifted to be administrators; some have the gift of helps, and lastly is listed the gift of tongues. After he listed the gifts, he talked about what he called the 'more excellent way' of love. He said that although he spoke with tongues of men and of angels, if he did not have love, he was merely a sounding brass or a tinkling symbol."

"Who is Paul?" Rufus asked.

"Paul is our apostle. He is our teacher," Cadmus replied. "John Mark gave me instructions to by all means find him when I am come to Rome. He wanted Paul to read his personal account of the gospel."

"That will be very dangerous," Antonina said. "When I met Paul he was ministering out of his own hired house, but now he has been accused of arson, and arrested on conspiracy charges as an enemy of the State. Now that Cæsar has begun persecuting us we will be found out for sure if we visit him."

"I want to meet this man," Rufus said.

Cadmus nodded in agreement. "I think we should pray and ask the Lord to open a door for us to go to him, but first let us take another look at Mark's Gospel. Then we will pray and ask God to give us an audience with the apostle Paul."

Reading by candlelight inside the workshop, the three brethren prayed together and hungrily devoured the treasured parchment that Cadmus had brought from Jerusalem. Cadmus and Rufus both read easily. Antonina read slowly. Cadmus and Rufus took turns helping her learn to read Greek. Some passages they read over and over, committing them to memory. Eg:

And when he had called the people unto him with his disciples also, he said unto them, Whosoever will come after me, let him deny himself, and take up his cross, and follow me.

For whosoever will save his life shall lose it; but whosoever shall lose his life for my sake and the gospel's, the same shall save it.

For what shall it profit a man, if he shall gain the whole world, and lose his own soul?

Before they knew it, the night hours had passed. The rooster crowed as the sun began to rise. Antonina wondered if she would get in trouble. She had never stayed out all night before. If she was lucky her master would be too drunk or too busy to notice. This was something that she needed to pray about.

If ever a time should come, when vain and aspiring men shall possess the highest seats in government, our country will stand in need of its experienced patriots to prevent its ruin.

— Samuel Adams

Beloved, believe not every spirit, but try the spirits whether they are of God: because many false prophets are gone out into the world.

The First Epistle General of John 4:1

IX

CONSTANTINE
THE GREAT

Constantine shocked the world when he declared, "I am a Christian!"

Constantine was the son of an emperor. Consequently, he felt he was the rightful heir to the throne. Through a series of military victories over his rivals, he was poised to become the next emperor. On October 28th, in 312 AD, he faced Maxentius on the battlefield. Constantine and his troops were outnumbered. At the stone Milvian Bridge on the Tiber River, Constantine had a vision. According to tradition, he beheld the sign of the cross in the sky, and the words "in this sign, conquer." Constantine defeated Maxentius, and converted to Christianity, based on his vision. He fixed the sign of the cross on the shields of his soldiers and baptized them. (Of course this did not make them Christians. It just made them wet.) He went on to stop the persecution of Christians and reorganize the empire. In 313 AD he issued the Edict of Milan, thereby legalizing Christianity. Assuming the title of Pontifex Maximus, he became the head of the State Church in the Roman Empire, as well as the head of the pagan temples.

Constantine knew what the politicians of today know. That the best thing to do when you have a grass-roots movement that threatens your power is to co-opt it so you can control it. The Republicans did it with the Tea Party and the Democrats did it with the Occupy Wall Street movement. (The Tea Party, for example, was actually started by Alex Jones and Ron Paul. It was neither Republican nor Democratic. It was made up of people across the political spectrum who were against the expansion of government that is squelching civil liberties and raising taxes.) Constantine did it with the church. The new religion that arose out of Constantine's 'conversion' was an establishment attempt to control what it could not kill. The pagan holidays were merged into Christianity. Confession booths, prayer beads, a celibate priesthood, each of which were pagan and originated from Babylon (and found nowhere in Scripture), were amalgamated into Christianity. The old Roman way of using the priesthood to augur the decisions of the empire was still intact.[1] Although Constantine claimed to be a Christian he refused to be baptized. In 337 AD, as he was dying, Constantine was baptized on his deathbed, which was displayed publicly. He was arrayed in his royal robes for the ceremony. It was suspected that by the time the water was sprinkled, he was already a corpse. Constantine's State Church would eventually give birth to a leviathan that would be much more oppressive and tyrannical than pagan Rome ever hoped to be — the Holy Roman Empire.

The modern day parallels are so well hidden that it is easy to miss them. The Christians were awake in the nineties. I recall sitting in a congregation of around 2000, in a normal Wednesday-night Bible study, as the speaker would calmly discuss the Clinton dead list. Americans were not yet afraid to tell the truth. The gun prohibitions of the nineties had awakened many non-Christians to the threat to our Constitution. An unprecedented slew of scandals (Chinagate, Filegate, Whitewater, Mena AR, Travelgate, Vince Foster, Paula Jones, Jennifer Flowers, Monica Lewinsky, etc.) had many seriously wondering if Clinton would be our last

[1] Eg, Pope Gregory compared the Church to the sun [Jesus in biblical typology, Ps 19, Mal 4] and the State to the moon which reflects the light of the sun. See Schaff, *History of the Christian Church*, Vol V, (Grand Rapids, MI, Eerdmans Publications, 1907), pp. 28–32.

president. Although Clinton claimed to be a Christian the church was not convinced. Then after the age of Clinton, the Christians breathed a sigh of relief when the next president, George W. Bush declared he was a Christian. Although it may be a bit of a stretch to compare Bush to Constantine, Bush did something similar to Constantine when he announced the fusion of the federal government with faith-based organizations. This went virtually unnoticed by the general public.

Because their president was a Christian, the church did not question the wars in Iraq and Afghanistan, or the rise of the police state. September 11 had clouded our vision. However, the process of tearing down the old world to make way for the new one had begun long before September of 2001.

By the time George Bush took office in 2001, the vestiges of our once great Republic were straining under the heavy burden of the new plutocracy. With the introduction of the Patriot Act following 9/11, the architects of the New World Order had succeeded in dismantling the foundation of the Republic with the stroke of a pen. Those of us who received mail and solicitations for support from the office of John Ashcroft in the 90s, to help him with legislation protecting privacy and civil liberties, watched in disbelief as he used his authority as attorney general to ram the Patriot Act through Congress. What is blatantly obvious now, is that the two-party system is a facade. Barack Obama continued all of the same unconstitutional policies Bush had implemented: the bailouts, the wars of aggression, continuation of the Patriot Act (and going even farther with the NDAA), appointing a Goldman Sachs executive as Secretary of the Treasury, etc. — and also claiming to be a Christian. What has been in the planning stages for years, is now in your face. The careful planning of the New World Order was written about in 1966 by Bill Clinton's mentor, the late Dr. Carroll Quigley:

> There does exist, and has existed for a generation, an . . . international network which operates to some extent in the way the radical Right believe the Communists act. In fact, this

network, which we may identify as the Round Table Groups, have no aversion to cooperating with the Communists or any other group, and frequently do so. I know of the operation of this network because I have studied it for twenty years and was permitted for two years in the early 1960s, to examine its papers and secret records. I have no aversion to it, or to most of its aims and have, for most of my life, been close to it and many of its instruments. I have objected, both in the past and recently, to a few of its policies . . . but in general my chief difference of opinion is that it wishes to remain unknown, and I believe that its role in history is significant enough to be known.[2]

— Carroll Quigley, *Tragedy and Hope*

Following the introduction of the Patriot Act, the fusion centers were set up. These join local police together with federal government. Then the FEMA camps were set up. These are concentration camps that will inevitably be used to intern political dissidents. Then the clergy were recruited. Clergy Response teams now work in tandem with FEMA and the federal government, telling their congregants they must obey the government, even if that means going to a FEMA camp. (See Chapter XIII.) This was tested during Hurricane Katrina, resurrecting Constantine's strange relationship between church and state.

In order to achieve their goals, the architects of the New World Order would have to orchestrate a grand illusion. They would have to create a false reality that would be presented to the unwitting public, and lull them to sleep as their rights were being taken from them. For lack of a better term, we will call this process 'mind control'. Throughout most of history mind control was handled very much in the same way that it was in the Roman republic. The Catholic Church, operating as God's representative on earth, with

[2] *Tragedy and Hope* (Macmillan, 1966), p. 950, as cited in Des Griffin, *Forth Reich of the Rich* (Clackamas OR: Emissary Publications, 1976), p.15.

the pope as the Vicar of Christ, demanded absolute devotion and submission from all subjects throughout the Holy Roman Empire. Just as with the pre-Christian Roman Empire, dissidents were punished with torture and death. The Bible was included in the *Index Librorum Prohibitorum,* the list of forbidden books. No free thought of any kind was allowed.

With the proliferation of the Bible, and the birth of America, things changed. The Inquisition officially ended in 1806 AD. Freedom was spreading. People were becoming much less superstitious, and much more willing to challenge authority. Although the early United States were religious, even in government, the idea that adherence to religion could somehow be mandated was absolutely foreign to the new Republic. Americans believed in freedom of conscience above all. While Christianity was largely accepted as the one true philosophy,[3] it was well understood that believing in Christianity was a voluntary act of the will and could not be forced on anyone. It was also understood that those who rejected Christianity were allowed to worship whatever god they pleased, or no god at all if they so chose. At the time of the founding of the Republic, America was vastly Protestant, with only about 2% being Roman

---

[3] For example, Benjamin Rush began his 1830 pamphlet, A Defense of the Use of the Bible in Schools as follows:

Dear Sir:

It is now several months since I promised to give you my reasons for preferring the Bible as a schoolbook to all other compositions. Before I state my arguments, I shall assume the five following propositions:

I . **That Christianity is the only true and perfect religion**; and that in proportion as mankind adopt its principles and obey its precepts they will be wise and happy.

2. That a better knowledge of this religion is to be acquired by reading the Bible than in any other way.

3. That the Bible contains more knowledge necessary to man in his present state than any other book in the world.

4. That knowledge is most durable, and religious instruction most useful, when imparted in early life.

5. That the Bible, when not read in schools, is seldom read in any subsequent period of life. [Emphasis added.]

Catholic. With the Inquisition fresh in everyone's mind, it was well understood that Catholicism was antithetical to freedom. This sentiment continued into the 20th century, and can be easily seen by examining books and encyclopedias from that era. In short, America created a radical shift in thinking from that of the Old World. In Europe, allegiance was made to a king who was the head of the Protestant Church, or the pope, who was the head of the Catholic Church. In America, there was no central figure who represented the head of the church, or required any special allegiance. But these ways persisted in Europe. In 1933, an extension of the Holy Roman Empire emerged, with the full backing of the pope. It was known as the Third Reich. The civil leader of this movement was Adolf Hitler. The religious leader of this movement was Pope Pius XI. In 1933, Germany and Italy both signed concordats with the Vatican. The signer was German Cardinal Pacelli, who would later become Pope Pius XII. To this day, Adolf Hitler has not been excommunicated from the Catholic Church.

The Revelation of St John the Divine was written circa 96 AD. The Greek word for Revelation, *Apocalypse*, literally means 'unveiling'. While the popular view of the Revelation is that the seven seals fit neatly into the final seven years of world history as we know it, there is an equally valid interpretation that the opening of the seven seals begins early on at the beginning of the fourth century. (Most passages in the Bible are pregnant with information and by no means limited to one interpretation.) Historically, Constantine was the first pope. He may be seen as the rider on the white horse that comes out of the first seal in Revelation 6. The following three seals can be seen as being fulfilled in the centuries to follow. Through the middle ages, the Church grew in power and the world was engulfed in war (second seal). Famine and plagues followed, as the Church assumed complete legal authority (third seal). The Church set up tribunals and persecuted the believers in the true gospel (fourth seal).

The Holy Roman Empire is also known as The First Reich. The Second Reich is considered Protestant by historians, but Wilhelm II traveled to Rome and had private conversations with Pope Leo XIII in 1888, 1895, and again in 1903. The Third Reich was Catholic, as was the First Reich. It was backed by the pope, and bound to the Church by an official concordat. In the case of the First Reich, its power was greatly shaken by the gospel and the proliferation of God's word. The Reformation was largely responsible for ending the Holy Roman Empire. After Napoleon defeated the Austrians 1806, the Holy Roman Empire was ended. (Napoleon himself, however, also went on to sign a concordat with Rome, and made himself emperor.) In the case of the Third Reich, it was the military defeat of Hitler by Protestant England and Protestant America that sealed its fate. Communist Russia was an Allied nation as well, but later collapsed after a long, cold war with the United States.

An important component of history, is God's hand moving through unbelievers. They are often the major players in terms of history, acting as his direct instruments. Although it is always Christians who are involved in the major advances in history involving personal freedom and liberty, sometimes God's hand moves unlikely instruments to accomplish his will. In the first century for example, the world had been perfectly prepared to receive the gospel through world events that transpired under pagan leaders. The Greeks unified the language and the Romans built the roads. Everything was set for the proliferation of the gospel.

Similarly, the American Revolution was influenced by Thomas Paine and his pamphlet, *Common Sense*. While Paine was a enlightenment thinker, who latter attacked the veracity of the Bible and the doctrines of the Christian faith in *The Age of Reason*, it is nevertheless true that Paine was raised in a Quaker family and received a Christian primary education. In *Common Sense*, he quoted Scripture and used illustrations from the historical narrative in the Bible to make his case for liberty. He argued that a monarchy is a terrible form of government, and the rights of the individual should supersede the authority of the state.

Thus, *Common Sense* was based on biblical principles, and appealed to clergymen and rank-and-file Christians alike, as well as other enlightenment thinkers like Benjamin Rush, who helped

Paine write *Common Sense*. Although they may not all have been what we think of as orthodox Christians, the enlightenment thinkers such as Paine, Rush, Jefferson and Benjamin Franklin did believe in God. Absolutely no one connected to the Revolution of 1776 was an atheist. Atheists have accomplished little if anything in terms of freedom or liberty. As a matter of fact, even though the founders were influenced by the enlightenment philosophy, which was popular in their day, they were much more heavily influenced by the Bible. The Bible was quoted more than any other document in the proceedings of the Continental Congress. Hard core enlightenment philosophy, which was the basis of the French Revolution, discounted the Bible entirely.

It is the prerogative of the church to be salt and light, and therefore to take the lead in setting the course in the direction that God is guiding. In 1776 that meant fighting a war for independence from Great Britain. If the church rises to the occasion, we can have a new Revolution as an extension of the first American Revolution, and without fighting a war. The government given to us by the founding fathers is still viable, but only if the church comes to terms with the fact that we have been lied to. Indeed, we have been deceived. We need to go back to the libertarian principles that were fought so hard for. It is not a mater of politics so much as philosophy. We have to make thinking cool again. That means we have to understand the philosophical underpinnings of our heritage as Americans. Consider the following quote by President Reagan:

Libertarianism is the heart and soul of conservatism.

— Ronald Reagan

Libertarianism simply means a return to the laws and ideals our nation was founded on. Although we do not necessarily (God help us) need to fight a physical war to achieve this end, we do need to fight a spiritual war, and we need to be prepared to exercise civil disobedience. II Corinthians 10:4 tells us our weapons are mighty. Things like the word of God, prayer, and the truth (Eph 6). Only when the church is ready to come to terms with the truth can this war be fought and won, and the truth is that during a very short period of time, while America was asleep, our government has been hijacked without most of us even noticing. Consider where we started and what we have come to:

No man has a natural right to commit aggression on the equal rights of another, and this is all from which the laws ought to restrain him.

— Thomas Jefferson

Rightful liberty is unobstructed action according to our will, within limits drawn around us by the equal rights of others. I do not add 'within the limits of the law,' because it is often but the tyrant's will, and always so when it violates the rights of an individual.

— Thomas Jefferson

In America, we have this strong bias toward individual action ... But individual actions, individual dreams, are not sufficient. We must unite in collective action, build collective institutions and organizations.

— Barack Obama

In the collective model it is not the individual that is important, but the group. The individual is told that for the welfare of the collective, he must set aside his individuality and conform. This is absolutely contrary to everything America was founded on. The American ideals of freedom and individual rights are what American soldiers fought and died to preserve. The enemies of freedom have been furiously trying to scrub these ideals from the hearts and minds of Americans for the last century. Mainly through the education system, but in other ways as well, the ideas of collectivism are being infused into the minds of

Americans, as can be seen by the quote above. The bitter fruit of these ideas can be seen in places like China, where Mao killed somewhere between 45,000,000 and 75,000,000 people who apparently did not conform well enough into the collective.

When America still believed in individual rights and free-market economics, we had the highest standard of living in the world. We were envied for our success and high standards, for honesty in government and justice in public affairs. Now however, we are trillions of dollars in debt. We are hated around the world because of our corruption and our human rights abuses.[4] [5]

Individualism means you reap the fruit of your labor. You are rewarded for your hard work. Collectivism means you will never be above average, no matter how hard you work. The rise of the corporation was the collectivization of the American economy. Corporations are not true capitalism. Adam Smith is largely credited as the father of capitalism. In the economics of Adam Smith, capitalism meant private ownership; it was free-market, and individual driven. In the New World Order, corporations gobble up local economies, then siphon the money out of the community and into the coffers of the global elite. In the beginnings of our great Republic, corporations were viewed with suspicion and frowned upon. Companies had to convince the state they operated in that their charter would benefit the public good. Their charter was limited to a specific duration, and could be revoked if the corporation was found to cause harm to the public. Today we are led to believe that corporations are as American as baseball and apple pie, part of free-market capitalism. This is not true. American business was built on the concept of private ownership, in which case money circulates in the community and benefits the local economy.

---

[4] For example, Madeline Albright defended America's responsibility in the deaths of 500,000 children in Iraq because of sanctions. She said, "We feel it's worth it."
[5] Another example is the use of depleted uranium. The most horrific birth defects imaginable are seen now in Iraq as a result of depleted uranium, not to mention the adverse health effects on the American troops. Terrible birth defects were also caused by the use of agent orange in Vietnam.

In the case of the corporation however, the money leaves the local economy and benefits corporate interests, while adversely affecting the local economy by driving local companies that cannot compete out of business. Economic freedom is suppressed and diversity is suppressed, as everything is assimilated into the collective of the corporation. Someone may protest, saying that collectivism divides money equally and corporations do not, but that is part of the con of collectivism. It never works in practice as it is supposed to in theory. At least corporations do not try to hide the fact that their pay scale is pyramid shaped, with the rich executives at the top in the capstone. The general principles of collectivism are still present — uniformity, assimilation, everyone is forced into the mold. Collectives are the result of bullies telling people that they have to be like them. They have to think like they want them to think, dress like they want them to dress, do as they are told, take their wages, and conform without making waves.

Nearly all facets of our modern society are geared toward collectivism. Collectivism hates anyone who is different, anyone who can think for themselves, or refuses to comply. Collectivism fears anything it does not understand or cannot control.

Catholicism is a form of collectivism. Again, it forces the individual into a group. He is forced to interpret Scripture as defined by the group and its leadership. Individualism is discouraged. Freedom of thought and expression is not allowed. If one refuses to submit to the canon law and dogma of the Church, he is 'anathema'. By contrast in a Christian church, the individual is encouraged to study the Bible for himself, and allow the Holy Spirit to guide and teach him (II Pet. 1:20).

Constantine did not have a full spectrum control grid, like the emperors of today. The Roman citizens did not carry around GPS devices that could be tracked by satellite, or used to spy on them via the built-in microphones. Constantine did not have drones with heat seeking missiles. He did not have cameras on the street corners, and microphones in the street lamps. He had a town crier, but he did not have a box in every house he could use to brainwash the masses while they munched on GMO corn and aspertame, in a highly suggestible alpha state of consciousness induced by the soothing glow of the TV screen, with all of its small movements and carefully crafted flicker-rate. Constantine did not have the NSA and Facebook to compile dossiers on the plebs profiling their "personal details, 'pattern of life,' connections to associates, [and] media."[6] The Romans did not have smart meters and home appliances that bugged their homes. Constantine did not have a massive NSA data mining program that could monitor anyone, anywhere, anytime. We have nearly come to see Orwell's prophecy fulfilled. On August 1, 2013, the main-stream media finally admitted what those who have been paying attention have known for a long time. The TV can spy on you.[7] According to the *New York Post* the FBI can access the web cam on your personal computer any time they want, and view whatever is on the screen of your computer as well.[8] And what about your smart meter? The power companies like to say that their smart meters emit less radiation than your cell phone, but that is simply not true. Depending on different factors your phone emits anywhere from 50 to 1000 mW/M^2. Your smart meter on the other hand, emits 30,000 mW/M^2. That is at a minimum 30X, and at a maximum 600X as much as your cell phone! Dr. Laura Pressley took these measurements after she and her husband (who is also an engineer, like her) noticed that they were both twitching in their sleep, every 25 seconds. Measurements taken from the smart meter determined that the smart meter was sending out a 30,000 mW/M^2 pulse every 25 seconds. Through a long process she and her husband eventually

[6] "How the NSA and the FBI made Facebook the Perfect Mass Surveilance Tool", Harrison Weber, *Ventura Beat*. http://venturebeat.com/2014/05/15/how-the-nsa-fbi-made-facebook-the-perfect-mass-surveillance-tool/

[7] "Your TV might be watching you", Erica Fink and Laurie Segall @CNNMoney, August 1, 2013. http://money.cnn.com/2013/08/01/technology/security/tv-hack/index.html

[8] "FBI can turn on your Web cam, and you'd never know it", Pedro Oliveira Jr., *NY Post*, Dec 8, 2013. http://nypost.com/2013/12/08/fbi-can-turn-on-your-web-cam/

persuaded the power company to come out and temporarily turn off the smart part of the meter. The twitching stopped. Smart meters emit radio waves in two different bands, 900 mHz, and around 2.45 GHz, the same frequency as your microwave oven! Dr. Pressley recommends using STETZERiZER® Filters as an easy way to filter out this radiation.

After Constantine issued his Edict of Toleration in 313 AD, the persecution stopped. Nevertheless, the Christians knew that Constantine's state-sponsored Church was a counterfeit. Some of them moved up into the northern Alps of Italy where they protected the word of God and kept the faith. They became known as the Waldenses. (*Halley's Bible Handbook* and other sources claim they were named after Peter Waldo [Pierre Vaudès], but their name literally means "men of the valley." They migrated from the Alps to the high valleys of Piedmont, then into France.) The pure Scriptures they preserved were used by Olivétan for his French translation of the Bible.

The Waldenses were Christians who resisted the establishment. They refused to compromise. They believed in the commandment to *earnestly contend for the faith which was once delivered unto the saints.* They believed their faith was *much more precious than of gold that perisheth.* They believed they needed to continue *stedfastly in the apostles' doctrine and fellowship.* They rejected the new religion of Constantine. In the ages to follow many of their progeny paid the ultimate price for their rebellion, which was in reality a crown of glory. They fought the good fight, they finished their course, they kept the faith.

I am not suggesting we retreat to the mountains. I believe God probably directed the Waldenses to do so, but I do not believe that is what God is telling his church to do today. I do believe we are to resist tyranny and spread the gospel. I do my best to evangelize but there is always room for improvement. I have a friend who stood up in McDonald's last Easter, and made rounds approaching everyone in the restaurant, and personally invited them to church. Some of them came, and two of them responded to the altar call!

He is doing his part to spread the gospel.

The governor of Wisconsin recently signed legislation making them the first state in the Union to require that there must be an independent investigation when the police kill somebody. He is doing his part to resist tyranny.

West Point graduate, veteran, and activist, Antonio Buehler films bad cops who commit acts of brutality, and uploads the video to YouTube. He is doing his part to resist tyranny.

Rey Collazo wrestled the phone from the hand of a TSA marshal who was taking pictures up the skirts of passengers. The TSA agent was fired. Collazo is doing his part to fight tyranny.

Stacey Armato sued the TSA and won, when they illegally detained her and tried to make her radiate her breast milk. She is doing her part to fight tyranny.

Ron Paul has developed an excellent home schooling program to counter the Common Core program that is designed to dumb down America's children. Ron Paul is doing his part to fight tyranny.

People came out in droves when the Bureau of Land Management (BLM) sent snipers to the Cliven Bundy ranch in Nevada and stole his cattle. Supporters brought their guns and stood up to the BLM, who were operating more like Nazis than an American bureau that is supposed to manage land. These brave Americans did their part to fight tyranny.

But many in America seem to be suffering from Stockholm Syndrome. They have fallen in love with those who are trying to steal our rights and hold us captive. Although *Infowars*, *Drudge*, and even *Fox News* took the side of the Cliven Bundy supporters who stood up to the tyranny of the government snipers who tried to steal his cattle, Glen Beck took the side of the BLM, and gave the liberal talking points. He parroted the false claim that Bundy was a racist. Even if he was, what does that have to do with government snipers on his land because of grazing fees? (See Chapter XVI on mind control.) Although Beck is himself a Mormon, he is wildly popular among Christians who seem strangely mesmerized by him as he deviates from his conservative bent at key opportune moments, like when it's time to demonize courageous freedom loving Americans, or attack Ron Paul just as he was rising in the polls, or to demonize Alex Jones (a Christian), all the while using Jones' material for his own show, so he can pose as a libertarian.

Edward Snowden risked his life and his liberty to expose the tyranny of the New World Order, when he released documents detailing their illegal surveillance and data mining to the media. He is doing his part to fight tyranny. What about you? These and countless others are ordinary people just like you. They have courage, and care enough to take a side. Are you willing to stand for what is right and what you know in your heart is true? Your friends and family may snicker and poke fun, but Jesus knows it is no laughing matter, and he will stand with you.

The wicked flee when no man pursueth: but the righteous are bold as a lion.

Proverbs 28:1

T he Suebian ranks were circling. Gaius wondered if this may be the end. Rough territory, Germania. They had been on half rations for weeks. They had already lost a lot of men. Now they were surrounded and outnumbered. They rallied back to back and awaited the order to attack. Seventy-seven men were left. They had been separated from their legion for days now. They still had their centurion. As the enemy closed in it was getting unnerving. Gaius had seen his share of war. It was not that. He wondered if he would be able to make one last sacrifice to Mars before he died. The Suebians were closing in fast now. He decided they would be his sacrifice. Gaius prayed and asked for the strength to die honorably. The centurion blew his whistle, as the battle ensued. Gaius and what was left of the centuria thrust their swords and parried with their shields, then doubled back in their ranks on command as the next wave took the front line. Suebians advanced like madmen. Some jumped over the front line like gazelle, daggers flailing. One by one, Roman legionaries fell. Suebians kept coming. The day dragged on. Gaius lost count of how many Suebians he had killed. Now his hand clave to his sword. He had a fair amount of wounds and he was bleeding. He was starting to feel weak. *I will not be able to last much longer*, he thought to himself. Then he saw a flash of light. *This must be the afterlife*, he thought, but he lost consciousness before he could continue his thought process. When Gaius awoke the sun had set and twilight was giving way to darkness. Gaius slowly realized he had collapsed and lost consciousness. The battle was over. He saw some figures walking around in the fading twilight, and knew from their speech that they were the enemy. His head felt like it was going to explode and his body felt like it had been hit with a lucerne hammer. He also felt like he was being crushed. Gaius realized he was beneath a pile of corpses. He had been taken for a corpse passed over. He was lucky to be alive. He waited until there were no enemy soldiers nearby and dragged himself out from under the pile of dead flesh that had been his camouflage, then snuck off into the night until he was at a safe distance where he could tend to his wounds and rest.

When Gaius woke the next morning he realized why his head hurt so badly. An arrow had pierced his helmet. The shaft had broken off, but the arrowhead was still lodged in the bronze, just above the left face-guard. It had just missed his temple, leaving a deep gash above his ear. He thanked Mars and dislodged the arrowhead with the tip of his sword. He then went to work on mending his helmet. As he was tinkering with it he heard something move in the brush very near to him. Wasting no time, he charged and prepared to attack. As he neared the thicket, a Suebian leapt at him from a tree. Gaius noticed him just in time to thrust with his sword and grab the enemy's wrist with his other hand, stopping his dagger as the warrior landed squarely on top of him. After a short skirmish, Gaius arose. His adversary was dead. He approached the thicket to find his commanding officer, tied to the same tree that his attacker leapt from. As Gaius ungagged him and severed his bonds, Artellies started giving orders.

"Take what you can from their camp. Let us be going. There are more of them and they will be returning soon. If we are lucky we can outrun them and shake them off our trail."

"Aye aye sir," Gaius said, as he and Artellies made their escape. They had five days rations, weapons, all their limbs, and a dagger with a bejeweled golden haft, that Gaius had lifted off the Suebian that attacked him. It looked to Gaius like it had come from Persia. How the Suebian had come by it was anyone's guess. Artellies did not know he had it. If they could make it back to Rome, Gaius would be set after finding a buyer. Maybe his luck was changing. Little did Gaius know that what he had was a prized treasure that belonged to the king of Germania. The solider he had killed was the king's son. He had taken his father's dagger before going to battle. Having captured a centurion, he was ready to proudly present him to his father. Then Gaius showed up.

The day wore on as Gaius and Artellies evaded their pursuers. In the later hours of the afternoon they began to relax a little. Having found an old trail that looked like it had not gotten any use for some time, they walked at a normal pace as their thoughts drifted to other things besides mere survival.

"Some luck 'eh?" Gaius said. "You and I escaping that hoard."

"I do not believe in luck," Artellies said.

"Well what would you call it?" Gaius asked. "My coming along just when your captors were mostly off foraging for food, and rescuing you from that Suebian bastard? I suppose the gods may have had something to do with it. I never could figure that lot. They don't seem to have any rhyme or reason to what they do if you ask me."

"The Jews call it providence," Artellies said.

"The *Jews*?? Do you mean to tell me you have bought into that one true God nonsense?" Gaius protested.

"Watch your tone soldier," Artellies said. "I am still your superior officer. Even if you did save my skin today."

"Do you mean to tell me you have bought into that one true God nonsense, sir?" Gaius said, correcting himself.

"Something like that. The Jews know more than you think."

"How so?" Gaius asked. Not that he was really interested but it passed the time.

"I was stationed in Antioch back in DCCC VII. There was something of a revolution going on there. Many of the Jews believe their Messiah has come."

"And this Messiah, you pray to him now?" Gaius asked.

"I do," Artellies confessed.

"But you're a Roman, a centurion no less." Gaius thought this was very strange.

"Have you ever thought that maybe you need to be forgiven Gaius?"

"For what?"

"Something like, deserting in battle for example?"

"I am not a deserter!!" Gaius protested. "I lost consciousness! When I awoke the battle was over!"

"Alright don't get excited. What about stealing?"

"The Jewish law. Yeah. Well Mars isn't concerned with such things," Gaius retorted.

"What about our Roman virtues?" Artellies asked. "Do you ever lie?"

"I'm no worse than the next man I suppose," Gaius answered.

"Alexander thought there was something to the Jews' wisdom."

"Alexander?"

"That's right. When he conquered Jerusalem he worshiped their God. The Jews had prophesied Alexander's coming."

"I always thought the Greeks were of a mind to believe in a lot of nonsense," Gaius said.

"Yeah? Well I have news for you. Some of the men I knew in Antioch, Roman men, men of the standard — they told me that after we Romans crucified their Messiah, he rose from the dead. A lot of people saw him."

"Nobody can come back from a crucifixion," Gaius said.

"I know," Artellies said. "Nobody, except God."

"What? You believe this Messiah is God??" Gaius had never heard such talk. Certainly not from a centurion, anyway.

"His disciples wrote about him. One of their writings says, The wages of sin is death, but the gift of God is eternal life, through Iesus Christus our Lord," Artellies said.

Gaius did have something in his heart that bothered him. He felt guilty about it. He had never told anyone about it. He wondered if the gift of God might be available to him. "What do you mean gift?" Gaius asked. "You don't have to make any sacrifices to him?"

"No, Messiah sacrificed himself for us. All you have to do is stop worshiping our Roman gods and dedicate yourself to the him." Gaius did not know what to make of it. It sounded strange.

I am the eye in the sky
Looking at you
I can read your mind
I am the maker of rules
Dealing with fools
I can cheat you blind
And I don't need to see any more
To know that
I can read your mind, I can read your mind

— Eric Woolfson, 1982

Yea, they opened their mouth wide against me, and said, Aha, aha, our eye hath seen it.
The Book of Psalms 35:21

For of this sort are they which creep into houses . . .
The Second Epistle of Paul the Apostle to Timothy 3:6a

Also take no heed unto all words that are spoken; lest thou hear thy servant curse thee:
Ecclesiastes 7:21

THE FUTURE IS NOW

The Doomsday Clock, at the University of Chicago, has been evaluated by a panel of scientists and set to the estimated countdown to nuclear holocaust since 1947. The most recent officially announced setting — five minutes to midnight — was made on January 14, 2014.

In his classic work, *1984*, George Orwell acknowledged that the Catholic Church was a system of control and oppression that had become outdated. Orwell's prophetic work told of a future system of complete government control. One that would dwarf the intrusive nature of the Church.

In 1961, in *The Obsolete Man*, Rod Serling described it this way: "You walk into this room at your own risk, because it leads to the future; not a future that will be, but one that might be. This is not a new world; it is simply an extension of what began in the old one. It has patterned itself after every dictator who has ever planted the ripping imprint of a boot on the pages of history since the beginning of time. It has refinements, technological advances, and a more sophisticated approach to the destruction of human freedom. But like every one of the super-states that preceded it, it has one iron rule: Logic is an enemy, and truth is a menace."

The Obsolete Man is fiction, but what it prophetically made reference to is not. In fact, there are many messages embedded into popular culture, that have been warning us about what is coming for years now. The first song to tell of the rising technocratic police state was Electric Eye, performed by Judas Priest in the early 80s. By that time is was well known that the U.S. intelligence community could read Russian newspapers by way of spy satellites with powerful telescopes:

Up here in space
I'm looking down on you.
My lasers trace
Everything you do.
You think you've private lives
Think nothing of the kind.
There is no true escape
I'm watching all the time.
I'm made of metal
My circuits gleam.
I am perpetual
I keep the country clean.

— Rob Halford, 1982

A decade later in 1992, Dave Mustaine of Megadeath, who incidentally is a born again Christian, released "Symphony of Destruction," which went straight to the heart of the matter and exposed the endgame:

You take a mortal man,
And put him in control
Watch him become a god
Watch peoples heads a'roll
A'roll...

Just like the Pied Piper
Led rats through the streets
We dance like marionettes
Swaying to the symphony ...
Of destruction

— Dave Mustaine, 1992

We have made it to the future Eric Woolfson of the Alan Parsons Project wrote about in 1982, but we haven't quite come to the future that Dave Mustaine wrote about in '92, *yet*. (The Judas

Priest lyrics describe Satan's propaganda campaign justifying mass surveillance, which is a lie.) Music is powerful. It was a major force in the social movements in the sixties. It was a major part of the revolution in South Africa. A careful examination of today's music shows that the elites understand this, and therefore they have co-opted all the major record labels for themselves. Ancient iconic imagery is embedded into the acts of the artists, as they display the all-seeing eye in the capstone of the pyramid with their hands forming the triangle. The elites have their own troubadours now, championing their cause of world domination. Jay-Z's label is even named after one of the elites' most high profile families, "Roc-A-Fella Records." Lauren Hill has publicly stated that the music industry suppresses free expression by the artists, and purposely protects the establishment. Here are a couple of excerpts from her public statement on tumbler in 2012:

> "For the past several years, I have remained what others would consider underground. I did this in order to build a community of people, like-minded in their desire for freedom and the right to pursue their goals and lives without being **manipulated and controlled** by a **media protected military industrial complex** with a completely different agenda.
> . . . I entered into my craft full of optimism (which I still possess), but immediately saw the suppressive force with which the system attempts to maintain its control over a given paradigm.
> . . . Over-commercialization and its resulting restrictions and limitations can be very damaging and distorting to the inherent nature of the individual. I Love making art, I Love making music, these are as natural and necessary for me almost as breathing or talking. **To be denied the right to pursue it according to my ability, ... in an attempt to control, is manipulation directed at my most basic rights!**

The entire statement is worth reading, but not as elegant and rhythmical as the lyrics to her song against the illuminati, called "I get out." http://www.youtube.com/watch?v=0HdzTvH8mvw

Katy Perry said in a candid interview that she sold her soul to the devil, in order to make it in the industry.[1] Kanye West told the audience at a concert that he sold his soul to the devil.[2] Anthony Kiedis of the Red Hot Chili Peppers thanked

Satan at the MTV Music Awards.[3] These modern examples fit with the rock legend of Robert Johnson selling his soul to the devil. Nicole Sherzinger, the former lead singer of the Pussycat Dolls, cited this as the reason she did *not* make it big. She said "To make it, you really have to sell your soul to the devil." Sherzinger went on to say in the interview that she did not sell her soul. Judging by her recent work, it would appear that Sherzinger is telling the truth, and that God is making good on his promise to bless those who trust in him (see Genesis 15:1). If you have never heard Sherzinger sing "The Phantom of the Opera," or "Don't Cry for Me Argentina," the trip to YouTube is well worth it. The big lie they tell people in the industry is that you have to compromise, or completely sell out. Scott Stapp of CREED did the opposite, and made a deal with God. In a candid interview on CBN, Stapp related how he felt the Holy Spirit whenever he would write lyrics. He told about how he made a deal with God, stipulating that if he made it big, he would never stop using inspired lyrics in his songs. God blessed him and catapulted him into super-stardom, before he even started walking closely with him.

The secret to navigating these last days is trusting God, wherever he has you. According to Philippians 4:22, the apostle Paul had Christian friends who were *of Cæsar's household.* Ie, Cæsar Nero. Those in the music industry or other high profile segments of society have the same invitation to receive Christ as everyone. And incidentally, selling your soul to the devil is not an irreversible act. Jesus can break *any* bondage the enemy places on you; he can set *anybody* free. God gave us his only begotten Son. What more could he have done to prove his love to you? *[T]he blood of Jesus Christ his Son cleanseth us from all sin.*

The main point in all this is that those who control the music industry are purposely manipulating the music to suit their

---

1 http://www.youtube.com/watch?v=lKquBixWL24

2 http://www.youtube.com/watch?v=bbmiOBN3U7Y

3 http://www.youtube.com/watch?v=AzXHnHIb2Z0

agenda. They are using the music as a tool for mind control. They understand all too well that impressionable fans are heavily influenced by the music. Therefore, they carefully control what is produced, and the message it conveys. For example, Ke$ha tweeted that she was *forced* to do the song Die Young:

ke$ha
@keshasuxx
i understand I had my very own issue with "die young" for this reason. I did NOT want to sing those lyrics and I was FORCED TO.
7:05pm - 18 Dec 12   (Her tweet was immediately removed.)

Beyonce has publicly stated that she "felt a power come into her," and indeed looked like she became demon possessed during her Superbowl performance. Aristotle said, "If one listens to the wrong kind of music, one will become the wrong kind of person." Satanic music used to be only for those who wanted to listen to a caustic melody with heavy power chords and guttural vocals. But now, the powers that be have made Satanism 'cool'. Gorgeous women with soft voices and catchy melodies trumpet the New World Order, as their videos are peppered with satanic images and occult symbols. Upside down crosses, inverted pentagrams and above all, the all-seeing eye of Horus are liberally incorporated into the video and concert presentations of the most popular performers. Think about it.

Finally, brethren, whatsoever things are true, whatsoever things are honest, whatsoever things are just, whatsoever things are pure, whatsoever things are lovely, whatsoever things are of good report; if there be any virtue, and if there be any praise, think on these things.

The Epistle of Paul the Apostle to the Philippians 4:8

If you tell a lie big enough and keep repeating it, people will eventually come to believe it. The lie can be maintained only for such time as the State can shield the people from the political, economic and/or military consequences of the lie. It thus becomes vitally important for the State to use all of its powers to repress dissent, for the truth is the mortal enemy of the lie, and thus by extension, the truth is the greatest enemy of the State.

— Joseph Goebbels, Nazi Minister of Propaganda

The individual is handicapped by coming face-to-face with a conspiracy so monstrous he cannot believe it exists.

— J Edgar Hoover, discussing communism

America no longer has a functioning democracy.

— Jimmy Carter, 2013

The wicked walk on every side, when the vilest men are exalted.
The Book of Psalms 12:8

When the righteous are in authority, the people rejoice: but when the wicked beareth rule, the people mourn.

The Proverbs 29:2

XI

THE LATE GREAT AMERICAN REPUBLIC

The story of our first-century Christians is mostly fictional, but there were undoubtably similar, much more dramatic stories than this one, that happened in real life in the first century. I wrote about Rufus and Antonina because to them Christianity was not just a social club. The idea of a 'seeker friendly' sort of evangelism would have never entered their mind. Christianity was not a separate part of their lives that they could compartmentalize. It *was* their life. We are entering a time much like the time that Rufus and Antonina lived in. We are witnessing the end of America and the rise of the one-world Church, referred to in Scripture as the *falling away* (II Thess 2:3).

There has been a strange role reversal. Now people who tell the truth and run from tyranny defect from the USA to Russia, instead of visa-versa. 'Made in China' used to indicate inferior quality, but now it is China that is telling the United States they do not want our GMO grain exports, which have been proven to cause cancer. That should tell us we need to examine ourselves and get to the bottom of what is going on. It requires a radical self evaluation. One of the hardest things for a man to do is admit he was deceived. It requires humility to admit that. It requires investigative thinking to determine what is wrong. There is a term that the establishment has invented to keep people from questioning them, and that term is 'conspiracy theory'. Yet every day people are brought up on conspiracy charges. If conspiracies are not real, then why are people being charged with conspiracy and tried in our courts every day? The word conspiracy appears in the Bible several times, and the Bible gives several examples of people conspiring to commit acts of evil. In fact, recent studies have shown that people who believe 'conspiracy theories' are more well adjusted than people who do not. Gina Loudon of *World Net Daily* cited several of these studies in an article[1] showing that people with strong intellects are more willing to hear things that challenge their worldview, and to look at things from all angles.

Paul Craig Roberts is the father of Reaganomics. He has called it what it is, a coup d'état. Roberts has said the best we can hope for now is collapse, but perhaps that is only because he does not know the miracle working God the Christian serves. (Not to mention the *blessed hope* of Titus 2:13.) The recent string of scandals, in government and business, have exculpated the 'conspiracy theorists', inasmuch as the things they have been warning the public about for decades have now turned into front page news. The scandals however are just the tip of the iceberg. Not only have powerful forces restructured the legal and political landscape, and implemented a full-spectrum surveillance apparatus; the powers that be have reengineered and taken control of the machinery by which society operates. They now control education, politics, the courts, entertainment and the media, business and industry, and essentially all other aspects of society as well, from the food we eat to the health care we receive.

Susan Lindauer was the chief CIA asset covering Iraq at the United Nations before September 11. She attempted to testify before Congress about advanced knowledge the Bush Administration had about September 11, and the peace option that had been on the table with Iraq, all of which the Administration was trying to suppress. Shortly after she approached Congress to testify, she awoke to hear

---

[1] http://www.wnd.com/2013/10/are-conspiracy-theorists-really-the-sane-ones/

the FBI pounding on her door with an arrest warrant under the Patriot Act. She was accused of being a spy, and accepting bribes from her Iraqi contacts. Since her release, she has publicly stated that "They had already decided that if the 9/11 conspiracy maximized damage on the towers, that there would be a perfect pretext for war." Iraq's response prior to September 11 was that the FBI was more than welcome to investigate within Iraq, and that Iraq wanted only to cooperate to preserve the peace option.

Since it is admitted and well known now that Iraq had nothing to do with September 11, Lindauer's testimony proves that the agenda from well before September 11 was to use the terror attack as a pretext for the war. She has written a book chronicling how she was indicted under the Patriot Act. In her book, *Extreme Prejudice, the Terrifying Story of the Patriot Act and the Cover Up of 9/11 and Iraq*, Susan Lindauer reveals how the Patriot Act was used against her. She was the second non-Arab American to be indicted under the Patriot Act:

1. The Patriot Act stripped her of her basic rights as an American Citizen. She was falsely accused of accepting bribes from her Iraqi contacts, and denied a trial by a jury of her peers.

2. She was held in prison at Carswell Airforce base for a year. She was held under indictment for *five years* with *no trial*. She was forced to go into court with *no attorney* present.

3. She was nearly given a "chemical lobotomy," but only because of the high-profile exposure given to her by the alternate media, and the fact that her cousin was White House Chief of Staff, was she finally released.

4. The Patriot Act has criminalized dissension. Free speech itself is now criminalized by the Patriot Act.

5. She stated "I can tell you that for several years, within a 10 mile radius of every home in the United States in the most isolated rural areas and the most remote areas, there is someone listening to your phone calls and reading your emails. And we've known this for a long time."[2]

---

[2] Susan Lindaurer, July 01, 2013, *RT News*.

The Rutherford Institute, a non-profit Christian organization dedicated to defending civil liberties and human rights, has reported that the federal government, in coordinated operations with local police, are now routinely detaining returning veterans — over 20,000 in Virginia alone in 2011. Many of these vets are guilty of nothing but exercising their free speech rights by posting political comments in public forums like Facebook and Twitter. Such was the case with Rutherford Institute client and Marine veteran, Brandon Raub.

These recent events are strikingly similar to the state of affairs in Nazi Germany preceding WWII. Yet the most significant similarity to the rise of the Nazi party correlates to Hitler's covert operation in which he bombed the Reichstag building, and blamed it on the Communists. This is actually a common technique that has been used several times throughout history, and is known as a 'false flag attack'. The U.S. has a history of false flag attacks as well. The most widely known now, is probably the Gulf of Tonkin incident, which was used as a pretext for the war in Vietnam. Defence Secretary Robert McNamera later admitted that the U.S. was not in fact attacked in the Gulf of Tonkin by the North Vietnamese. NSA documents declassified in 2005 confirmed that "no attack happened that night." There is another event which affected the United States just as much or even more so than the Gulf of Tonkin incident. Not only was it used as a pretext for wars overseas, but an ambiguous 'war on terror' which will never end. But what's more, this event was used as a pretext for the police state, where Americans now willingly submit to being groped by low-paid workers who have very little training in the security business. They submit to surrendering their firearms. They submit to being spied on by the government, and a lot of other things that they would have never agreed to if it were not for this event. You have probably guessed by now what I am talking about. Consider:

Did you know that over 1000 architects and engineers have signed a petition to Congress, stating that the official version of events explaining the fall of the Twin Towers is not scientifically possible?[3]

Did you know only a few dozen architects and engineers have openly supported the NIST and WTC reports (the official version)? *Did you know* that Solomon Bros. Tower 7, which also collapsed into itself on September 11, in the same controlled-demolition like manner as the twin towers, was not hit by any plane?

Did you know that before September 11, no steel-frame skyscraper in history had ever collapsed because of a fire, or from being hit by a plane? (Many skyscrapers have had much longer burning and wider ranging fires. The Empire State Building was hit by a B-25 bomber in 1945, yet did not collapse.)

Did you know that Jet fuel does not burn hot enough to melt steel? Jet fuel burns at less than 1600° F. Steel melts at 2700° F. And, most of the jet fuel burned off in the initial explosion.

Did you know that 7X the normal number of investors sold short on American Airlines stock the week before September 11?

Did you know that no plane parts from flight 77 were found at the Pentagon? The two six-ton jet engines were completely missing. There was no fuselage. This is an unprecedented occurrence. There are always plane parts after a crash. The turbine that was recovered from inside the Pentagon, was not a part from a Boeing 757. According to Major General Albert N. Stubblebine, "It looked like a turbine from a missile."

Did you know that Flight 93 completely disappeared as well? An entire 757 seemingly evaporated, as no discernible parts were found at the Pennsylvania crash site. No bodies of the passengers were found. No blood. No jet fuel. However during the trial of Zacarias Moussaoui, the prosecution magically produced key items recovered from the crash site. Among them a red bandana — exhibit PA00111, and a Saudi ID card — exhibit PA00101. (The FBI released pictures showing a jet engine and two small fragments of fuselage, *but never explained where they were found*.)

Being confronted with information like this can be very unsettling to people. It is painful to think that fellow Americans could betray us, and be capable of such evil. However, psychologists tell us that the

3 http://www2.ae911truth.org/downloads/AE911Truth-Petition&Names.pdf

best way to heal and recover from traumatic events such as 9/11, is to search for the truth, and uncover it. The Germans did this after WWII. The South Africans did this after Apartheid. After the Holocaust, the Jews felt the best way to honor and value the victims was to make sure the truth about the Holocaust was known. A common thread in all of the reasons that people use to deny something other than the official version of events transpired on 9/11, is fear. People fear being ostracized. They fear having to change their worldview. They fear feeling helpless or vulnerable. However the Bible tells us over and over not to be afraid. Psychologists tell us that the best way to recover from trauma is to identify the source of our anxiety, gradually uncover the truth, and accept it. People fear that questioning the official versions of events will mean they are not patriotic Americans. But in fact, it is very patriotic to question things, and what we need now more than ever are patriotic Americans who will stand on our founding principles and confront what we are facing.

There are many other facts, and a vast amount of evidence, proving what we were told about the events of September 11 simply does not add up. (Much more at https://vimeo.com/31428815) According to investigative reporter Ben Swan, the official version of September 11 is now questioned by the majority of Americans. His special report on 9/11/2013 cited credible poles and statistics verifying this. Nevertheless, after September 11, the Patriot Act was signed into law, we went to war in Afghanistan and Iraq and we were given the TSA.

> If tyranny and oppression come to this land, it will be in the guise of fighting a foreign enemy.
> — James Madison

The founding fathers knew very well how tyranny worked. Not only did they fight a war to be free of it, but many of them were philosophical giants in their own right, a fact their writings bear out. It was their understanding of these things that gave them the wisdom to craft the Declaration of Independence, and the Constitution with its Bill of Rights. These three documents form a three fold cord, not easily broken, that restrains tyrants from harassing and injuring the American people.

According to Suetonius, when Cæsar Nero was still a young man he said, "How I wish I had never learned to write," before he singed his first death warrant. Nero spiraled out of control in his blood lust, and it looks as if history is repeating itself. Today it seems nobody is safe across the entire political spectrum, whether Right or Left, from Andrew Breitbart to Michael Hastings. Much like the days of the Third Reich, all opposition is targeted. Whistle blower Edward Snowden wised up and left the country before they could get him, after he leaked documents proving that the government is wiretapping every American citizen — in every aspect of their data — with the complicity of the Big Data names like Google, Facebook, Microsoft and Apple. His *Guardian* interview is like a civics lesson from a libertarian professor. After Snowden brought the discussion to the forefront, the main stream media went into damage control and started to spin the narrative to discredit Snowden. They did so by cherry picking parts of the interview that were the least embarrassing to the intelligence community, and by falsely implying that he was a not a high-level intelligence operative. These parts of the interview were typically left out in the mainstream media:

"I've been a systems engineer, a systems administrator, a senior advisor for the Central Intelligence Agency, solutions consultant and a telecommunications information systems officer.

"I sitting at my desk certainly had the authority to wiretap anyone, from you or your accountant, to a federal judge, to even a president if I had a personal email.

"You don't have to have done anything wrong. You simply have to eventually fall under suspicion, from somebody, even by a wrong call. And then they can use the system to go back in time and scrutinize every decision you've ever made.

"The greatest fear that I have regarding the outcome for America of these disclosures, is that nothing will change. People will see in the media all of these disclosures. They

will know the lengths that the government is going to grant themselves powers unilaterally to create greater control over American society, and global society, but they won't be willing to take the risks necessarily to stand up and fight to change things; to force their representatives to actually take a stand in their interests. And in the months ahead and the years ahead it's only going to get worse, until eventually there will be a time where policies will change. Because the only things that restricts the activities of the surveillance state are policy; even our agreements with other governments, we consider that to be a stipulation of policy rather than a stipulation of law. <u>And because of that, a new leader will be elected; they'll flip the switch; say that, because of the crisis, because of the dangers we face in the world, you know- some new and unprecedented threat. We need more authority. We need more power. And there will be nothing the people can do at that point to oppose it, and it will be turnkey tyranny.</u>"

— Edward Snowden

While this statement by Snowden seemed to get little attention, comparatively speaking, to minor details like the thumb drive he used to obtain his leaked documents, it was probably the most important thing he said. People who have limited worldviews would naturally overlook this statement. However if you know history, if you understand human nature as revealed in Scripture, if you know Bible prophecy as foretold in the books of Daniel and the Revelation, in short, if you have an accurate worldview, then you will recognize this statement by Snowden as being truly prophetic.

Shortly after the Snowden story broke, *Investors Business Daily* broke a story revealing that the NSA surveillance program exempts Muslim mosques.[4] The truth was revealed. They are not

---

[4] http://news.investors.com/ibd-editorials/061213-659753-all-intrusive-obama-terror-dragnet-excludes-mosques.htm

looking for Muslim terrorists, at least not exclusively. They are looking for freedom-loving Americans, who threaten the New World Order with their old fashioned ideas.

A well-rounded worldview is one that incorporates not just religion, philosophy, history, and current events, but politics as well — a reasoned view of politics. In order to truly understand an organization, one needs to understand its roots. Although the Democratic Party has styled itself as the party of civil liberties, their true roots are such that they were indeed the party of slavery. This is what they stood for historically. The Republicans, the party of Lincoln, started out well but have been co-opted in the twenty-first century by the 'neocons', a name they adopted for themselves. The neocons no longer represent American values as defined by the founding fathers. The anti-slavery stance for example was a founding-father value. Many of the founding fathers were abolitionists. The Declaration of Independence itself attacked slavery by declaring that all men are created equal. However the neocons are now championing the end of civil liberties by destroying the Bill of Rights, and by subjugating the modern populations of the world. The Democrats are complicit with them.

It looks like Ed Snowden's "greatest fear" is going to come true. Both Democrats and Republicans let out a big yawn after his blood-curdling testimony about turnkey tyranny. The only one to speak up was Senator Rand Paul (R-KT), who is a champion of libertarian causes and the son of Ron Paul, a leader in the liberty movement.

I highly recommend listening to Judge Andrew Nepalitano's great speech, which has come to be known as "How To Get Fired in Five Minutes" because it got him fired from his popular Fox News program. It can be viewed on YouTube, and it gives an excellent synopsis of what is going on today in America politically: http://www.youtube.com/watch?v=edNmwmKRLeA

From an economic standpoint it was a Democrat, Clinton, who deregulated the banks in the 90s and threw out the Glass-Steagall Act. This brought about the housing bubble that led to the crash of 2008, thus leading to quantitative easing[5] and economic subjection. It was the neocon Republican, George W. Bush, who struck a major blow to civil liberties by signing the Patriot Act. Then Obama, a Democrat, renewed the Patriot Act, despite campaign promises to reform it. But Obama went even further. On Dec 31, 2011 he signed the 2012 National Defence Authorization Act, making it possible to secretly arrest and indefinitely detain Americans, *suspected* of 'terrorism'. He has utilized secretive procedures for his 'kill lists' that target American citizens with no due process. This new power has already been used on an American citizen in Yemen, merely because he was related to a known terrorist, his father. The White House defended their actions by saying "he should have picked a better father." Instead of calling foul, Congress is attempting to set up a yet another secret court, to legitimize this Nazi practice of killing citizens at will. Perhaps worse, Obama has expanded aggressive worldwide military campaigns beyond even that of the Bush-Cheney White House. By aiding Al-Qaeda rebels in Libya and Syria, and supporting the Muslim Brotherhood in Egypt, Obama has shown he is even more hawkish than his Republican predecessor. Americans were told that the wars we have engaged in since 9/11 were taking down tyrants and spreading democracy, yet they are beyond any shadow of a doubt installing worse dictators than the ones they deposed and stealing what little freedom the peoples of those countries had to begin with. After the coup d'etat in Libya and the death of Gaddafi, the al-Qaeda flag was raised over the courthouse in Tripoli as Hillary Clinton triumphantly declared, "We came, we saw, he died," as if she was Julius Cæsar. Some of the Syrian rebels that America is supporting have even taken the name, The Osama bin Laden Birgade.

Historically, America has not been for meddling in the affairs of other countries around the world. George Washington made this abundantly clear in his farewell address, which used to be taught as textbook American foreign policy in the public schools. Democrats, who have styled themselves as the 'peace party' have

---

5 Quantitative easing is the practice of the Fed pumping fiat currency it into the economy. (Ie, the Federal Reserve purchases financial assets from commercial banks.) Since our fiat currency system has nothing to back the value of the notes, this leads to inflation, which is a hidden form of taxation.

done an about-face. Not only that, but civil liberties for normal Americans have been drastically altered by both parties since September 11. The Bush Administration created the TSA, but under Obama the TSA has become much more aggressive in the airports, harassing and groping people at will, whether they be invalids in wheelchairs, infants, or more commonly pretty women. Former Miss USA Susie Castillo gave a tearful YouTube testimony about her molestation by the TSA after one of their agents stuck her hand down her pants and "touched my vagina." Then there are the scores of other abuses by the TSA, ripping away colostomy bags to the shock of crippled people in wheelchairs, groping men, women, and children, and generally being bullies. Some TSA agents have been hired despite having histories as sex offenders. To date over 500 TSA agents have been suspended or fired for stealing. How many others have stolen from passengers and not been caught? It basically amounts to psychological conditioning. This same technique was used by the Nazis, in which they employed 'brownshirts' to harass and bully people. These brownshirts later became the SA, commonly referred to as the Storm Troopers. With the TSA preparing to make extremely large ammunition purchases,[6] it looks like it is only a matter of time before this same transition is made with the TSA. People are being systematically and methodically trained to not resist. This is how Nazis took over Germany without any opposition, even though only a small percentage of the people actually belonged to the Nazi party.

It has been thoroughly documented that the legislative and political events leading up to the dark days of Nazi Germany are in many ways chillingly similar to events taking place in the U.S. It is often asserted that the Nazi party was right wing, but their full name was Nationalsozialistische Deutsche Arbeiterpartei (National **Socialist** German Workers' Party). The shortened name, Nazi, was derived from the first two syllables of the German word for "national." Therefore, being Socialist, the Nazis were obviously not 'right wing'. Fascism in Nazi Germany employed a mixed economy, with free

[6] http://www.infowars.com/tsa-to-purchase-24-million-rounds-of-duty-ammunition/

health care and government handouts. The private sector served at the pleasure of the Nazi Party. After the night of the long knives,[7] Hitler consolidated his power and took complete control of the economy. It looks as if we may soon be entering this stage in America. They are currently making preparations to arm the TSA, and expand their jurisdiction from the airports into many other segments of society.

We Americans can be so smug when we talk about Hitler's Germany, as if we would never let anything like that happen here. I wish that were true. Two of the most prominent companies involved in financing the Nazi war machine were General Electric and Standard Oil.[8] [9] [10] Much more shocking than that fact of history however, is that there is currently a holocaust in America, happening right now. Aborted babies are being chopped up and sold for money. Selling human tissue is supposed to be illegal under federal law, but it happens every day. Here is a price list from Opening Lines, a West Frankfort, IL company that sells baby parts to research companies after it buys them from Planned Parenthood:

Unprocessed Specimen (>8 weeks) $70
Unprocessed Specimen (≤ 8 weeks) $50
Livers (≤ 8 weeks) 30% discount if significantly fragmented $150
Livers (> 8 weeks) 30% discount if significantly fragmented $125
Spleens (≤ 8 weeks) $75
Spleens (> 8 weeks) $50
Pancreas (≤ 8 weeks) $100
Pancreas (> 8 weeks) $75
Thymus (≤ 8 weeks) $100

---

[7] The night of the long knives happened in 1934 when Hitler had about 100 of his political opponents assassinated, and around 1000 more arrested. This has been happening on a smaller scale in America for quite some time. It is now becoming so common that the mainstream media are forced to cover it, and spin the narrative. Michael Hastings was killed in a way intended to intimidate; rather than attempting to conceal the crime they made it obvious, to be an example to others who may dare to oppose them.

[8] Q.v. Antony C. Sutton, *Wall Street and the Rise of Hitler* (Buccaneer Books, Inc., 1976).

[9] http://www.reformation.org/wall-st-hitler.html

[10] http://www.youtube.com/watch?v=J3nDbJooPu0

Thymus (> 8 Weeks) $75
Intestines & Mesentery $50
Mesentery (≤ 8 weeks) $125
Mesentery (> 8 weeks) $100
Kidney with/without adrenal (≤ 8 weeks) $125
Kidney with/without adrenal (> 8 weeks) $100
Limbs (at least 2) $150
Brain (≤ 8 weeks) 30% discount if significantly fragmented $999
Brain (> 8 weeks) 30% discount if significantly fragmented $150
Pituitary Gland (8 weeks) $300
Bone Marrow (≤ 8 weeks) $350
Bone Marrow (> 8 weeks) $250
Ears (≤ 8 weeks) $75
Ears (> 8 weeks) $50
Eyes (≤ 8 weeks) $75
Eyes (> 8 weeks) $50
Skin (> 12 weeks) $100
Lungs & Heart Block $150
Intact Embryonic Cadaver (≤ 8 weeks) $400
Intact Embryonic Cadaver (> 8 weeks) $600
Intact Calvarium $125
Intact Truck (with/without limbs) $500
Gonads $550
Cord Blood (Snap Frozen LN) $125 2
Spinal Column $150
Spinal Cord $325

Whereas the Nazis made things like lamp shades out of their victims, at least they didn't make FOOD out of them, which is exactly what has happened here. Pepsi, Ocean Spray, Tropicana, and Gatorade are all on the list of companies that are using fetal tissue in research to enhance their flavorings. When the stock holders of PepsiCo found out about this they tried their best to put a stop to it, but the U.S. Securities and Exchange Commission (SEC) ruled that the stockholders could not stop the company from engaging in "normal business practices" which apparently include using aborted babies for flavoring, according to the SEC.

PepsiCo claims that the aborted fetal tissue is not actually used as an ingredient in their flavoring, but even if it is not, do you really want to drink a soda knowing that a dead baby was used to research and develop the recipe?

You can also bet that a good portion of these aborted babies are being sold to the big pharmaceutical companies. Anyone who has been studying the landscape of American politics knows that the corporations are now running the country. The CEOs of these corporations, many of them foreign owned and operated, are the new Roman emperors. Bill Gates, Eric Schmit and Baron Rothschild have replaced Charlemagne, Pepin and Cæsar. The old aristocracy is still in control, together with corporate CEOs. Government officials and bureaucrats are beneath them and do their bidding. They control armies, sway economies, and make sweeping global policies that change the course of history. At the top of the pyramid is the Vatican (Rev 17:18), which has always wanted to destroy America.

Our national debt currently stands at about 17 trillion. (Of course it is really much higher than that.) It is virtually impossible for this debt to ever be paid off. Governments can not create money; they can only collect money through taxes. This means the government's ability to control the economy has its limits in the absence of nationalization of all revenue producing activity.[11]

When a government becomes too overextended, one of the solutions it has available is to start printing money — essentially what the Fed is doing now, and calling it 'quantitative easing'. This causes hyper-inflation. I lived in Zimbabwe in 2001-2002. At that time they introduced the $500 note, and consequently everybody knew that hyper-inflation was coming. By the time the Zim dollar was sacked in favor of switching to foreign currency, the $100 Trillion note had been introduced — and it was absolutely worthless. With the amount of American dollars in circulation, it will take a lot longer for that to happen here. Nevertheless, figures do not lie. Numbers, mathematics and economic principles are absolutely honest. The end result of the course we are presently on always ends the same way. For this reason, David M. Walker, Controller General of the Government Accounting Office from 1998-2008, has likened the United States to the Roman Empire in its decline. In the introductory comments to this chapter I included a recent quote from former president, Jimmy Carter. Although the national news media ignored this statement by a former president of the United States, that "America no longer has a functioning democracy," *Der Spiegal* published it in German. For those who may think only right-wing fanatics are concerned about the state of the Union, this should serve as a wake up call.

Maybe we cannot make America repent, but we can repent as individuals. The prophet Jeremiah was spared by Nebuchadnezzar, because he refused to go along with the apostasy of Israel (Jer 40). His fellow citizens were carried away into captivity. Likewise Ezekiel was caught up into heaven and saw visions of God (Ezek 1), while his fellow countrymen wept by the rivers of Babylon (Ps 137). Daniel, Ezekiel, Jeremiah, these were men who were willing to stand up to the bullies of their day. They were willing to take a side. They did not just tell the truth, they shouted it from the rooftops. They prayed prayers of repentance and acknowledged their sin.

There was once a wicked queen in Israel who had the nobles who were the true heirs to the throne murdered, in order to set herself up as queen. God's servants hid the last heir to the throne in the temple, and after six years they presented him to the nation in a public coronation. Wicked queen Athaliah cried *Treason, Treason*, when Joash was anointed king. Likewise the Athaliahs of today cry treason when patriots defend the Constitution and stand for liberty, that justice may be done, and that we may continue to be a free and independent people.

Truth is treason in the empire of lies.

— Ron Paul,
The Revolution: A Manifesto

Heaven has no rage like love to hatred turned, nor hell a fury like a woman scorned.

— William Congreve, 1670-1729
English Playwright and Poet

But she that liveth in pleasure is dead while she liveth.

The First Epistle of Paul the Apostle to Timothy 5:6

XII

SEXTA'S FURY

After a night of prayer and meditation in the word, Rufus, Cadmus, and Antonina were in agreement that it was God's will for them to seek an audience with the apostle Paul. After a light Mediterranean-style breakfast of bread and oil with orange juice, they set out to meet him. Rufus left the shop with a closed sign on the door. He figured his father could open for business if he felt like it when he awoke. Antonina had no idea what she would tell her master. She had never stayed out all night before. Cadmus was the only one who was not taking the day off from his secular responsibilities, as his master was at his side and no longer seemed to be a master at all, but a brother. Neither Rufus nor Antonina really cared about the responsibility they were shirking. They were concerned with much more important things today.

Sexta had a sleepless night as well, but for different reasons. Her slave checked in on her after the sun had been up for a time, and helped Sexta slip into her stola. "Perhaps my lady should take some meat," Anna said, thinking this would lift her mistress's spirits.

Sexta's father also noticed that she was not in the best of

spirits. She sat at the breakfast table, looking at her juice, but not drinking. He had lived with his wife and two daughters long enough to know that there are times when you need to watch what you say, and times when it is best not to say anything at all. "Sweetheart, why don't you tell Papa what is on your mind?" he said as bent down to lower his face to her level.

"It's nothing Papa, I am just tired," she said in a tone that was almost matter-of-fact enough to be convincing. Picking up her pink grapefruit juice she said "I think I will have my breakfast alfresco today," and walked to the atrium. But Sexta knew she was lying. Away from the prying eye of her father Sexta began to frown, and wonder, *What went wrong? Why did he grow so cold last night? What happened to the surprise he told me about?? WHY IN THE NAME OF DIS PATER DID HE NOT PROPOSE TO ME????* When Sexta's father heard the sound of his daughter's cup smashing against the patio tile, he went to her again and tried to console her, holding her shoulders in his large hands as she turned away and cried.

"What is it Sweetheart? You can tell me," he said.

"No Papa, it's nothing — I will be fine," she said as she pulled her shoulder away and went back to her room. After a time in front of her polished bronze mirror she decided to walk down to the Circus. She took her servant Anna with her for company. There was always something interesting going on there — especially lately. Before Nero started persecuting the Christians, Sexta's favorite was the chariot races. But Nero had brought the Circus to a new level. The Christians were torn apart by wild animals, sometimes even tortured! It was all so exciting; she loved it. The old games had grown too boring. And Sexta was certainly not the only one who was happy with the changes; it seemed they had quelled the civil unrest that Rome had been suffering from. The people had stopped rioting. Now they had something to pacify them. They could go to the Circus and forget about their troubles, watch their heros the gladiators, and get drunk with the blood of the souls who fell prey to claw or sword.

As chance would have it, Rufus and his friends had to pass by the Circus on their way to find Paul. Antonina was the only one who had actually met Paul, and she knew where he was being held. When they neared the Circus they noticed that there was more of a crowd than usual. "What is all the fuss about?" Rufus asked a fellow citizen.

"That leader of the Christians, Paul the apostle," He replied with a grin. "Nero is going to throw him to the lions!"

"Is it?" Cadmus replied, hiding his shock and disgust. "I have to see this." Pushing their way through the crowd the three made their way through the arched entrance. Rufus normally would have taken his place in the section that distinguished his status as a first-class pleb, just below the women. But now it did not seem so important to him. He wanted to stay close to his friends.

Rufus caught Sexta's eye, and she observed as the three continued up the stairs past the women's section and stood in the servants' area at the very top of the amphitheater. *Why is he slumming?* Sexta wondered to herself. She continued to observe with great interest.

Rufus and his friends spied three young men leave their seats to follow three young women who passed by in front of them. They grabbed the empty seats and sat down as the master of ceremonies entered the arena.

"Fellow Romans, let us all rise and hail our gods!" came the cry from the master of ceremonies, as images of Venus and Jupiter were paraded from one end of the arena to the other on large litters borne by bands of eunuchs.

The crowd cheered as the images passed them by, "Ave Venus!! Ave Jupiter!!!"

As the images left the arena, the master of ceremonies once again hailed the crowd to calm down and introduced the guest of honor. "Fellow Romans, lovers of our Lord and his magical harp, let us now all hail the one, the only, NERO . . . CLAUDIUS . . . AUGUSTUS . . . GERMANICUS . . . CÆSAR!!!" With that the crowds cheered even louder as Nero emerged and waved to his fellow Romans from his balcony.

"This is just awful," Rufus said. "How could I have been so blind? I used to think that Roman justice was the will of the gods."

Cadmus looked up at Nero, flanked by the Praetorian Guard, his chin proudly raised. "When I was in Jerusalem, the apostle John once told me that the whole world lies in wickedness," Cadmus said.

"Now without further adieu, let the games begin!!" As the crowd continued to cheer, Rufus, Antonina, and Cadmus huddled and conferred with one another.

Rufus and Antonina were both looking to Cadmus now. "Listen to me," Cadmus began, "I do not believe it is God's will for Paul to die today. Brother James taught us that the effectual fervent prayer of a righteous man avails much. Without being too obvious we all need to pray in one accord for God to deliver him."

"I know I am new at this," Rufus said, "but are you saying prayer can actually stop the mouths of those lions?"

"Yes I am!" Cadmus replied. "God has done it before and he can do it again if he chooses to. Let us stop talking and start praying." Both Antonina and Rufus felt a new faith surge through them, a sort of change in their state of mind, persuading them that God would work a miracle. As their eyes turned from one another to the arena where Paul was being led by the guards into plain view for all to see, they each prayed silently.

"Paul of Tarsus," the master of ceremonies began, "you stand accused of being a Christian, a member of that notorious cult that is known to engage in the most abominable of practices, which meets in secret to do their mischief, which continues to spread their poison throughout our blessed empire. This crime is punishable by death, but moreover, you are guilty of conspiring and committing incendiary crimes that have caused great loss of life and property to our Republic. Cæsar's judgment is that you be given to the lions." The master of ceremonies wore a white toga, adorned with scarlet and purple, the colors or Rome. Paul's clothes were plain, old, and worn. "However," the master of ceremonies continued, "Cæsar is not without mercy. . . If you will recant from following that way, and proclaim as all good Romans do that Cæsar is Lord, renounce your attachment to your ridiculous 'one true God', and confess your crimes against the empire, you may be spared some of the torture that awaits you and be given a more expedient death." The spectators did not react well to that, and the master of ceremonies had to wait until his voice could be heard above the din. "So what say you Paul of Tarsus?"

Paul looked to the sky and said a silent prayer. *Father in Heaven, I thank you that I have been counted worthy to suffer shame and persecution for your name. You know my innocence in these matters, save only the accusation of my devotion to thee. May these things be used for your glory and the furtherance of the gospel of Yeshua Ha'Mashiach whom I serve, my Lord and my God. Amen.* It was a clear day. The sky was blue. Surprisingly, the crowd did not boo at Paul's refusal to recant, but remained silent.

"So be it!" proclaimed the master of ceremonies, and with that he climbed into his chariot and exited the arena. Roman soldiers walked out and uncoupled Paul's shackles. They then exited, as the gates that stood between the man-eaters and Paul were slowly lifted. The growls of the lions stirred the crowd and the noise level began to rise until the gates opened wide enough for the beasts to enter the arena. Then as they slowly sauntered toward where Paul was standing, front and center, the sound died down again and grew almost quiet. The anticipation and lust of the crowd was a sharp contrast to the how the Christians, Rufus, Antonina, and Cadmus were faring. Cadmus and Rufus were both stone faced. Antonina was crying, and when she could not take it anymore she grabbed Rufus and clung to him. Cadmus was busy in fervent prayer. He could feel the Spirit interceding inside him with groanings that could not be uttered. Rufus had waited nearly his entire life for Antonina to hold him that way. He had fantasized about holding her for almost as long as he could remember, and now he was, but he felt terrible. He caressed and comforted Antonina as she wept in his bosom. Little did he know that Sexta was watching from afar, as he kissed Antonina on the top of her head. Then Rufus remembered the dream. Or maybe it was a nightmare, at least that was how it began. He was a slave. He remembered a feeling of absolute despair. It seemed so real.

He felt so helpless. He was overwhelmed with the awareness that he was someone else's property. They owned him. It as terrifying. Then *she* was there, and she was a freeborn citizen. Even though she was a slave when he met her the next day in real life, he knew it was her. Her image had been burned into his psyche. But in the dream she was an aristocrat of the highest order, yet she did not treat him like a slave. She maintained eye contact with him. He saw approval in her countenance, acceptance. She had a scroll in her hand, which she held against her heart as she smiled at him. He looked down and saw that he was holding a scroll too. She said, "Go ahead, eat it." He ate the scroll, then suddenly the nightmare part of the dream was over. They were both freeborn Roman citizens. She was weeping in his bosom as he held her. He kissed her on top of the head. Then he awoke.

The lions approached Paul, growling and sauntering. They circled him, then . . . then they sat on their haunches. Four lions, compassing Paul about — each reverently sat, watching him pray. The crowd was displeased to say the least. Some shouted in protest, others booed, and soon the boos turned into what was almost a full-blown uproar. Then once again the crowd began to quiet down to a dull roar when they saw soldiers enter the arena with whips and spears to chastise the beasts and force them to do their duty. However, the soldiers did not get far before the lions rose up and ran to where they were, and leapt on them, having the mastery over them and rendering their weapons useless. The crowd could not have been more pleased. They got what they came for. The sound of cheers and whistles filled the Circus as the lions dismembered their prey.

Now it was time for Cæsar to render a decision. Since Paul had escaped the mouths of the lions it was up to Cæsar to decide whether to grant him a pardon with a thumb's up, or to order him executed with a thumb down. Everyone looked to Nero as he rose to render his decision, which was a thumb's up. This pleased the crowd. Paul had won their favor if not their hearts. When the gods favored the prisoners so did the Romans. And so it was, that the weeping of the Christians was turned to tears of joy for their leader and their answered prayers. Everybody was happy; everybody that is, except Sexta.

Just who does he think he is anyway? Casting me aside for that slave trash? It would be bad enough to be slighted for a pleb, but a slave? Sexta left the Circus and made her way to the Temple of Veiovis, the wrath inside her still building. *Just who does he think I am? I am Sexta Vitellia. I come from a long line of proud equestrian Romans. There are many Roman men who would kill to have me. I would not even let that slave trash of his empty my piss-pot. I will fix her. I will fix both of them. That little creep. That little plebis creep. That little plebis Christian creep . . . wait until my father gets through with him . . .*

Sexta made her way into the temple and presented the priests with a young kid as a sacrifice. After a brief ceremony of chanting and prayer to Veiovis, the priests anointed Sexta with the blood of the sacrifice, and she was prayed over. Then it came to her. It was so simple; the best way to fix Rufus was to report his little whore to the Praetorian Guard. If that did not bring him back to her with his tail between his legs, then nothing would. She wasted no time. After they were back home, Sexta instructed Anna to fetch Africanus for her. When he arrived he bowed and addressed her. "What is thy pleasure Domina?"

"I have a job for you," Sexta replied. "There is a trollop who has been seen associating with my Rufus. I want to know her name and station. I believe her to be a slave but I need that verified. I need to know where she squats, and anything else you can find out about her."

"Of course Domina," Africanus replied. "I will attend to it at once."

"Keep a record of any coin you need to pay for bribes," Sexta said. "She is young, long brown hair, from Hispania by the looks of her; light brown complexion, stands not much more than III cubits high."

"A little thing, huh?" Africanus said.

"She is not bad looking, in a trashy kind of way. That is all the information I have. I want this taken care of quickly. Do not worry about getting your hands dirty if need be."

"As you wish Domina." Africanus knew exactly what was meant by that. He not only attended most of the important affairs of the house but was also in charge of security. In Rome, that sometimes meant "getting your hands dirty."

Africanus changed out of his slave tunic and donned something that made him look like more like a citizen so he could blend in. After he made his way to where Rufus stayed, he found a place where he could observe from a distance and see what was going on at Rufus's shop. After a time he noticed that there were some children playing knucklebones out in the street. *This is going to be easy*, he told himself.

"Ah, knucklebones, my favorite game," Africanus said. "I am pretty good at it. I have a semis here that I will bet."

"We don't have any money," one of the children replied.

"No money?? Well then, maybe there is something else we can play for. If I win, I will ask you some questions, and you can answer them for me."

"If we win, do we each get a semis?" The children asked.

"Of course," Africanus replied. After a few rounds Africanus was running out of change. He decided to change his strategy. "I'll tell you what," he said, "you have XII semissis there. How would you like to double your money."

The children nodded enthusiastically.

"Okay, but you have to keep all of this a secret. I am looking for an old friend who lives here and I want to surprise him. I happen to know he likes a young slave girl, from Hispania. She is about this tall, kind of cute..."

The boys interrupted and said, "That's Antonina. She's not cute. She's a goddess."

"Ah, good," Africanus said. "Do you know where she stays?"

It was not long before Africanus had all the information he needed. He then reported back to his mistress. Having obtained the information she needed from her servant, Sexta made her way to the scriptorium and had them scribe a letter for her:

TO THE MOST HIGH AND HONORABLE
PRÆTORIAN GUARD,

I HAVE IT ON GOOD AUTHORITY, THAT ANTONINA
THE SLAVE, PROPERTY OF GAIUS LUCANUS VIBIDIUS,
IS OF THE JEWISH SECT CALLED THE CHRISTIANS, AND
HAS BEEN PROSELYTIZING ROMAN CITIZENS INTO
THAT WAY. ID EST, SHE HAS BEEN SEEN ASSOCIATING
WITH ROMAN FREEBORN MEN, AND CORRUPTING
THEM WITH HER CROOKED BELIEFS. I THEREFORE
BESEECH THAT SHE BE APPREHENDED AT ONCE AND
BROUGHT TO JUSTICE FOR HER CRIMES AGAINST
CÆSAR OUR LORD.

SEXTA VITELLIA,
DAUGHTER OF APPIUS VITALLIUS TRAJANUS

The devil can cite Scripture for his purpose.

— William Shakespeare, 1564-1616
From *The Merchant of Venice*

Study to shew thyself approved unto God, a workman that needeth not to be ashamed, rightly dividing the word of truth.

The Second Epistle of Paul the Apostle to Timothy 2:15

"Once mighty, once glorious, a nation that was established under God. A nation that stood forth in the world as a Christian nation, but has become so totally corrupt, obscene, and has sought to just rule God out of our national life. I'm appalled by the rulings of the Supreme Court, and by the local courts, in the issues that relate to freedom of worship. Separation of church and state, it only works on one side, it doesn't work on both sides. And even by my saying this I'm jeopardizing myself, because they've started a new system now, if ever you speak out against it, then soon you have all kinds of harassment."[†]

— Chuck Smith, Calvary Chapel Costa Mesa
Circa 1980

[†] Sermon on II Chron 10, about 15 min in.
http://resource.cccm.com/c2k/c2075.mp3

ⅩⅢ

ROMANS XIII

Tyrants all recognize how the church is a threat to their power, as well as how it can be used as a tool to exercise their despotic power. For this reason the founding fathers placed the free exercise of religion and free speech in the *First* Amendment to the Constitution. However, the wisdom of the day in many Christian circles says that we must not say anything critical and obey the government above all else, based on Romans 13. But since Jesus and the apostles were executed by the government for what amounted to civil disobedience, how do we reconcile this with Romans 13? Romans 13 tells us this:

> *Let every soul be subject unto the higher powers. For there is no power but of God: the powers that be are ordained of God.*
>
> *Whosoever therefore resisteth the power, resisteth the ordinance of God: and they that resist shall receive to themselves damnation.*
>
> *For rulers are not a terror to good works, but to the evil. Wilt thou then not be afraid of the power? do that which is good, and thou shalt have praise of the same:*

For he is the minister of God to thee for good. But if thou do that which is evil, be afraid; for he beareth not the sword in vain: for he is the minister of God, a revenger to execute wrath upon him that doeth evil.

Wherefore ye must needs be subject, not only for wrath, but also for conscience sake.

For for this cause pay ye tribute also: for they are God's ministers, attending continually upon this very thing.

Render therefore to all their dues: tribute to whom tribute is due; custom to whom custom; fear to whom fear; honour to whom honour.

Romans 13:1–7

This is one of those portions of Scripture that is loved by unbelievers who take it out of context for their own advancement. This was Hitler's favorite passage of Scripture. There are many portions of Scripture that can be easily twisted, if taken out of context and used in the mouth of the enemy. For example, I often hear critics of the New Testament claim that it is anti-Semitic, and cite how the Jewish Pharisees stirred up the people and ultimately caused the crucifixion of Jesus. So, such a statement, unchecked, creates the misconception that Christians and indeed the New Testament must in fact be anti-Semitic. But in the larger context, when carefully examined, this false claim is easily proven wrong. First of all, Jesus himself is Jewish. Second, all the apostles were Jewish. Third, Jesus at times slighted Gentiles and told them he was only sent to the house of Israel, and even called the Gentiles dogs (Matt 15:22-28). Fourth, the New Testament makes it clear that the gospel is extended *to the Jew first, and also to the Gentile* (Rom 1:16; 2:9,10). Fifth, even though it was clear during the time of the writing of the New Testament that the nation of Israel had by and large rejected Jesus, the New Testament writers made it clear that the promises of the Old Testament are still in effect, and that *touching election* the Jews are still *beloved for the fathers' sakes* (Rom 11). Many other examples could be given to show how easily the enemy can twist Scripture to suit his own needs. Therefore, we must carefully examine Romans 13.

As Christians we are servants of all, including those in government. Paul said it this way in his first letter to Timothy:

> *I exhort therefore, that, first of all, supplications, prayers, intercessions, and giving of thanks, be made for **all men**;*
>
> *For kings, and for all that are in authority; that we may lead a quiet and peaceable life in all godliness and honesty.*
>
> *For this is good and acceptable in the sight of God our Saviour;*
>
> *Who will have **all men** to be saved, and to come unto the knowledge of the truth.*
>
> *I Timothy 2:1-4*

We wrestle not with flesh and blood, even when a tyrant like Nero is in power. Nero had a spirit behind him. We should respect all in authority, following the example of Jesus and the apostles. Yet it is clear that although they went about doing good, they often got into trouble, and refused to back down when faced with the decision to obey God or obey government. When Peter and John were brought before the rulers of their day and commanded to quit preaching they responded, *Whether it be right in the sight of God to hearken unto you more than unto God, judge ye.* Jesus was crucified by the Roman government. This, for upsetting their vassal Jewish government. (Of course, the deeper reason was to pay for the sins of the world.) Many of the apostles were martyred by the government, for their defiance of their perceived authority. That is where the crux of the issue is. Romans 13 makes it clear that the rulers themselves are under the authority of God.

In WWII, Corrie ten Boom was arrested by the Nazis, together with her sister Betsy and her father, who everyone affectionately called Opa (lit. Grandfather). A Nazi picked up Opa's Bible and said, "I see you are a man who studies Scripture. Tell me, what does Scripture say about obeying the government?" Then Corrie records that ". . . the life giving words came from Opa's mouth, strengthening us all; *Fear God. Honour the queen.*" The Nazi protested that it did not say that, and Opa admitted that it did in fact say *Fear God. Honour the king* (I Pet 2:17), but in their case in Holland, it was a queen. By quoting Peter, Opa pointed out to the Nazi that it was he who was in fact was resisting the *power* (Gk. *exousia*) that was ordained by God, by invading Holland and rebelling against the *ruler* (Gk. *archōn*). He was also pointing out that although we are to give honor to who honor is due, we are to *fear God*, who is the highest *power* as well as the highest *ruler*. By engaging in an aggressive war against Holland, the Nazis were being disobedient to Scripture on several levels. At that point the Nazi's attempt to bully them with the Bible was thwarted. All he had left was his brute power, but Corrie had the moral high ground, because when understood in context, Romans 13 is by no means an endorsement of everything any government does, and it is certainly not a blanket commandment to obey anyone in the government regardless of the circumstances. In Exodus 1 for example, the midwives who disobeyed Pharaoh were commended by God for their civil disobedience when they refused to murder the Hebrew babies. John the Baptist rebuked King Herod for his sin and was ultimately beheaded for it, and yet Jesus said, *Among those that are born of women there is not a greater prophet than John the Baptist* (Luke 7:28). Saul's soldiers disobeyed him when he commanded them to kill his son, Jonathan. Shortly afterwards, Samuel informed Saul that God had rejected *him* for *his* disobedience. God told Samuel to anoint David to be king in Saul's stead, and instructed him to make up a story if he got caught while he was on his way to anoint David. This was in direct disobedience to Saul, but in obedience to God. Samuel risked his life to obey God, and the methods he used were what Jesus meant when he said [*B*]*e ye therefore wise as serpents, and harmless as doves* (Matt 10:16b).

The missionaries who smuggle Bibles into China do not ask the government for permission. The most important government official is King Jesus, and it is him we are to obey. We are a *chosen generation, a royal priesthood, an **holy nation**, a peculiar people,* and we are to take our orders from the King of Kings.

It is often pointed out, and rightly so, that Nero was ruling when Paul wrote Romans. I say rightly so because a Christian should always follow the truth, wherever it may lead. I wondered about this as a younger Christian, and when I brought it up with older, presumably wiser, Christian scholars, I found no satisfactory explanation. After some study of the subject however, it becomes clearer why Paul would make such statements, at the very moment when a tyrant such as Nero was ruling. To begin with, Paul wrote Romans circa 57 AD, around 3 years after Nero began his reign. At this time Nero was winning the hearts and minds of the Roman people. He had not yet begun to display his erratic and perverse behavior. He was being guided by his tutor Seneca, and Agrippina, his mother. Nero had not gone mad yet at the time Paul had written Romans, or else Paul would never have appealed his court case to him a short time later. Paul believed in the rule of law and due process, which is what Romans 13 is really all about. In America, as in the common law tradition, the law is king, not vice versa. In America, *We the People* are the government. We have a responsibility to govern ourselves. The president is merely a steward of that tradition; he is a citizen who performs a civic duty, by serving in office. It is the job of the church to educate the citizens of this great nation about our civic duty to govern ourselves and hold our elected representatives accountable for their actions. Yet the church appears to be AWOL. Where are the Black Regiment pastors today? Why are so many pastors afraid to preach against corruption in government, not to mention sin? It's because they are afraid of the government. The Bible says, *The fear of man bringeth a snare.* Liberty is like a muscle, if you do not exercise it, it becomes weak and begins to atrophy. We are becoming weak and anemic. Our muscles are becoming thin and emaciated. Only by exercising our spiritual authority and preaching truth can we restore our spiritual health, and by God's grace save our Republic.

The scope of church activities used to encompass a much wider range than it does today. Pastors used to take on all issues, however controversial. Nothing was off limits. *Changeling* with

Angelina Jolie tells the true life story of Rev. Gustav Briegleb, a Presbyterian minister played by John Malkovich. Dr. Briegleb took on the corruption in the LAPD in the first half of the 20th century. Around this same time, pastors in Texas were taking on corruption in politics. There was one politician in particular who was getting not a little annoyed with them — Lyndon Johnson. Johnson came up with an idea. Although churches were always exempt from taxes from the founding of the Republic, LBJ neutered the churches by making them 501 C3 for tax exemption purposes. The churches were told they must sign contracts that stipulated they were not allowed to discuss anything political, or they would lose their tax exempt status. *www.hushmoney.org* has instructions on how to take back our spiritual authority as the church, and get out of the straight jacket that LBJ has forced us into. As mentioned in Chapter VII, another website resource is *www.biblicallawcenter.com.*

We have lost our concept of freedom. True political freedom means much more than being able to vote. It means that you can own land, and do as you choose to with the land you own. It means that nobody can tell you what to do on your land. It means that nobody is allowed on your land without your permission, except for a very good reason, and then only by due process. It means that nobody can tell you what to say, or what not to say. It means that you have the right to defend yourself and others, by force if necessary. It means that you are always secure in your papers, person, and effects, and nobody can harass you, or even question you, without probable cause. It means that you can pursue whatever goals or endeavors you choose. It means that you can believe whatever you want, and worship in any way you choose. It means you can come and go as you please, at any hour of the day, without being asked why or where. It means you are innocent until proven guilty, by a jury of your peers, and if you are accused of a crime you have the right to a speedy trial. It was not all that long ago that all these things were taken for granted in the United States. I certainly remember things being this way when I was a young man. How fast things change. The due process in our courts is one of our greatest treasures as Americans. The fact that we are innocent until proven guilty, and must be convicted by a jury of our peers is a stalwart safeguard against tyranny. As a member of the jury, a citizen is an officer of the court, and has the authority to override the law when it is misapplied or inappropriate. It's called *jury nullification*, and it is the duty of the jury to invoke it when a fellow citizen is being wrongly charged with a crime.

In communist countries they have none of these freedoms. The state tells them when they can come and go, what their goals and endeavors will be, where they will work, etc. But, they are told they have the 'right' to work. So the government gives them a job. Nobody will ever make more money that anyone else, because that wouldn't be fair, according to the state. Never mind that you work twice as hard as the deadbeat in the next cubicle. The state gives you everything you need, but first they take everything you have. This is where we are headed in the U.S.

If indeed this is the endgame of unchecked authoritarian rule, why would Romans 13 declare that we must obey the government? Does it really say that? The Romans 13 debate is an old one, and one that has been thoroughly explored by theologians for ages. The subject had already been debated and preached on for centuries by the time of the American Revolution. At that time, Quakers took the side that today's mainline preachers have adopted, believing that government should be obeyed without exception, while most of the other denominations, Baptists, Presbyterians, Methodists, Congregationalists, by and large adopted the view that governments are to be submitted to God, and when that sacred trust is broken, and when said government becomes a terror not to the evil but to those that are good, then it is the duty of the Christian to resist that government. Jesus taught that under the old covenant, the kingdom of God allowed for violence, and the violent took the kingdom of God by force. He taught that John the Baptist would be the last old covenant prophet to operate under this system (Matt 11:12,13). But Jesus never commanded his disciples to be in blind submission to corrupt and unjust governments either. For this reason, the colonists were careful to follow legal avenues and not to engage in insurrection against Great Britain. It was only after their petitions fell on deaf ears, and after being physically persecuted and attacked, that they were forced to defend themselves. Today we commonly hear that the reason for the Revolution was taxation without representation, yet that was only one of twenty-seven reasons listed in the Declaration of Independence for the separation from Great Britain, and it was not even one of the primary reasons. I encourage the reader to read the full Declaration for themselves in Appendix E. In some ways the tyranny they were under by the British was not as severe as the tyranny we have today. Their taxes were certainly much lower. Basically, the Crown had stripped the colonists of their rights as British subjects, and made them their enemy by openly firing upon and killing them, among many other sore grievances.

Christians have for a long time now in America, had the luxury of not having to worry about persecution, or corrupt and oppressive regimes that twist the truth and stifle freedom of religion. However, things are changing fast here in America. The recent IRS scandals targeting and harassing Christians, conservatives, and libertarians prove it. Although internal emails proved that the targeted persecution was happening, with the Christian groups being denied tax exempt status, nobody went to jail. Lois Lerner, one of the main people involved, and who perjured herself before Congress, was allowed to resign without consequence. And now the IRS is training with AR-15 assault rifles. Representative Jeff Duncan (R-SC) witnessed IRS agents training with AR-15s at a federal firing range. Is the IRS training with assault rifles to take their targeted persecution of Christians to the next level? And if so, who is really resisting the *power* Paul wrote about in Romans 13?

It is the church that is by and large responsible for the birth of America and the freedoms we enjoy. Yet this has been forgotten, and the responsibility the Christian bears to be a defender of freedom is under attack. First, the truth that the founders were Christians is under attack, next the truth that the founders were acting righteously in fighting the tyranny of Great Britain is under attack, and third, the idea that Christians have a responsibility to act in civil disobedience against tyranny is under attack.

Thomas Paine was by far the least religious person connected to the American Revolution, yet Paine was not in fact a founding father. He never served in office, and he did not sign any founding document. It is true however, that he authored an important pamphlet that inspired people to join the cause. As an 'enlightenment' thinker, Paine was a believer in the power of reason and rational thinking. This philosophy heavily influenced many of the founders. But Paine also believed in God, and in creation. Although he did not believe in the inspiration of Scripture or the deity of Jesus Christ, Paine was definitely no atheist. His pamphlet *Common Sense*, was steeped in Bible references. Paine's pamphlet inspired many Christians to fight for the cause, people like the clergymen known as the Black Regiment. These were preachers who wore military uniforms under their black robes, and inspired their congregations to join the Continental Army and fight for freedom. The theological application of Romans 13 was written about, preached on, and thoroughly examined by the theologians of that day, and with much more insight, prayer and deliberation than that of the theologians of today, who tell us we should blindly obey the government. Colonial preachers who took the superficial view of Romans 13 quickly changed their mind, when their churches were raided by British regulars.

Maybe the debate should not be so much whether Christians should obey the government, but whether they should *be* the government. We know about the nonreligious founders like Benjamin Franklin and Thomas Jefferson — even Jefferson considered himself a Christian, attended church, and required the Bible to be taught in D.C. public schools — but what about the others, like these for example:

Abraham Baldwin, *Signer of the Constitution*:
Chaplain in the American Revolution for two years.

Rufus King, *Signer of the Constitution*:
Manager of the American Bible Society.

Alexander Hamilton, *Signer of the Constitution*:
Proposed formation of the Christian Constitutional Society to spread Christian government to other nations.

Francis Scott Key, *Attorney; Author of "The Star Spangled Banner"*:
Manager and Vice-President of the American Sunday School Union.

John Langdon, *Signer of the Constitution*:
Vice-President of the American Sunday School Union.

John McHenry, *Signer of the Constitution*:
President of the Baltimore Bible Society.

Robert Trent Paine, *Signer of the Declaration*:
Military Chaplain.

Charles Cotesworth Pinchney, *Signer of the Constitution*:
President of the Charleston Bible Society; Vice-President of the American Bible Society.

Benjamin Rush, *Signer of the Declaration*:
Founder and manager of the Philadelphia Bible Society.[1]

The Revolution was a beacon of hope, a light that transformed the modern world. It brought liberty to those in slavery. (Eight States almost immediately abolished slavery.) It opened the doors to the oppressed of the world. Consider for example, the sonnet by Emma Lazarus, on the placard on the Statue of Liberty:

---

[1] David Barton, *Original Intent* (Aledo, TX: Wallbuilder Press, 1996), pp. 139–143.

The New Colossus

Not like the brazen giant of Greek fame,
With conquering limbs astride from land to land;
Here at our sea-washed, sunset gates shall stand
A mighty woman with a torch, whose flame
Is the imprisoned lightning, and her name
Mother of Exiles. From her beacon-hand
Glows world-wide welcome; her mild eyes command
The air-bridged harbor that twin cities frame,
"Keep, ancient lands, your storied pomp!" cries she
With silent lips. "Give me your tired, your poor,
Your huddled masses yearning to breathe free,
The wretched refuse of your teeming shore,
Send these, the homeless, tempest-tost to me,
I lift my lamp beside the golden door!"

The Colossus of Rhodes was an image of the Greek Titan Helios (Roman counterpart: Sol, the sun god, ie Satan), constructed to celebrate Rhodes' military victory over Cyprus. The Statue of Liberty is a peaceful French lady, donning a Roman stola, modeled after Libertas, the Roman goddess of liberty. The Colossus of Rhodes stood 99 feet high (149 including the pedestal). Our French lady stands 151 feet tall (305 including pedestal). She welcomes all who come to America seeking freedom by way of New York. Yet, it is actually preached by some that America was a mistake and the colonists should have just rolled over to the tyranny of King George. Those same preachers seem to be oblivious to the tyranny that has hijacked our constitutional form of government. They kneel in ready submission before the tyrants of our present age, without ever considering that Christianity is the only hope of the world. If we as God's people do not stand for freedom, then who will? Besides, we stand in a much different position than did the colonists, and certainly than the Romans did. The president is elected to represent us. He is not a neo-aristocratic monarch who is above the law, who has grapes fed to him by slaves as he rules from a throne with SPRQ engraved in marble above him, in mockery of the old Republic. Paul wrote his letters to different Christians in different cultures, and what was good for one culture may not necessarily be good for another culture. For example, Paul wrote that in Corinth, the women should not shave their heads, because that is what the shrine prostitutes did in Corinth (I Cor 11). They were to have a covering. That would not necessarily apply to women today in say, Zimbabwe, where many women shave their heads, but prostitutes typically have long hair. In Paul's letter to the Hebrews, he said things about people who leave the faith, and it being impossible to renew them again to repentance (Heb 6). This applied to their specific culture at that time, and to coming out of a system of works, and accepting the Jewish Messiah, Yeshua Ha'Mashiach, only to forsake him and return to dead works, and trying to earn salvation through keeping the law. There may be some cultures where Hebrews 6 would apply today, but generally that does not apply to any other Christians except those to whom it was written, the Hebrews. Paul wrote Romans to a specific culture at a specific point in history. That being said, I believe the principles of Romans 13 are more relevant than ever today, as we are looking more and more each day like pagan Rome. Yet I do not believe Paul taught the Romans to blindly obey Nero. Paul did not blindly obey Nero, and he was beheaded for it. But if Romans 13 does not teach blind submission to everyone in the government, what does it mean?

Dr. G. Campbell Morgan would not write a commentary on a book of the Bible until he had read it fifty times. I recommend reading and re-reading Romans 13 in prayer, and it should become clearer with the aid of the Holy Spirit. For starters, the passage is a treatise against anarchy. Jesus is a God of order. He ordained government institutions to keep society civil, and to protect it from spiraling out of control into chaos. All the problems addressed in this book could probably be solved by an informed church that engaged in targeted intercessory prayer, in conjunction with grass-roots petitioning of the appropriate public servants for a redress of grievances. The Christian is never to resort to rebellion and insurrection, but to follow the lawful system of due process. Such a system existed in some form in Paul's day (Acts 19:38, 39, et al). Romans 13 is about due process and order in Government. It is acknowledged by all that the Constitution is the highest law of the land in America. Therefore, whoever resists the Constitution, resists the *power*. It is those who are trying to reorganize our Republic into a new global empire that are not following Romans 13.

Before we read Romans 13, let us consider Luke 4. In Luke 4 (and Matt 4) Satan offers Jesus the kingdoms of the world. He claims that they belong to him, and he can give them to whosoever he will. Jesus does not dispute this. In order for it to have been a temptation, it must have been true. Therefore, the doctrine that all rulers are appointed by God is faulty doctrine. Romans 13 teaches that governments are ordained by God, not necessarily individual rulers (*cf* I John 5:19; the leading cause of death by far is democide, or death by government). We do see examples of people being divinely appointed by God in the Bible, yet even in those cases, they were often examples of God's permissive will, not his direct will. God allowed the people of Israel to have a king, Saul, only because they rejected God's rule over them through his servant Samuel. The idea of the divine right of kings can be traced back to Augustine of Hippo (354-430 AD). The Catholic Church incorporated this into their canon law and dogma. They crowned Pepin king of the Franks in 754 AD, claiming it was decreed by none other than St Peter himself, based on a forged heavenly document. The decree extended to Charlemagne, Pepin's son, and all subsequent descendents. This was the beginning of the Holy Roman Empire. It was bolstered by another forged document, *The Donation of Constantine*. Thomas Aquinas (1225-1274 AD) solidified the doctrine of the divine right of kings into Catholic dogma, and the idea still pervades Christian theology today.

Now, having reviewed Romans 13, slowly reading it in prayer, asking the Lord for understanding and discernment, note how the passage begins in Romans 13:1:

*Let **every soul** be subject the higher powers. For there is **no power but of God**: the powers that be are ordained of God.*

Every soul would include those in government, whether it be an emperor in Rome or a mayor in Culver City. One of the new and revolutionary aspects of the American experiment, was that our rulers were not royalty, but public servants, and we hold our public servants accountable. They are subject to the same laws that we are. When they break those laws they suffer the consequences the same as anyone else. After the articles of the Constitution were drafted, which detail the legal basis on which the federal government operates, the Bill of Rights was added, which details the rights of all citizens. The Constitution with its Bill of Rights, is the form of government that God has ordained for America, and it is what our elected representatives swear by oath to uphold. Many public servants take this oath, from police officers to the president, as well as those in the armed services. Therefore, whosoever resists the Constitution is in breach of Romans 13:1. The first ten amendments to our Constitution are in what appears to be a divinely inspired order:

The *First* Amendment protects our freedom of religion, our free speech, and our free press. This threefold cord is a strong check against government tyranny.
The *Second* Amendment gives teeth to the First Amendment, and all the others that follow, by arming the public. That is the reason we were given the Second Amendment; it has nothing to do with hunting.
The *Third* Amendment sets the premise that a man's house is his castle, and not even the army can not infringe on that. (This principle was further refined with the Posse Comitatus Act. Just as the Romans had a law that kept standing armies on the other side of the Rubicon River, the Posse Comitatus Act makes clear that the military can not be used against U.S. citizens.)
The *Fourth* Amendment guarantees our right to privacy, and to be secure in our person, papers and effects.

The *Fifth* Amendment guarantees our presumption of innocence, right to due process, and protects us from double jeopardy. These principles were by and large uniquely American at the time of the Revolution. They are like crown jewels in the tiara of the Statue of Liberty, and have taken root in other Western countries as well.

The *Sixth* Amendment guarantees our right to a speedy trial by jury.

The *Seventh* Amendment grants the right of jury trial in civil suits.

The *Eighth* Amendment protects us from excessive bail, fines, and cruel and unusual punishments.

The *Ninth* Amendment: "The enumeration in the Constitution, of certain rights, shall not be construed to deny or disparage others retained by the people."

The *Tenth* Amendment guarantees States' rights, and guards further against overreach by the federal government. I encourage the reader to read the entire Bill of Rights in Appendix E.

Now, having established that *everyone* is subject to the *powers* that are ordained of God, Paul continues is verse II:

*Whosoever therefore resisteth **the power**, resisteth the ordinance of God: and they that resist shall receive to themselves **damnation**.*

Christians are to obey the law. The *power* ordained by God in America is our constitutional system of a separation of powers, regulated by checks and balances, along with the Bill of Rights to protect the citizens. Verse III details what the responsibilities of rulers are:

For rulers are not a terror to good works, but to the evil. Wilt thou then not be afraid of the power? do that which is good, and thou shalt have praise of the same:

The ultimate Ruler is God himself. He has ordained that those in authority are to punish (be a terror to) evil doers, and to reward those that do good with praise. Therefore, when a public servant begins to persecute the good guys, and to receive bribes from the bad guys, it is he himself who is being disobedient to Romans 13. Now verse IV:

> *For he is the **minister of God** to thee for good. But if thou do that which is evil, be afraid; for he **beareth not the sword in vain**: for he is the minister of God, a revenger to execute wrath upon him that doeth evil.*

This verse shows that those in government are *servants*, not "officials." Minister, as they are still referred to as in Europe, literally means servant. They have been granted by God the authority to kill under due process of law. A ruler is a servant of God, who is supposed to punish evil doers. The problem is that we have a government with no fear of God. This is virtually unprecedented in Western history. Ever since the *Magna Carta* (1215 AD), rulers have always understood that they act under the authority of God. This was certainly understood by the founding fathers, and was a continuation of the tradition of Europe. The marked difference was that in America, it was the pure gospel of Jesus Christ that they served, not the Church of England, or the Catholic Church, or any denomination.

> The only foundation for . . . a republic is to be laid in Religion. Without this there can be no virtue, and without virtue there can be no liberty, and liberty is the object and life of all republican governments.
>
> — Benjamin Rush

> Christianity is the only true and perfect religion...
>
> — Benjamin Rush

> The Declaration of Independence laid the cornerstone of human government upon the first precepts of Christianity.
>
> — John Adams

The highest glory of the American Revolution was this: it connected, in one indissoluble bond, the principles of civil government with the principles of Christianity.

— John Quincy Adams

I have always said and always will say that the studious perusal of the Sacred Volume will make us better citizens.[2]

— Thomas Jefferson

Indeed, Jefferson remarked that the First Amendment had thrown a "wall of separation" between church and state. The true meaning of that phrase — which Jefferson used to assure the Baptists in Danbury, Connecticut — was that their religious freedom was God given, not granted by the state. Not that we were not a Christian nation — everybody knew we were — but that there was no national denomination and people were free to worship as they pleased, free from government interference. Now verse V:

Wherefore ye must needs be subject, not only for wrath, but also for conscience sake.

Christians are to be good citizens, not only because it is the right thing to do, but there is also the practical reason that they may suffer the wrath of the government authorities if they stray from the law. Of course this applies to those who serve in office as well. Verse VI:

*For for this cause pay ye tribute also: for they are **God's ministers**, attending continually upon this very thing.*

Jesus said we should *render unto Cæsar that which is Cæsar's,* yet our tax code has mutated into a 73,608 page monstrosity that

---

[2] David Barton, ~~Unconfirmed~~ *Confirmed Quotes.*
http://www.wallbuilders.com/libissuesarticles.asp?id=138585

nobody has ever read in its entirety. At the time of the Revolution the taxes owed to King George were only about 1 - 2.5% of total income. Of course there was no income tax per se, only a tax on tea, sugar, paper, and certain imports. This is about the same amount as the taxes paid to Rome in the New Testament time period. Although it is difficult to determine exact amounts, taxes in the first century probably amounted to around 4% or less of gross product. Today however, we have income tax, sales tax, employment tax, property tax, inheritance tax, import tax, export tax, gasoline tax, cigarette tax, alcohol tax, and around forty other taxes, which all amount to 30 - 50% or more of our total income. The Grace Commission, appointed by Reagan in 1982, exposed the unnecessary waste of our tax dollars, which registers in the trillions. Jesus told us to *render unto Cæsar*, but before we willingly render everything we have let us remember that in America, We the People are Cæsar, and it is our duty as good stewards to rein in wasteful spending using proper legal channels.[3] Finally, let us examine verse VII:

> *Render therefore to all their dues: tribute to whom tribute is due; custom to whom custom; fear to whom fear; honour to whom honour.*
>
> *Romans 13:7*

I pay my taxes. I pray for all who are in authority. I do not just mean that I pray the president will do what I want him to do. I mean that I pray for him, personally, and for his wife and his children. When I get a ticket I pray for the officer who wrote it. If I have one handy, I give her a gospel tract. I pray that God will give those in places of authority wisdom to govern rightly. I recognize that as a Christian I am a servant of all and I do my best to respect everyone, whether they be in government or in jail. Sometimes the greatest respect you can offer someone is telling him the truth, when no one else will.

---

[3] A good documentary about the legalities of the tax code is Aaron Russo's *America: Freedom to Fascism* (2006). https://youtu.be/O6ayb02bwp0

S exta could not resist getting a note for Rufus as well while she was at the scriptorium, to inform him what had become of his little friend. Having heard about Antonina's arrest, Rufus wasted no time. He had to see what he could do to save her. He prayed out loud as he ran to the Castra Prætoria. When he arrived he had to stop and catch his breath.

Rufus scaled the outer wall and slipped between the battlements at the top, then made his way down the scaffolding, moving quickly but quietly to avoid being detected by the guards. He moved in the shadows until he made his way to the entrance of the stockade. He picked out the one in charge by his centurion helmet.

"My name is Rufus Licinius," Rufus said. "And I am here to secure the release of Antonina the slave."

"How did you get in here?" the centurion demanded.

"What is more important than that Centurion, is what I can do for you," Rufus said. "I can pay coin."

"I could have you arrested for sneaking in here," the centurion said. "Why did you not present yourself at the front gate?"

"Let's settle this man to man," Rufus countered. "I'm a man, and you're a man. I can pay V aurei now, and D sestertii tomorrow after the girl is released." Rufus had cashed in his notes from the partners he traded with in imports and exports. This was all he had left, but it made no difference at this point. It did not matter if he was ruined. His journey was over.

"M sestertii is of no use to a dead man.[4] Get lost before I lose my patience, citizen."

"I have a way where you can get your coin, and keep your life."

"Go on," the centurion replied.

"She was brought in just hours ago, on your watch, correct? Nobody but you and your men knows that she is here correct? Put my name on the manifest," Rufus said. "You still have your prisoner. Just exchange me for her. It's a perfect plan. Why not profit from it?"

"You would exchange your life, for the life of a slave?"

"I will."

---

[4] V=5, D=500, M=1000, 5 aurei is equivalent to 500 sestertii.

Without debate, without criticism, no Administration and no country can succeed — and no republic can survive. That is why the Athenian lawmaker Solon decreed it a crime for any citizen to shrink from controversy. And that is why our press was protected by the *First* Amendment — the only business in America specifically protected by the Constitution — not primarily to amuse and entertain, not to emphasize the trivial and sentimental, not to simply "give the public what it wants" — but to inform, to arouse, to reflect, to state our dangers and our opportunities, to indicate our crises and our choices, to lead, mold, educate and sometimes even anger public opinion.

— President Kennedy, April 27, 1961

The kings of the earth set themselves, and the rulers take counsel together, against the LORD, and against his anointed, saying,

Let us break their bands asunder, and cast away their cords from us.

He that sitteth in the heavens shall laugh: the Lord shall have them in derision.

The Book of Psalms 2:2–4

THE
NEW WORLD ORDER

The original 9/11 occurred on September 11th, 1990, when George H.W. Bush, rallied an international coalition to come to the aid of Kuwait. During his speech, he introduced the "New World Order":

> Out of these troubled times, our fifth objective — a *new world order* — can emerge: a new era — freer from the threat of terror, stronger in the pursuit of justice, and more secure in the quest for peace.[1] [Emphasis added.]

Ask yourself, how is that working out? Are we freer from the threat of terror? Are we stronger in the pursuit of justice? Are we more secure in the quest for peace? The New World Order promises great things, but delivers nothing but lies. When governments forsake their Romans 13 mandate, deny God, and actively pursue programs of destabilization that cause countries to become war zones where the local government has no control,

---

[1] Bush Library Archive: http://bushlibrary.tamu.edu/research/public_papers.php?id=2217&year=1990&month=9

like has happened in Iraq, Afghanistan, Egypt, Libya, and now Syria, then it is clear that the governments that are doing so are the ones that are 'resisting the *power*' (Rom 13:2). I remember watching President Bush's speech on September 11, in 1990. I was impressed. It sounded pretty good. Little did I know at the time that I was being deceived. Now we see a pattern in their design: The term New World Order was introduced to the public on September 11 in 1990; their master plan to roll it out was executed on the same date in 2001, 11 years later. 9/11 was used as a pretext to bring in the police state and to go to war in the Middle East, all in the name of the 'War on Terror' — an endless war with no visible enemy that can never be won. It is the perfect government crisis. It's perpetual. It instills fear in the mind of the public. It calls for huge budgets, reduced liberties and increased power.

The plan for restructuring in the new millennium was published in a document by The Project For a New American Century (PNAC). PNAC was a neoconservative think tank, that outlined a plan for the U.S. to take over seven Middle-Eastern countries and reorganize the Middle East. Jeb Bush was a member, and seventeen of the of the PNAC's participants would take positions in the administration of GWB. Up until Syria, their plan was going forward perfectly. 9/11 was the event that kicked it off. The PNAC stated in its published documents that this plan would require a very lengthy process of implementation, absent a "catalyst" event like a "new Pearl Harbor." The PNAC was made up of powerful establishment elites who move in and out of government, while intermittently working for fortune 500 companies. Much to his disbelief, Four-Star General Wesley Clark was informed of this plan to go into seven countries in the Middle East following 9/11. He wrote about it in his book, *Winning Modern Wars* (Public Affairs, 2003), and has spoken publicly about it:

> About ten days after 9/11, I went through the Pentagon and I saw Secretary Rumsfeld and Deputy Secretary Wolfowitz. I went downstairs just to say hello to some of the people on the Joint Staff who used to work for me, and one of the generals called me in. He said, "Sir, you've

got to come in and talk to me a second." I said, "Well, you're too busy." He said, "No, no." He says, "We've made the decision we're going to war with Iraq." This was on or about the 20th of September. I said, "We're going to war with Iraq? Why?" He said, "I don't know." He said, "I guess they don't know what else to do." So I said, "Well, did they find some information connecting Saddam to al-Qaeda?" He said, "No, no." He says, "There's nothing new that way. They just made the decision to go to war with Iraq." He said, "I guess it's like we don't know what to do about terrorists, but we've got a good military and we can take down governments." And he said, "I guess if the only tool you have is a hammer, every problem has to look like a nail."

So I came back to see him a few weeks later, and by that time we were bombing in Afghanistan. I said, "Are we still going to war with Iraq?" And he said, "Oh, it's worse than that." He reached over on his desk. He picked up a piece of paper. And he said, "I just got this down from upstairs" — meaning the Secretary of Defense's office — "today." And he said, "This is a memo that describes how we're going to take out seven countries in five years, starting with Iraq, and then Syria, Lebanon, Libya, Somalia, Sudan and, finishing off, Iran." I said, "Is it classified?" He said, "Yes, sir." I said, "Well, don't show it to me." And I saw him a year or so ago, and I said, "You remember that?" He said, "Sir, I didn't show you that memo! I didn't show it to you!"

— General Wesley Clark

As the popularity of sending troops overseas to fight wars in the Middle East wanes, the U.S. has turned to al-Qaeda to fight its proxy wars in the Middle East. The U.S. government is providing material support to al-Qaeda, and Jordan is the base camp. On Sept 10, 2013, Obama gave a speech in which he attempted to bolster support for a U.S. strike on Syria. In his speech, he claimed that the rebel forces in Syria — U.S. backed al-Qaeda forces — just want to be left alone to live in peace. That has got to be one of the biggest whoppers ever to come out of the mouth of a U.S. president. Since the rebel forces have invaded Syria, there have been well over 1000 documented murders of Christians. Hundreds of thousands have had to flee their homes. Christians have been forced to either convert or be dismembered, beheaded, or raped. The chemical weapons attack that Obama shamelessly cited in his Sept 10th, 2013 speech was clearly orchestrated by the rebels. AP reporter Dale Gavlak exposed the connection between Saudi Arabia and the gas attack in Syria (via their al-Qaeda proxies), and was subsequently "indefinitely suspended" (read fired), at the behest of the Saudi government.

Middle East politics can not even begin to be understood until one considers that it revolves around oil and petro-dollars. The Saudis have been the oil supplier of choice to the West ever since the beginning of the 20th century. The world's reserve currency is the U.S. dollar. As such, oil can only be traded in dollars on the world market. Any attempt to change this is a threat to the supremacy of the dollar. The dollars are created by the Federal Reserve, which is the U.S. wing of the Rothschild's banking cartel. The European Central Bank is the European wing, and issues euros. The Saudis work in concert with the U.S. and the West to stifle any dissent from the carefully crafted plan of the New World Order elite. Under this plan, the Saudis have the most-favored-nation status for oil exports as long as they accept the system of petro-dollars issued by the central banks. Each of the countries the U.S. has invaded since 9/11 had one thing in common; they did not have a central bank.[2] Ie, they created their own money, the way the United States are supposed to as outlined in Article I, Section 8 of the Constitution. The first thing that happened after the overthrow of Gaddafi in Libya was the creation of a central bank. All this as the al-Qaeda flag was raised over the courthouses in Tripoli and Benghazi, as well as Gaddafi's home town of Qasr Abu Hadi.

Al-Qaeda is simply the Arabic word for 'database'. In the 1980s the CIA began compiling a database of people in the Middle East that were willing to work with them. Out of these relationships grew the al-Qaeda network. Al-Qaeda has become the answer to all of the New World Order's problems. They blamed

---

[2] In addition to this, Iraq and Libya were making plans to start accepting payment for their oil exports in other currencies, instead of U.S. dollars. http://www.theguardian.com/commentisfree/cifamerica/2011/apr/21/libya-muammar-gaddafi

9/11/2001 on al-Qaeda. They used al-Qaeda to take down Libya. They used al-Qaeda for security for the consulate in Benghazi, which in turn raided the consulate on 9/11/2012, 11 years after the second 9/11. This was a cover up operation to get rid of Ambassador J. Christopher Stevens, who refused to cooperate with the New World Order by running heat-seeking missiles (called MANPADS) to Syria.

Al-Qaeda is now being used by the U.S. to fight a proxy war in Syria in an attempt to topple the government of Bashar al-Assad. Some of the 'database' are still using the name that they used when America began arming them to fight the Russians in Afghanistan back in the eighties — the Mujahideen. The terrorists who systematically killed Christians and released Muslims in the Westgate Mall shooting in Nairobi, on September 21 of 2013 went by this name. The truth about the CIA connection to al-Qaeda is well known. Osama bin Laden was part of the original network funded by the U.S. in the eighties, called the Mujahideen.

So to sum up, bin Laden, son of a Saudi billionaire, was part of the original U.S.-funded al-Qaeda network. The U.S., together with the Saudis, are still funding and arming al-Qaeda. The U.S., Saudi Arabia, and even Israel, are taking the side of the al-Qaeda rebels in the Syria conflict. All because of Oil. Why else would Israel take the side of their sworn enemies? Bashar al-Assad's government is secular. Al-Qaeda is militantly Islamic. In fact, many of the Syrian rebels follow the Wahhabi form of Islam of the Saudis — arguably the most radical form there is. In Assad's Syria, women are allowed to drive and lead normal lives, unlike Saudi Arabia. Christians and Bibles are welcome in Syria, unlike Saudi Arabia. Although Assad is by no means a saint, the emerging pattern is that of overthrowing a tyrant for an even worse one. The founding fathers warned that this kind of intervention would ultimately make us slaves. And so it is. The Saudis exert an enormous amount of influence on the U.S., as do the European central banks, as world players vie for supremacy.

In 2011 Iran announced its energy pipeline accord with Syria. This would allow Saudi Arabia's main competitor — Iran — to pipe natural gas through Iraq and Syria, strengthening Iran's economy. Since Iran competes with Saudi Arabia, and since Iran does not submit to the central banks of Europe, anything that strengthens Iran is forbidden. It was actually CIA meddling (and MI-6) that caused our problems with Iran in the first place. Operation AJAX deposed the democratically elected Prime Minister, Mohammad Mosaddegh in 1953. The Iranians are inclined to resent it. The New World Order is a relatively small group of people, who do not believe in God, who think they are gods, who think they can control the world, and through their incompetence and hubris are destroying the planet. They are control freaks. The good news is that many people are beginning to wake up out of their trance and stand up to the New World Order. In September of 2013, twelve U.S. intelligence officials told Obama that it was not Assad who launched the chemical weapons attack in Syria on August 21, but "a pre-planned provocation by the Syrian opposition and its Saudi and Turkish supporters."

The chess pieces are being positioned and everyone is taking sides. Syria is allied with Iran and Russia. Israel is allied with the West as are the Saudis, who want to shut down all their competition in the world oil market. The al-Qaeda network, which is used to fight proxy wars for the Saudi team, is funded and supplied by the U.S. and the Saudis. Therefore in September of 2013 President Obama waived a federal ban on arming terrorist groups, clearing the way for him to openly arm al-Qaeda in Syria. In 2011 Obama *waived a U.S. law banning assistance to countries that use child soldiers*, allowing millions in financing to flow to Yemen, the DRC, and Chad. This is the current state of affairs of the Middle-Eastern politics of the New World Order. In short, the rogue nations of the Middle East, that operate outside of the Rothschild's international banking system are being forced by the West to assimilate. These countries are not cooperating with the New World Order. This is how the New World Order is forming its world-wide monolithic control grid. At least that is how they are using military means to deal with the Muslim nations that have not yet submitted.[3]

Smaller less independent nations are forced into the New World Order through more subtle techniques. Major events in this process, already in its final stages, took place in 1999, the year of globalism. Veteran investigative journalist Greg Palast reported how after having repealed Glass-Steagall in the U.S. (which kept commercial banks and investment banks separate), the process of dismantling its equivalent in other countries and reorganizing the world banking system was executed by key people in the U.S. Treasury, and the banking sector. Under pressure to comply to the Financial Trade Agreement, countries around the world were forced to open their doors to J.P. Morgan and Citibank, as the World Trade Organization forced toxic derivatives into the world financial market. Countries were flatly told that their exports would no longer be accepted if they did not comply and accept the toxic assets. These were among the key events that led to the global economic meltdown in 2008.

The plan of the New World Order is total domination. Individuals are forced into economic slavery as economies crumble beneath the weight of the New World Order. Again, the repeal of the Glass-Steagall Act in the nineties allowed the merger of commercial banks with investment banks and made them 'too big to fail'. This paved the way for the massive bailouts that looted the American taxpayers in the new millennium.

The hijacking of America was a sophisticated program, but the way to resist it is decidedly basic and uncomplicated. First however, we have to recognize we have been taken hostage. How did we get here?

The beginning of the New World Order was in Genesis 11. After the flood, the earth was of one language. In Genesis 11 the great men of the earth said *Go to, let us build us a city and a tower, whose top may reach unto heaven; and let us make us*

---

3 The best laid plans of the global elite always fail. Al-Qaeda has gone completely rogue, and changed its name to the ISIS, or IS (Islamic State). Russia is also 'going rogue' so to speak, and top US diplomat Christopher R. Hill says Putin has betrayed the "new world order."
http://www.infowars.com/top-u-s-diplomat-russia-has-betrayed-the-new-world-order/

*a name, lest we be scattered abroad upon the face of the whole earth. And the LORD came down to see the city and the tower, which the children of men builded. And the LORD said, Behold, the people is **one**, and **they have all one language**; and this they begin to do: and **now nothing will be restrained from them**, which they have imagined to do.* This was not only the beginning of one world government; this was also the beginning of false religion, which goes hand in hand with the political structure of the New World Order. Nimrod was the leader of the one world government. Semiramis was his mother and wife. After Nimrod's death, Semiramis gave birth to Tamuz, who she claimed was the virgin-born reincarnation of Nimrod. She was worshiped as the **queen of heaven**, and Tamuz was worshipped as her immaculate child.[4] Semiramis was not only worshipped as the queen of heaven by the Babylonians, but also later by apostate Israel (Jer 7; 44). She was known by the Phoenicians as Astarte, as Aphrodite by the Greeks, as Isis by the Egyptians, and as Venus by the Romans, then later as Mary by the Roman Catholic Church. The real queen of heaven is the church (Rev 19:7-10), but neither Mary or the church receives worship according to the Bible.

God destroyed the tower of Babel and confounded the language. Communication was broken up into different languages. This forced them to obey the command to replenish the earth in Genesis 9:1. People were forced to find others they could communicate with. They regrouped and formed new communities.

The base of Nimrod's tower was found in Babylon by the famous Assyriologist George Smith. Just as the ruins of the tower remain today, so do the remnants of the religion. Although Nimrod was killed, there remains to this day in the hearts of men the desire to conquer and oppress others in world domination. The icon of the elite is the all-seeing eye peering out through the capstone. It symbolizes the rebuilt and finished tower of Babel, which has been the goal of the elite ever since God destroyed it.

Children need to be educated about the New World Order by

---

[4] Hislop, *The Two Babylons* (Neptune, NJ: Loizeaux Brothers, 1959), p. 69.

their parents. If they are not, they will be educated about it by the New World Order. The best place to start is the story about the tower of Babel in the book of Genesis. Another creative way to explain it is by using the Star Wars series. Young people are already familiar with the story and will readily engage in a discussion about it.

George Lucas's Star Wars is in many ways a metaphor for the New World Order. It is the tale of a far away galaxy that operated as a republic, long ago. (The United States operate as a republic.) The Jedi are the 'good guys' who are trying to preserve the old ways of the Republic (like those trying to preserve our Republic as outlined in the Constitution). In Star Wars, a group of "separatists," who rely on secrecy and espionage, attempt to usurp the authority of the Senate, the legitimate government. (The separatists are figurative of those in our day who are working towards world socialism. For years they worked in secret and kept much of their activity out of the public eye.[5]) The separatists are led by the evil "Sith." The Sith lord infiltrates the Galactic Senate under false pretenses. As a respected senator from Naboo, nobody suspects him to be an enemy. Using a false flag event which he himself orchestrated — the attack on Naboo — he becomes Chancellor. He gains sweeping new executive powers because of the war he created. (Barack Obama's real name is Barry Soetoro. He campaigned as a Christian but he is in reality a Muslim[6] and a Fabian Socialist. He posted a fake birth certificate on the White House website.[7] He also has a fake Selective Service card, and uses a fake Social Security number.) After the separatists have served their purpose,

---

[5] For more than a century, groups like the Fabian Society in England, and the Ford, Carnegie, and Rockefeller Foundations in America have worked in secret. Norman Dodd, chief investigator on the congressional Reece Committee, uncovered that these (American) foundations operated with the expressed purpose of engaging the U.S. in war, controlling education, and controlling the State Department, to work towards world government. https://www.youtube.com/watch?v=YUYCBfmIcHM

[6] http://www.conservapedia.com/Obama's_Religion

[7] Anybody with Adobe Illustrator can see that the birth certificate is a forgery. It has several different layers that have been put together piecemeal, in a cut an paste fashion. A legitimate file would be one single layer of the scanned document. (Continued overleaf.)

the Sith lord has them killed. (Those who support the New World Order — including Obama — will all be cast aside by the real Sith lord, Satan, after they have served their purpose.) The Sith lord reorganized the Republic into the Galactic Empire, which 'swept away the remnants of the old Republic'. (For a century now, we have been moving away from our original form of representative government, and George Washington's doctrine of non-intervention, to a centralized government, controlled by elite corporate interests like the industrial military complex, central banks, and mega-corporations, all bent on foreign wars.) In Star Wars Episode IV, the empire engaged in a false flag attack on the Jawas. The empire used a directed energy weapon called the Death Star. (There are some who believe the New World Order may have used a directed energy weapon on 9/11/2001.)[8] The empire replaces the legitimate government with their own regional governors. (By executive order, the U.S. has been divided into 9 FEMA sections, which will be controlled by 9 regional governors, in the event of a national crisis. The authority of the regional governors will supersede the authority of the legitimate state governors.) In Episode III, Padmé asks Anakin, "Have you ever considered that we may be on the wrong side? What if the democracy we thought we were serving no longer exists, and the Republic has become the very evil we've been fighting to destroy?" Anakin responds in

---

[7] (Continued) Not only has Sheriff Joe Arpaio provided exhaustive evidence proving that Obama's birth certificate and selective service card are both frauds, Investigative reporter Kenneth Timmerman stated a well-placed but unnamed source told him that the real point of the passport breach incidents was to cauterize the Obama file, removing from it any information that could prove damaging to his eligibility to be president. CIA Director John Owen Brennan is reported to be a Muslim. He speaks fluent Arabic. Before Obama was elected in 2008, henchmen who worked for Brennan's security firm (Stanley Inc., a company based in Arlington, Va.) broke into the Federal Passport Office and seized Obama's records to sanitize his passport records. Brennan subsequently became Security Advisor to the White House, and then later CIA Director in charge of counter terrorism. http://www.wnd.com/2013/01/did-cia-pick-sanitize-obamas-passport-records/#uoCbQ0gtc7RXXQyd.99

[8] Q.v. Judy Wood, PhD, *Where Did the Towers Go?* (The New Investigation, 2010).

true establishment character, refusing to consider that maybe he has been deceived. When the Sith lord infiltrates and dismantles the Senate, he says "In order to insure the security and continuing stability, the Republic will be reorganized into the First Galactic Empire! For a safe and secure society." Senator Padmé responds by saying, "So this is how freedom dies, to thunderous applause." The parallel here should be obvious. We were sold the New World Order for safety and security. When Barack Obama was inaugurated, he received an unprecedented amount of thunderous applause, even being called "the messiah." By signing the NDAA, effectively destroying the Bill of Rights, and continuing the policy of military aggression, he has shown himself to be a counterfeit of everything he stood for while campaigning. He has continued reducing civil liberties and expanding the police state. In reality of course, Obama is merely a puppet. Those who are truly in power stay out of the public eye, using politicians to do their bidding. When Obi-Wan confronts Padmé with the reality of what has happened with Anakin and the attack on the Jedi Temple, he says, "He was deceived by a lie; we all were. It appears the chancellor is behind everything, including the war." After the rapture of the church, when the New World Order starts to fall apart, and the red horse of apocalypse brings World War III, there will be many like Padmé and Obi-Wan, who will discover the truth too late. They will discover the world leaders they looked up to have led them into a trap. In Star Wars the Sith attempt to rule the galaxy. The goal of the New World Order elite is to rule the world.

George Lucas' fictional story about good and evil has been talked about for a long time in terms of its deeper meanings. Although it's made for kids, these and other hidden subtleties touch on deep subjects. There are deep philosophical ideas that are woven into the beliefs of the characters. For example, in Episode V, Obi-Wan Kenobi says to his pupil, Skywalker, "What I told you was true, from a certain point of view . . . you will find that many of the truths we cling to depend greatly on our point of view." This is the essence of existentialism, which is the philosophy of the leaders of the New World Order. Parents must talk to their kids about the ideas they get from movies, whether it be Star Wars or any other film or program. The similarities between the religion of the Jedi and Hinduism were noted early on by Christians, who saw the seductive nature of the movies for kids who could be made more susceptible to cults, through the glamorizing of "the force." (q.v. Dan 11:38, KJV) The deceptive nature of the New World Order is woven into the most unsuspecting places, yet the subtle Hindu references in Star Wars are fairly benign compared to the outright satanic assault on children today through the media. Parents, talk to your children about what they see. You cannot hide everything from them but you can give them practical wisdom and instruction, as well as spiritual protection through prayer. By discussing what they see, children will be better equipped to recognize propaganda, and they will be prepared to build on their biblical and historical knowledge as they grow into adulthood.

The first significant advances towards the New World Order were made by Woodrow Wilson. Wilson, a supporter of the KKK, gave us Income Tax and the Federal Reserve Act. He signed the Espionage and Sedition Acts, which criminalized free speech. His tax acts made the top tax bracket 77%. Although he was elected on a peace platform, Wilson changed American foreign policy from non-intervention, to set up the draft and get us involved in WWI. To accomplish this he set up a massive propaganda campaign using a select group of elite intellectuals called the Committee on Public Information. It was Wilson who created what became known as the military-industrial complex. Wilson was also a key architect of the League of Nations, which was the predecessor to the United Nations. WWI was supposed to be the war to end all wars, which of course turned out to be a lie. WWII was supposed to make the world safe for democracy (a Wilson claim from WWI, recycled for WWII), which of course turned out to be a lie. Every war comes with a promise. People are killed and maimed, while the money men get rich. Just as the League of Nations utterly failed in stopping WWII, the United Nations is going to fail in stopping WWIII.

On July 4th, 1918, as WWI was coming to an end, Woodrow Wilson made a speech at George Washington's tomb on Mount Vernon:

> "It has been left for us to see to it that it shall be understood that they [the founding fathers] spoke and acted, not for a single people only, but for all mankind. We are in this war to fulfill the promise of their vision; having achieved our own liberty we are to strive for the liberties of every other people as well."

Claiming that WWI was a fulfilment of the founders' vision, while standing in front of Washington's tomb has got to be the height of arrogance (especially for a historian, which Wilson was). Washington set the tone of America's foreign policy for years to come in his farewell address:

> Observe good faith and justice towards all nations; cultivate peace and harmony with all ... In the execution of such a plan, nothing is more essential than that permanent, inveterate antipathies against particular nations, and passionate attachments for others, should be excluded; and that, in place of them, just and amicable feelings towards all should be cultivated. [...]

> The nation which indulges towards another a habitual hatred or a habitual fondness is in some degree a slave. [...]

> So likewise, a passionate attachment of one nation for another produces a variety of evils.

> — George Washington, Farewell Address, 1796

The New World Order, with its intervention policies that erode national sovereignty, used to only appeal to the left. Then along came the neocons. The neocons have been in control of the Republican Party ever since George H.W. Bush. Irving Kristol is the "godfather of neoconservatism." This is what Irving Krostol's Wikipedia page says: "As a former *Trotskyist*, Irving was indeed himself mugged by the "reality" of conservative philosophy and enfolded leftist policies such as a lack of objection to welfare programs, international "revolution" through nation-building/ militarily imposed "democracy" and application of *Fabian Socialism*/Keynesianism coupled with a socially conservative viewpoint. These concepts lie at the core of neoconservative philosophy to this day." [Emphasis added.]

While most politically astute observers would readily affirm that Barack Obama is a Fabian Socialist, few Republicans would ever dream that George W Bush is one. Reality check: Not only George W Bush, but all neocons in general are Fabian Socialists. Yet the church was none the wiser, as we blindly supported the neocons in their global conquest following 9/11. The endgame is worldwide economic control.

The mark that this system will use to implement the universal electronic currency will actually be a mark of allegiance to the one-world dictator, Antichrist. Many different elements have been working in concert towards this end, without even knowing the real reason why. Many of them undoubtably believe they are doing what is right. I suppose that even Wilson felt he was doing right, in creating the Fed. The Federal Reserve was supposed to 'stabilize the economy'. Epic fail. The Federal Reserve and its effect on our economy is a somewhat complex subject. G. Edward Griffin's classic book, *The Creature From Jekyll Island* examines this subject in detail. In short, the Fed took control of our currency from Congress, and placed it in the hands of a private central bank, which the American people are now forced to borrow from. The central bank prints the money, which costs them nothing, but We the People have to work to pay it back with interest. If any of We the People were to do this, it would be called counterfeiting, and rightly so. A small secretive group of people have conned America (and the world) into using Monopoly money, and they can print as much as they want for themselves.

Michael Snyder @ *The American Dream* has listed 25 facts that show exactly what the fruit of the Federal Reserve has been:

#1 The greatest period of economic growth in U.S. history was when there was no central bank.

#2 The United States never had a persistent, ongoing problem with inflation until the Federal Reserve was created. In the century before the Federal Reserve was created, the average annual rate of inflation was about half a percent. In the century since the Federal Reserve was created, the average annual rate of inflation has been about 3.5 percent, and it would be even higher than that if the inflation numbers were not being so grossly manipulated.

#3 Even using the official numbers, the value of the U.S. dollar has declined by more than 95 percent since the Federal Reserve was created nearly 100 years ago.

#4 The secret November 1910 gathering at Jekyll Island, Georgia during which the plan for the Federal Reserve was hatched was attended by U.S. Senator Nelson W. Aldrich, Assistant Secretary of the Treasury Department A.P. Andrews and a whole host of representatives from the upper crust of the Wall Street banking establishment.

#5 In 1913, Congress was promised that if the Federal Reserve Act was passed that it would eliminate the business cycle.

#6 The following comes directly from the Fed's official mission statement: "To provide the nation with a safer, more flexible, and more stable monetary and financial system. Over the years, its role in banking and the economy has expanded."

#7 It was not an accident that a permanent income tax was also introduced the same year when the Federal Reserve system was established. The whole idea was to transfer wealth from our pockets to the federal government and from the federal government to the bankers.

#8 Within 20 years of the creation of the Federal Reserve, the U.S. economy was plunged into the Great Depression.

#9 If you can believe it, there have been 10 different economic recessions since 1950. The Federal Reserve created the "dotcom bubble", the Federal Reserve created the "housing bubble" and now it has created the largest bond bubble in the history of the planet.

#10 According to an official government report, the Federal Reserve made 16.1 trillion dollars in secret loans to the big banks during the last financial crisis. The following is a list of loan recipients that was taken directly from page 131 of the report...

Citigroup - $2.513 trillion
Morgan Stanley - $2.041 trillion
Merrill Lynch - $1.949 trillion
Bank of America - $1.344 trillion
Barclays PLC - $868 billion
Bear Sterns - $853 billion
Goldman Sachs - $814 billion
Royal Bank of Scotland - $541 billion
JP Morgan Chase - $391 billion
Deutsche Bank - $354 billion
UBS - $287 billion
Credit Suisse - $262 billion
Lehman Brothers - $183 billion
Bank of Scotland - $181 billion
BNP Paribas - $175 billion
Wells Fargo - $159 billion
Dexia - $159 billion
Wachovia - $142 billion
Dresdner Bank - $135 billion
Societe Generale - $124 billion
"All Other Borrowers" - $2.639 trillion (It is still unknown who.)

#11 The Federal Reserve also paid those big banks $659.4 million in fees to help "administer" those secret loans.

#12 The Federal Reserve has created approximately 2.75 trillion dollars out of thin air and injected it into the financial system over the past five years. This has allowed the stock market to soar to unprecedented heights, but it has also caused our financial system to become extremely unstable.

#13 We were told that the purpose of quantitative easing is to help "stimulate the economy", but today the Federal Reserve is actually paying the big banks not to lend out 1.8 trillion dollars in "excess reserves" that they have parked at the Fed.

#14 Quantitative easing overwhelmingly benefits those that own stocks and other financial investments. In other words, quantitative easing overwhelmingly favors the very wealthy. Even Barack Obama has admitted that 95 percent of the income gains since he has been president have gone to the top one percent of income earners.

#15 The gap between the top one percent and the rest of the country is now the greatest that it has been since the 1920s.

#16 The Federal Reserve has argued vehemently in federal court that it is "not an agency" of the federal government and therefore not subject to the Freedom of Information Act.

#17 The Federal Reserve openly admits that the 12 regional Federal Reserve banks are organized "much like private corporations."

#18 The regional Federal Reserve banks issue shares of stock to the "member banks" that own them.

#19 The Federal Reserve system greatly favors the biggest banks. Back in 1970, the five largest U.S. banks held 17 percent of all U.S. banking industry assets. Today, the five largest U.S. banks hold 52 percent of all U.S. banking industry assets.

#20 The Federal Reserve is supposed to "regulate" the big banks, but it has done nothing to stop a 441 trillion dollar interest rate derivatives bubble from inflating which could absolutely devastate our entire financial system.

#21 The Federal Reserve was designed to be a perpetual debt machine. The bankers that designed it intended to trap the U.S. government in a perpetual debt spiral from which it could never possibly escape. Since the Federal Reserve was established nearly 100 years ago, the U.S. national debt has gotten more than 5000 times larger.

#22 The U.S. government will spend more than 400 billion dollars just on interest on the national debt this year.

#23 If the average rate of interest on U.S. government debt rises to just 6 percent (and it has been much higher than that in the past), we will be paying out more than a trillion dollars a year just in interest on the national debt.

#24 According to Article I, Section 8 of the U.S. Constitution, the U.S. Congress is the one that is supposed to have the authority to "coin Money, regulate the Value thereof, and of foreign Coin, and fix the Standard of Weights and Measures". So exactly why is the Federal Reserve doing it?

#25 There are plenty of possible alternative financial systems, but at this point all 187 nations that belong to the IMF have a central bank. Are we supposed to believe that this is just some sort of a bizarre coincidence?

Ron Paul has written a book called *End the Fed* (Grand Central Publishing, 2009), that addresses these problems and what should be done about them. Left unchecked, the central banks and their policies will prepare the way for black horse of apocalypse (Rev 6).

The recent LIBOR scandal has revealed that the global elite have been manipulating markets amounting to somewhere around 500 *trillion* dollars. Yet nobody went to jail, for manipulating multi-trillion dollar markets for the benefit of the elite. The U.S. Attorney General claimed that those guilty were too important to bring to justice.[9] Thus, the mainstream media now admits what we have known for decades. There is in fact a shadowy elite controlling the world's wealth, and they are above the law.

Again, not only did Wilson give us the Fed, but also the League of Nations. When the League of Nations ziggurat crumbled, the propagandists went to work. Wilson's Committee on Public Information began to mold public opinion. Then they started over with the United Nations. This is how the New World Order works, whether at the global level through the mass media, or at the local level through Agenda 21, elites make the decisions, then brainwash the public to accept it, while actually convincing them

---

[9] *www.rollingstone.com/politics/news/everything-is-rigged-the-biggest-financial-scandal-yet-20130425*

that the ideas and policies are their own. The technique is very subtle, but incredibly effective. Most of the supporters of the New World Order do not use the term NWO. They use terms such as globalization or democratization. This kind of Orwellian language conditions those involved to truly believe that they are doing good, and that they will make America a safer place.

Satan has a similar method he uses to inject thoughts into people's minds. Even Christians are susceptible to this, which is why it is so important to bring *into captivity every thought to the obedience of Christ* (II Cor 10:5b). Only then can you identify these thoughts as being foreign and not your own. Then you can readily reject them and refuse to entertain them when they arise. Likewise, you do not have to accept the programing of the NWO. This is why I do not own a TV. I see no reason to allow the NWO to influence my thoughts and opinions.

How one views the NSA data scandal has primarily to do with one's worldview. If one believes in the humanistic philosophy of Carl Rogers, that people are basically good, then one is inclined to be trusting of the government, and not to get upset that he is being spied on. If one has a biblical worldview, or even a Machiavellian worldview for that matter, in which the human heart is *deceitful above all things, and desperately wicked*, then she is inclined to believe that the government can not be trusted, and to demand a redress for her grievances. It is vitally important to understand the nature of our democratic republic, and our role in it. A subject believes what he is told. A citizen believes what he knows to be right.

It seems to be the younger generation by and large that has accepted that the government is spying on them. One of the last entries in Anne Frank's diary reads, "In spite of everything, I still believe that people are truly good at heart." Unfortunately that statement was proven false soon after she wrote it. The older generation has memories of people like Hitler, Stalin, Pol Pot, Idi Amin, and other reminders, that people are not basically good. That was not the prevailing philosophy in their day. But it is the prevailing philosophy today. Aside from the humanistic indoctrination in the public schools, the population is also being conditioned to submit to authority, however idiotic said authority may be. It was beyond reason that in the nineties students were being suspended if they were found to be in possession of an aspirin, but now the schools have gone from unreasonable to stark-raving mad, as we see students expelled for being in possession of a Hello Kitty bubble-gun, or for taking bites out of a Pop Tart to form it into the shape of a gun, or for just uttering the word 'gun'. Jesus is not a pacifist, yet *even pacifists* who are thinking individuals recognize the importance of the right to bear arms. For example, Mohandas Gandhi, who was indeed a pacifist, wrote,

> Among the many misdeeds of the British rule in India, history will look upon the Act depriving a whole nation of arms as the blackest.[10]
>
> — Mohandas Gandhi

Remolding the minds of the American people was a deliberate process. They started over 100 years ago, first by lowering the education standards with the methods of John Dewy. The Bible and biblical materials were displaced by less weighty books. Then along came Dick and Jane. Instead of black and white text containing a wealth of wisdom and information: *In the beginning, God created the heaven and the earth*, the bar was lowered to a color picture and one line of disgustingly simple text: See Spot run. God was scrubbed from the curriculum. The *law* of biogenesis — the proven science that life comes from life — was replaced with the *theory* of evolution. When kids were told they were animals, they began to act like animals. Hence, the next step, training them to be submissive and obedient, was easily achieved. America went from producing the best and brightest, who were learned in philosophy, literature, and all kinds of advanced education, to producing subpar students through 'outcome based education' and 'values clarification'. SAT scores have plummeted in math

---

[10] Gandhi, Mohandas K. "Mahatma", *An Autobiography: The Story of My Experiments with Truth*, tr. Mahadev Desai, Part V., Ch. XXVII

and reading, and we now have a population that does not question anything, all by design. Common Core is the final step in this process. It is clear that Common Core has nothing to do with "more rigorous standards" and everything to do with statism.[11] Common Core excludes certain Algebra II and Geometry content that is currently a prerequisite at almost every four-year state college. Young people, it's you against them. Abraham Lincoln's total time in school only amounted to about one year, but he educated himself. He would walk for miles to borrow a book that he would read over and over. His pioneer schools in Indiana did not have arithmetic books, but he did not let that stop him from learning math. He set himself to the task of finding some paper, which was hard to come by, and made his own 'sum book'. If Lincoln had not educated himself and become a lawyer, is it possible we may still have slavery today?

In Chapter IV we looked at how the corporation squeezed out the true free market capitalism that America was built on. The undisputed Guru for shaping and guiding this new system was Peter Drucker. Drucker also heavily influenced another trend that emerged in the 20th century — the megachurch. Drucker's philosophy is that there are three legs to the stool of society: a public sector of government; a private sector of businesses (corporations); and a social sector of community (churches and charitable organizations). The elite saw in this model a way to restructure America and render the church, their arch enemy, weak and ineffective. It was Drucker, a man of little if any faith, who has shaped the trend for the new megachurches in America. His main disciple was CFR member, Rick Warren. I believe a church can be big and still maintain a model of New Testament integrity, but more often than not, that is not what happens. The gospel is watered down and truth is compromised. Social programs replace evangelism. Paul Smith, brother of Chuck Smith, wrote extensively about this in *New Evangelicalism: The New World Order* (Calvary Publishing,

---

[11] Common Core is the name of the K-12 Federal curriculum for public schools. https://www.youtube.com/watch?v=d1Ubjg_o8vg

2011). Chuck Smith wrote the forward. There is a strange hypnotic trance falling on the church today, where Christians fall prey to fatalism and call it Christian theology. Some Christians now accept F bombs from the pulpit. Some have keg parties after church. There is a spiritual deadness creeping in, as the Bible is cast aside for books by popular authors, conversation topics turn to movies instead of what God is doing, and psychology replaces theology.

> The empires of the future are empires of the mind.
>
> — Sir Winston Churchill

Since the decline and fall of the Roman Empire, and the end of the Holy Roman Empire, people have lost many of the old superstitions that the Roman emperors preyed on. Since people no longer worship men as gods, and many do not feel obligated to obey the pope, what tyrants do instead now, is claim that the individual must surrender his rights for the good of the state.

> A communist ... should be more concerned about the Party and the masses than about any individual.
>
> — Mao Tse-tung

> To be a socialist is to submit the I to the thou; socialism is sacrificing the individual to the whole.
>
> — Joseph Goebels

> If the nineteenth century was a century of individualism it may be expected that this will be the century of collectivism and hence the century of the State.
>
> — Bennito Mussolini

In essence this is what is being sold to the American people now by the establishment. We are told we need to surrender the Bill of Rights for the good of the nation. It is sold as a necessary step to keep us safe. But it is a big lie. It is a lie that leads to death. The Bill of Rights protects us from the government, and the greatest cause of death throughout history has unquestionably been democide — death by government. According to political scientist R. J. Rummel of the University of Hawaii, 262 million people were victims of democide in the 20th century. This includes genocide, politicide, and mass murder.

1st Century
Nero: Their [the Christians] execution was made into a game: they were covered with the skins of wild animals and torn to pieces by dogs. They were hung on crosses. They were burned, wrapped in flammable material and set on fire as darkness fell, to illuminate the night. Nero had opened his gardens for this spectacle and put on circus games. He himself mingled with the crowd dressed as a charioteer or stood up high on a chariot. Although these people were guilty and deserved the severest penalty, all this gave rise to compassion for them, for it was felt that they were being victimized, not for the public good, but to satiate the cruelty of one man.[12]

20th Century
13. Enver Pasha, Turkey (1913-1918). Killed in battle.
Killed 1.1 million to 2.5 million. Worst offense: Armenian genocide
Type of regime: Military

12. Kim Il Sung, North Korea (1948-1994). Died of heart attack.
Killed 1.6 million. Worst offense: Korean War
Type of regime: Communist

11. Ho Chi Minh, North Vietnam (1945-1969). Died of heart failure.
Killed 1.7 million. Worst offense: Vietnam War
Type of regime: Communist

10. Pol Pot, Cambodia (1975-1979). Cause of death unconfirmed.
Killed 1.7 million to 2.4 million. Worst offense: Cambodian genocide
Type of regime: Communist

9. Saddam Hussein, Iraq (1969-2003). Killed by execution.
Killed 2 million. Worst offense: Kurdish genocide
Type of regime: Authoritarian

8. Yahya Khan, Pakistan (1969-1971). Cause of death unknown.
Killed 2 million to 12 million. Worst offense: Bangladesh genocide
Type of regime: Military

7. Tojo Hideki, Japan (1941-1944). Killed by execution.
Killed 4 million. Worst offense: WWII civilian genocide
Type of regime: Military

6. Vladimir Lenin, USSR (1917-1924). Died of cerebral hemorrhage.
Killed 4 million. Worst offense: Russian Civil War
Type of regime: Communist

5. Hirohito, Japan (1926-1989). Died of cancer.
Killed 6 million. Worst offense: Nanking Massacre
Type of regime: Monarchy

4. Chiang Kai-Shek, China (1928-1949). Died of kidney failure.
Killed 10 million. Worst offense: 228 Massacre
Type of regime: Military

3. Adolf Hitler, Germany (1934-1945). Committed suicide.
Killed 17 million to 20 million. Worst offense: The Holocaust
Type of regime: Fascist

2. Joseph Stalin, USSR. (1941-1953). Died of heart attack.
Killed 40 million to 62 million. Worst offense: Gulag camps
Type of regime: Communist

1. Mao Zedong, China (1943-1976). Died of heart attack.
Death toll: 45 million to 75 million. Worst offense: Great Chinese Famine
Type of regime: Communist[13]

---

[12] Tacitus, *Annals XV.44*, as quoted in *The Early Christians*, by Eberhard Arnold, pp. 61-62.

[13] Daily Beast, 13 Deadliest Dictators, October 21, 2011.

21st Century[14]

Antichrist, Worldwide Dictator. Everlasting punishment: Lake of fire.
Death toll: Billions. Worst offence: Worldwide genocide
Type of regime: Worldwide dictatorship

The use of the FEMA style camps has begun. Columbia,
South Carolina has passed a law that makes it illegal to be
homeless. Vagrants are to be jailed, but 250 were given
the option to be taken to an internment center outside of town,
where they will only be allowed to leave by appointment on
a shuttle. Is this a test run for the FEMA camps? How long
before it is not voluntary anymore?

Certain theologians who hold to the 'preterist' view of eschatology
maintain that the prophecies in the Revelation concerning the one
world leader were fulfilled in the person of Cæsar Nero. This
simply can not be true in light of Jesus' prophecy in John 5:43:

> *I am come in my Father's name, and ye receive me not:*
> *if another shall come in his own name, him ye will receive.*

— Dragon Slayer Jesus Christ

The Jews never received Nero as their Messiah. Not by any
stretch of the imagination. Therefore, the Antichrist must be
someone other than Nero. As dark as things are, there is a time
coming which will be far worse. There will be a one-world leader
who will surpass all other dictators in his thirst for blood and his
powers to deceive. His brutal empire will be unlike any other,

---

[14] To believe that Jesus is most likely coming back soon is not 'setting a date'.
I acknowledge he may tarry through the 21st century. However when one
considers the amount of fulfilled Bible prophecy in our day, eg, the rebirth of
Israel, the rise of the New World Order and the one world Church, the rise of
the cashless society, the rebuilding of the temple in Jerusalem, the vast amount of
fulfilled prophecies in the Olivet Discourse, Daniel, and all of the other prophets
(specific signs Jesus said would point to his soon return), it is only reasonable to
obey Jesus' command to watch for him to come back. (Mark 13:35-37)

absorbing the world's wealth crushing all dissent:

> *After this I saw in the night visions, and behold a fourth*
> *beast, dreadful and terrible, and strong exceedingly; and*
> *it had great iron teeth: it devoured and brake in pieces, and*
> *stamped the residue with the feet of it: and it was diverse from*
> *all the beasts that were before it; and it had ten horns.*

The Book of Daniel 7:7

It should be plain to see that preparations are being made for the final world empire to be rolled out. We must submit ourselves to God, and resist the devil. If we cave into the pressure to conform and do not resist the evil, we will be without excuse. The Germans who did not resist Hitler were without excuse. Benedict Arnold thought the British would win and he switched teams. He died alone in Great Britain without any friends. He was without excuse. Following the liberation of France in 1944, de Gaulle's Free French Movement assumed control and the Vichy French were executed for treason. They were without excuse. It is time for the Christians in America to decide where they stand.

> It doesn't say 'lick the devil's boots' and he will flee
> from you.
> — Alex Jones

The enemy will tell you not to listen. It is a conspiracy theory. Danger. Sadly, some never listen. They choose to believe the lies. Like the people who were told on 9/11, "The fire in the North Tower is under control. Go back to your offices." They went back to their offices and then they died.

On December 7, 1941, the soldiers in Hawaii chose to ignore the blips on the radar that clearly showed them the Zeros were coming. They ignored the warning and Pearl Harbor was decimated.

In the thirties the Jews in Germany were given warning after warning. Some were wise, and left the country. But there were many who ignored the warnings, and perished in concentration camps.

The people of East Germany stood idly by and watched as the Communists built a wall separating East Berlin. After the wall was finished, some tried to climb over it, but it was too late. They were shot.

The signs are all around us. The New World Order is getting ready to clamp down. Why is the federal government arming to the teeth and purchasing billions of rounds of hollow point bullets? Why are police departments acquiring armored vehicles and looking more like standing armies than public servants who protect and serve? There is only one safe place to be at this time and that is in Christ. Proverbs 22:3 says, *A prudent man foreseeth the evil, and **hideth himself**: but the simple pass on, and are punished.* Psalm 119:114 says, ***Thou art my hiding place** and my shield: **I hope in thy word**.* See, the hiding place is not a location, but a person. Jesus exhorts us in Revelation 3:18, *[A]noint thine eyes with eyesalve, that thou mayest see.*

The evils of tyranny are rarely seen but by him who resists it.

— John Jay, First Chief Justice of the United States

What country can preserve its liberties if its rulers are not warned from time to time that their people preserve the spirit of resistance?

— Thomas Jefferson

Rebellion against tyrants is obedience to God.

— Benjamin Franklin

If a law is unjust, a man is not only right to disobey it, he is obligated to do so.

— Thomas Jefferson

Cowards die many times before their deaths; The valiant never taste of death but once.

— William Shakespeare

One has a moral responsibility to disobey unjust laws.

— Dr. Martin Luther King, Jr.

The doctrine of nonresistance against arbitrary power, and oppression, is absurd, slavish, and destructive of the good and happiness of mankind.

— New Hampshire Constitution

If we are ever going to change things it is going to require a God-sent revival. God has done it many times before. We need to recapture our frontier spirit. Alexis de Tocqueville is often quoted as saying, "America is great, because America is good. If America ever ceases to be good, she will cease to be great." Although people have searched in vain to find the source of that often quoted statement, it does indeed capture the spirit of what Tocqueville was saying in his classic work, *Democracy in America*. Over the course of two volumes, Tocqueville praised the Americans for their many virtues; among them their piety, their ingenuity and their freedom. For example:

It is not impossible to conceive the surpassing liberty which the Americans enjoy; some idea may likewise be formed of the extreme equality which subsists amongst them, but the political activity which pervades the United States must be seen in order to be understood. No sooner do you set foot upon the American soil than you are stunned by a kind of tumult; a confused clamor is heard on every side; and a thousand simultaneous voices demand the immediate satisfaction of their social wants. Everything is in motion around you; here, the people of one quarter of a town are met to decide upon the building of a church; there, the election of a representative is going on; a little further the delegates of a district are posting to the town in order to consult upon some local improvements; or in another place the laborers of a village quit their ploughs to deliberate upon the project of a road or a public school. Meetings are called for the sole purpose of declaring their disapprobation of the line of conduct pursued by the Government; whilst in other assemblies the citizens salute the authorities of the day as the fathers of their country. Societies are formed which regard drunkenness as the principal cause of the evils under which the State labors, and which solemnly bind themselves to give a constant example of temperance. *c

c

[At the time of my stay in the United States the temperance societies already consisted of more than 270,000 members, and their effect had been to diminish the consumption of fermented liquors by 500,000 gallons per annum in the State of Pennsylvania alone.]

The great political agitation of the American legislative bodies, which is the only kind of excitement that attracts the attention of foreign countries, is a mere episode or a sort of continuation of that universal movement which originates in the lowest classes of the people and extends successively to all the ranks of society. It is impossible to spend more efforts in the pursuit of enjoyment.

The cares of political life engross a most prominent place in the occupation of a citizen in the United States, and almost the only pleasure of which an American has any idea is to take a part in the Government, and to discuss the part he has taken. This feeling pervades the most trifling habits of life; even the women frequently attend public meetings and listen to political harangues as a recreation after their household labors. Debating clubs are to a certain extent a substitute for theatrical entertainments: an American cannot converse, but he can discuss; and when he attempts to talk he falls into a dissertation. He speaks to you as if he was addressing a meeting; and if he should chance to warm in the course of the discussion, he will infallibly say, "Gentlemen," to the person with whom he is conversing.

In some countries the inhabitants display a certain repugnance to avail themselves of the political privileges with which the law invests them; it would seem that they set too high a value upon their time to spend it on the interests of the community; and they prefer to withdraw within the exact limits of a wholesome egotism, marked out by four sunk fences and a quickset hedge. But if an American were condemned to confine his activity to his own affairs, he would be robbed of one half of his existence; he would feel an immense void in the life which he is accustomed to lead, and his wretchedness would be unbearable. *d I am persuaded that, if ever a despotic government is established in America, it will find it more difficult to surmount the habits which free institutions have engendered than to conquer the attachment of the citizens to freedom.

d

[The same remark was made at Rome under the first Cæsars. Montesquieu somewhere alludes to the excessive despondency of certain Roman citizens who, after the excitement of political life, were all at once flung back into the stagnation of private life.]

— Alexis de Tocqueville, *Democracy in America*, Volume I, p. 246 - 247

If we can first recapture our spiritual heritage, then in turn recapture our love of freedom, knowledge and self governance, we can recapture our liberty. For example, the voting record of the Amash Amendment to stop NSA data collection should be used as a litmus test for who gets voted out in the next election.[15]

Tocqueville ended his critique on America with this prophetic and eerie statement:

Appendix Z

It cannot be absolutely or generally affirmed that the greatest danger of the present age is license or tyranny, anarchy or despotism. Both are equally to be feared; and the one may as easily proceed as the other from the selfsame cause, namely, that "general apathy," which is the consequence of what I have termed "individualism": it is because this apathy exists, that the executive government, having mustered a few troops, is able to commit acts of oppression one day, and the next day a party, which has mustered some thirty men in its ranks, can also commit acts of oppression. Neither one nor the other can found anything to last; and the causes which enable them to succeed easily, prevent them from succeeding long: they rise because nothing opposes them, and they sink because nothing supports them. The proper object therefore of our most strenuous resistance, is far less either anarchy or despotism than the apathy which may almost indifferently beget either the one or the other.

— Alexis de Tocqueville, *Democracy in America*, Volume II, p. 863, 864

As I said earlier, the way to resist the encroaching evil is decidedly basic and uncomplicated. We need to return to the simple morals and American values we had in days gone by. Tocqueville's description of proactive Americans who govern themselves may seem like ancient history that is too far gone to ever bring back, but it's not. They are doing it in New Hampshire, and it's working.[16] There is no backplate in the armor of God (Eph 6). We have a belt, a shield, boots, a helmet, breastplate, a sword, and prayer — but no backplate. We cannot run away from the enemy. We need to run

---

[15] http://www.govtrack.us/congress/votes/113-2013/h412
[16] http://www.youtube.com/watch?v=b_34jAsXe1k

straight at them! That is what we need to do if the Lord tarries. But what if he does not? What if he is in fact preparing to come back soon and the blood moon tetrad of 2014 – 2015 is our wake up call? Are you ready? In Ezekiel 8 and 9, the prophet Ezekiel was given a vision of all the abominations that were taking place in Jerusalem. God brought judgement for these things, but first he sent an angel through Jerusalem with an inkhorn, and he put a mark on the foreheads of all who were sighing and crying for the abominations which were taking place in the city. Only those who were grieved over the evil that was taking place were spared from God's judgement. It is my firm belief that Ezekiel's message is not just for the people of Judah in the sixth century BC, but for us, today. If we do not repent, we will be conformed to the world, and in this day and age, that means being conformed to the New World Order. God help us.

Watch ye therefore, and pray always, that ye may be accounted worthy to escape all these things that shall come to pass, and to stand before the Son of man.

— Dragon Slayer Jesus Christ

I t had been a tough three weeks. Artellies and Gaius had made their way through enemy territory, over mountains, and through bad weather. Considering the harsh winter weather, and the Alps in their way, they decided to head for Greece. It took them more than three months to make it to Macedonia, after which travel became much easier, with a proper Roman road to travel on. Macedonia was a welcome relief. Gaius wanted to stop at every village and hamlet they passed, but Artellies would not hear of it. "What about Thebes?" Gaius protested. "Surely we can stop and take some rest in Thebes?"

"No not Thebes either," Artellies said. "You can glut your flesh as much as you like when we reach Athens." Beholding the Acropolis on the horizon, Athens looked like more like a soft

208 • DRAGON SLAYER JESUS CHRIST

pillow for a weary head than a thriving Hellenistic metropolis. It would not be long now. Meals and beds awaited. By nightfall, they were there. Finding their way to the garrison, Artellies and Gaius reported to the tribune and made their presence known. After briefing the tribune on their misfortunes in Germaina, they took some meat and then a long rest. By the time the sun was hot the next day, Gaius was mixing with some of the other soldiers who were planing a visit to the temple of the Virgin.[17] Artellies was not interested. He decided to stroll down to the Agora and look around. He walked with Gaius and the other men since the Agora was on the way to the Acropolis. Everything was fine, until a couple of soldiers strolling by greeted them with a hearty salutation, exclaiming "Cæsar is Lord!"

Gaius and his new friends all reciprocated, "Cæsar is Lord!" as they gave the Roman salute with their fists to their chests. Artellies abstained, which did not go undetected.

The alpha male of the group spoke up. "Hey what is the matter with your friend?"

Making a beeline to his accuser, Artellies met him face to face as he donned his centurion helmet. "What is your name and rank soldier?" Artellies commanded. The younger opera vacans begged his pardon, not having seen his helmet. "Do not let it happen again," Artellies barked. As they left and went on their way Artellies wondered if this meant trouble for him. Silence hung in the air, but nobody said what he was thinking. *Why didn't Artellies want to say Cæsar is Lord?* They did not have to walk much further with the uncomfortable silence. As they made their way into the Agora, Artellies told his cohorts to enjoy the Parthenon. He then split off into the Stoa of Zeus on the upper northwest corner of the Agora. Gaius and the others continued on the Panathenaic Way that went through the center of the Agora and led to the Acropolis. Passing the altar of the twelve gods, the

---

[17] The Parthenon literally means 'The temple of the Virgin' in Greek. The same word (parthenos) is used in Matt 1:23 to translate the Hebrew 'alma' in Isaiah 7:14. The Parthenon was the temple of Athena, 'the virgin patroness of Athens'.

soldiers stopped and prayed to Ares.[18] Gaius thought about Artellies and the strange things he had told him. He tried not to think about it, but he could not help himself. The men decided they would stop at Areopagus,[19] and pray to Mars again on their way to the Acropolis.

"What is the story with your mate?" one of the soldiers asked Gaius, as they approached Mars' Hill.

"Story?" Gaius replied.

"Came a little unglued back there. Seemed a bit pensive about the whole Cæsar is Lord thing."

"Yeah I noticed that too," Gaius said. "The truth is he has some strange beliefs."

"Like what?"

"He seems to have taken a fancy to the Jewish Messiah," Gaius said. "Something he picked up in Antioch I guess."

"There have been some changes while you were away in Germaina, Mate. That kind of thing is forbidden now."

"What do you mean?" Gaius asked.

"Cæsar has outlawed that way. He has been throwing them to the lions, crucifying them. If your friend knows what is good for him, he will come to his senses — come back to the Roman way."

Gaius raised an eyebrow and nodded, a bit pensive himself now. "Thanks for the information," he said.

As they prayed to Mars on Areopagus, Gaius was experiencing new emotions, feelings he was unfamiliar with. As he and the others offered their petitions, he felt unclean, dirty. He kept thinking about the things Artellies had told him about the Messiah. His arguments were very compelling. Artellies seemed so sure of himself. *What if he was right? Why was Cæsar making such a fuss? Could it be because it was true?*

---

[18] Ares was the Greek god of war. His Roman name was Mars.
[19] Lit. Ares Rock, known to the Romans as Mars Hill.

We are grateful to the Washington Post, the New York Times, Time Magazine, and other great publications whose directors have attended our meetings and respected their promises of discretion for almost 40 years. It would have been impossible for us to develop our plan for the world if we had been subjected to the lights of publicity during those years. But, the world is more sophisticated now and prepared to march towards a one world government. The supranational sovereignty of an intellectual elite and world bankers is surely preferable to the national auto-determination practiced in past centuries.

— David Rockefeller, 1991 Bilderburg meeting in Germany

For though we walk in the flesh, we do not war after the flesh:
(For the weapons of our warfare are not carnal, but mighty through God to the pulling down of strong holds;)
Casting down imaginations, and every high thing that exalteth itself against the knowledge of God, and bringing into captivity every thought to the obedience of Christ;

The Second Epistle of Paul the Apostle to the Corinthians 10:3–5

MIND CONTROL
THE DARK SIDE
OF HISTORY

The establishment is losing control of the narrative. Seymour Hersh, the Pulitzer Prize winning journalist who broke the story about the My Lai massacre in Vietnam, recently went public with his professional opinion that modern journalism is a joke, the bin Laden assassination was a complete fraud, and the government is completely out of control. He asserts that the Obama Administration "lies systematically." He believes that 90% of the news editors should be fired. "The republic's in trouble, we lie about everything, lying has become the staple."[1] Shortly after Seymour Hersh excoriated the media for their lies in 2013, *Popular Science* announced it would discontinue comments on their online articles. *The New York Times* also indicated that it would be scaling back its comments, and removing them completely from some articles. This is obviously a reaction to the fact that people are waking up to the false news they are reporting. How many times have you read an article online,

---

[1] http://www.theguardian.com/media/media-blog/2013/sep/27/seymour-hersh-obama-nsa-american-media (Hersh later retracted his statements about the bin Laden raid, and the Guardian amended the story in Oct. of 2013. Nothing fishy there.)

only to see the premise of the article destroyed in the comment section? Removing comments is an attempt to maintain control of the narrative, and the power to lie with impunity. But the news media is only one part of the systematic mind control of the New World Order. In order to deconstruct the virtual reality they have created, we must begin at square one, with an honest self appraisal.

There is something of inestimable value which every person possesses. Like most things of value it can be taken or destroyed. Its value is vastly underestimated by most, yet there are those who realize its real worth, and they will stop at nothing to steal it from you. It is your *mind.* The Bible tells us that our thought life is a battlefield where we engage in spiritual warfare: *Casting down imaginations, and every high thing that exalteth itself against the knowledge of God, and bringing into captivity every thought to the obedience of Christ;* (II Cor 10:5) Therefore it is of the utmost importance to the Christian to not allow her thought life to be controlled. We are to take all necessary measures to insure we are in control of our own thoughts and opinions. We are going to look at a few simple questions now, and find out if you are really in control of your own mind, or if you are allowing others to control what you think.

1.) Do you often agree with people just because you do not want to 'make waves'?

2.) Do you sometimes find yourself going along with the popular opinion without thinking about why, or 'just because'.

3.) When you do express an opinion about something, can you back it up with good reasons why you feel that way?

4.) If you were challenged to articulate your opinion on a subject, would one of the first reasons you thought of to support why you felt that way be, 'because that is what everyone believes'.

5.) Would you possibly 'go along with the crowd' on an issue even if you were certain it was untrue or wrong?

6.) Do you sometimes worry about what other people think of you?

7.) Do you sometimes lie to people just to make it easier for yourself or for them?

8.) Can you think of anything that is worth dying for?

If you answered 'yes' to questions 1, 2, 4, 5, or 7, the truth is you can be manipulated fairly easily. If you answered no to these, and 6 too, you have a very strong mind. But if you answered 'no' to questions 3 or 8, you have little control over your own mind, if any. If you have made it this far in the book, the chances are you answered pretty well. However if you turned here first out of curiosity, and you did not answer so well, take heart; this book is designed to strengthen you, not discourage you. The first step in solving any problem is acknowledging it. If you realize that your answers to these questions reveal a need for you to strengthen your mind, then you have already taken an important step in the right direction. If this subject makes you uncomfortable, or even afraid, that is all the more reason you should continue reading. *Fear them not therefore: for there is nothing covered, that shall not be revealed; and hid, that shall not be known.* The dragon wants you, and if you are paralyzed by fear, he has you. The only way to free yourself from his clutches and defeat him is to face him head-on. The good news is you do not have to do it alone. As David said, *Yea, though I walk through the valley of the shadow of death, I will fear no evil: **for thou art with me;** thy rod and thy staff, they comfort me.* Christ is with you. He has his rod and his staff to protect you, and he certainly is not afraid of the dragon. He has delivered us, who *through fear of death* were *subject to bondage. If God be for us, who can be against us?*

The way to maintain control of your mind is to know and embrace the truth. This statement opens the door to an array of philosophical and religious concepts, all of which are important and need to be understood properly. Once understood, these ideas need to be fought for, guarded, and protected, which will require courage. That is why we began by testing our ability to resist peer pressure. Truth is not always popular. Truth makes people uncomfortable. People resist the truth. However truth always prevails in the end. Hungarian physician Ignaz Philipp Semmeiweis believed that doctors should wash their hands because there were microorganisms so small that nobody could see them, yet they could make people sick. Despite the unprecedented results he achieved in **reducing infant mortality**, nobody believed him until after he died. Eventually however, the truth prevailed, and he was vindicated. Arm yourself with knowledge. The best defence is a good offence.

Sometimes when the truth indicates that a change is going to occur, maybe a change that will upset the normal course of things, it is more comfortable to believe everything will continue as it is, and be 'okay'. Psychologists call this a 'normalcy bias'. It is a form of cognitive dissonance and most people are biased this way in their thinking to some degree. Yet history proves this is not the case. People who think critically and logically do not allow themselves to be affected by a normalcy bias. As we explore mind control and how it affects us, keep that in mind.

Early in the 20th century, people affected by the existential philosophy of Europe began exerting their influence on America in a major way. One of these individuals was Edward Bernays, the father of modern advertising, and nephew of Sigmond Freud. Bernays worked closely with both corporations and government. In his 1928 book, *Propaganda*, he posited that the manipulation of the public was a necessary part of democracy:

> The conscious and intelligent manipulation of the organized habits and opinions of the masses is an important element in democratic society. Those who manipulate this unseen mechanism of society constitute an invisible government which is the true ruling power of our country. We are governed, our minds are molded, our tastes are formed, our ideas suggested, largely by men we have never heard of.
>
> — Edward Bernays, *Propaganda*, 1928

It was Bernays who taught the tobacco companies how to convince women to start smoking. (*Just tell them they are liberated if they smoke!*)

It was Bernays who convinced the American people that they needed fluoride in their water. (*It's good for you!*)

It was Bernays who convinced the American people to eat bacon made from pork bellies. If you have ever had British-style bacon, that is not cut from the fatty part of the pig, you can see bacon for what it really is: a strip of fat with a little bit of meat in it. Bernays' methods are still being used today, and very effectively.

After WWII a number of Nazis came to America. Many settled in Pennsylvania among the German-speaking Dutch community. Others fled Germany to South America. Some fled to Egypt, converted to Islam, and joined the Muslim Brotherhood. Many of the Nazis that came to the U.S. went to work for the U.S. Government. The most famous is Werner Von Braun, who became a director at NASA. But there are also the Nazis that are not talked about, the ones who had histories as war criminals; these were secretly brought in to work for the intelligence community. They worked on projects like *MK Ultra*, which focused on mind control of individuals through programs like Artichoke, Monarch and Bluebird, as well as manipulation of the media through operation Mocking Bird. *Operation Paperclip* was a Top-Secret operation that brought more than 700 Nazis to the U.S. to work in clandestine ways with the intelligence community. Much of this information has been declassified and made available through the Freedom of Information Act. America had no idea, as Nazi war criminals joined our team, for 'the good of the country' to 'fight the communists'. Yet, however one may try to justify his actions, the truth is, when you deal with the devil you will always lose. 'The ends justifies the means' is the philosophy of the enemy.

A major component of MK Ultra mind-control manipulation involved the use of pharmaceuticals. Another major component was controlled trauma. The MK Ultra mind-control program used what is known as 'trauma-based mind control'.

The Nazis were the first to experiment with water fluoridation.

They used this technique in their concentration camps to make the prisoners more compliant.[2] Water fluoridation in the U.S. started immediately following WWII, at the same time the Nazis came to the U.S. through Operation Paperclip. Around this time sodium fluoride was being used as an insecticide, as was fluoro-DDT and other forms of fluoride. A Harvard study posted on the Environmental Health Perspectives website shows that drinking fluoridated water lowers IQ scores by 7 points on average in children. Could this by one of the reasons that on October 8, 2013, the *New York Post* reported that American adults scored low on a global intelligence test? According to the *Post*, "In math, reading and problem-solving skills using technology, . . . American adults scored below the international average." Adding sodium fluoride to drinking water has been banned in Sweden, Holland, Finland, France, Germany and Japan. Even Great Britain and Israel have stopped fluoridating their water because of the obvious health risks, and sheer lunacy of ingesting a toxic by-product of aluminum production. IG Farben was responsible for fluoridation at Auschwitz. Overseeing this project was Fritz ter Meer. He was convicted at Nuremberg, but his sentence was commuted, so after a few years in prison he went to work for Bayer. According to the Dr Rath Health Foundation, ter Meer went on to become one of the architects of the Codex Alimentarius Commission in 1963. Codex Alimentarius was created by the UN to develop "harmonised international food standards." According to a 2008 Alimentarius report, water containing more than 1.5 ml/L of fluoride should be labeled "not suitable for infants and children under seven-years old." So they admit it. If it is not safe for children, it is not safe.

Your dentist may have recommended toothpaste with extra fluoride, but what he probably did not tell you is that for children and adolescents, too much fluoride causes white spots on the teeth, called *fluorosis*. You may want to ask your dentist if he has

2 http://www.thyroid-info.com/articles/shamesfluoride.htm
Richard Shames, M.D. Dr. Shames graduated Harvard and University of Pennsylvania, did research at the National Institutes of Health with Nobel Prize winner Marshall Nirenberg, and has been in private practice for twenty five years.

read the National Academy of Science's 2006 report on fluoride. Or, maybe ask him if any studies have shown any reduction in tooth decay in areas that fluoridate water. (None have.) Fluoride-free toothpaste is easy to find at health-food stores, and even at some supermarkets. Above all, remember that you are not the crazy one. The system has been manipulated in multiple ways, over and over again, to convince the public to accept harmful ideas and practices, while labeling time-tested techniques and practices as crazy. They pretend nothing is amiss by saying 'there has always been high cancer rates' or 'it just seems like there is more violence because we have more information available', etc. It is called *gaslighting*, which is a form of strategic mental manipulation.[3] The Bible calls it *bearing false witness*, and by definition: *Sin*.

What do each of these companies have in common: BASF, IG Farben, Merck, Hoechst, and Bayer?

1.) They were all Nazi companies that helped Hitler with things like creating the gas chambers that killed innocent Jews, and experimenting on the Jews with deadly vaccines.

2.) These are the top chemical and pharmaceutical companies in the world today, leading in cancer-causing vaccines and cancer-causing GMO foods.

IG Farben was the corporation most heavily involved with backing the Nazi party. They actually had their own concentration camp, Auschwitz. They supplied 95% of the poison gas (including Zyclon B) that the Nazis used to in their gas chambers. They supplied 84% of the explosives and 70% of the gunpowder. IG Farben produced 100% of the synthetic rubber, methanol and lubricating oil used by the Nazis. After the war, the company was broken up into other companies, including Bayer, BASF, and Hoechst.

---

[3] Gaslighting is an elaborate and diabolical form of mental abuse. The abuser may deny events happened, although he knows they did, or purposely create confusing scenarios, while pretending nothing is wrong. This is done to make the victim question his or her own memory, beliefs, or sanity.

It is not a little unsettling to see the number of Holocaust-denying websites that are now on the web. They posit that the Nazis did not really make lamp shades and other items out of human skin. They posit that the Nazis did not really have paperweights made out of shrunken heads. These things really did happen and clearly demonstrate that the Nazis were pure evil. The history is true and the Holocaust really happened.

Except for the little country of New Zealand, there is only one place on earth that allows pharmaceutical companies to market their prescription drugs directly to the public: the USA. Once the citizenry is popping pills, and zoned out on television while their Bibles collect dust on the bookshelf, they are defenseless against media mind-control foisted on them by the powers that be. The one thing that almost all of the mass shootings have in common is that the perpetrators were on selective serotonin reuptake inhibitors (SSRI). Whether you are talking about Columbine, Virginia Tech, Newtown Conn, Ft. Hood, Aurora Colorado, etc, what all the shooters have in common in these cases are (a) SSRI pharmaceuticals. In the case of the Sandy Hook, Newtown Conn shooting, the State of Connecticut has refused to release Adam Lanza's medical records, claiming that identifying the psychotropic drugs he was taking would, "cause a lot of people to stop taking their medications," according to Assistant Attorney General Patrick B. Kwanashie. Maybe that would be a good thing, for people to stop taking drugs that cause them to have psychotic episodes that make them want to kill themselves or others. If you have been prescribed this sort of medication by a doctor, talk to him about tapering off, but *do not* quit cold turkey. And *do not* quit without consulting your doctor. (If he says no, you may want to ask for a second opinion.)

Other commonalities include (b) simultaneous drills that train for the exact same scenario (in some cases not simultaneous, but a few weeks preceding), (c) an official narrative that attacks political enemies and serves a political agenda, and (d) changes in the story as it unfolds, because initial reports contradict eye witnesses. Often the alleged killer was (e) part of a government psych program. In many cases (f) other accessories to the crime are reported by eye witnesses, but ignored by law enforcement and the media. Often there are (*g*) bizarre coincidences related to the names of the people and places involved, like their prior appearance in strangely related ways in movies or music videos. (*h*) In some cases law enforcement is told to stand down. Eg, in an interview with Jake Tapper of CNN, Rep. Michael McCaul (R-TX), told Tapper that during the 2013 D.C. Navy Yard shooting, the ATF was kept out of the loop, and a SWAT team was told to stand down. McCaul said his information came from a member of the rescue team. (*i*) The killers are often either unable to remember the event, or unable to talk afterwards. This last point (*i*) is a very key component. They always need a scapegoat. The September 11 hijackers were perfect patsies for the events of that day, but for the greater war on terror, they had to come up with new ones. Aldus Huxley's *Brave New World, Revisited*, explains the real reason we have indefinitely detained people for over 10 years now without a trial: "For the dictator and his policemen, Pavlov's findings have important practical implications. If the central nervous system of dogs can be broken down, so can the central nervous system of political prisoners. It is simply a matter of applying the right amount of stress for the right length of time. At the end of the treatment, the prisoner will be in a state of neurosis or hysteria, and will be ready to confess whatever his captors want him to confess." Huxley wrote that in 1958. Today, this is happening not in Red China, but under the direction of the U.S. Government in Guantanamo Bay. In 1957, the USAF issued a report by Albert D. Biderman: *Communist Attempts to Elicit False Confessions from Air Force Prisoners of War*. In the report was a chart which detailed methods the communists used to elicit *false confessions* from American POWs in the Korean War. Personnel at Guantanamo Bay are now using the ***exact same chart*** from Biderman's 1957 report, for "interrogation training." Only the name of the chart has been changed. "Communist Coercive Methods For Eliciting Individual Compliance" has been changed to "Coercive Management Techniques." Again, the only change to the chart is the title. This may explain the bizarre photos that were leaked of the detainees in the supposed war on terror. Maybe the inmates at Abu Ghraib were not being interrogated? Were they being brainwashed through trauma-based mind control to confess to crimes they did not commit?

D.C. Navy Yard shooter Aaron Alexis had 'my ELF weapon' carved into the stock of his gun. Alexis was working with advanced weapons, and worked in an ELF area. ELF is an acronym for Extremely Low Frequency, which is an advanced technology used in mind control research. It works by beaming thoughts into the mind. Eg, ELF was used in New York for an advertisement for an A&E program called 'Paranormal Activity'. ELF beamed the thought into the heads of pedestrians, *"It's not your imagination, who's there?"* By fine-tuning the audio message, people can be manipulated to think the thoughts are their own. Dr John Hall, MD, has done extensive research in this area, which he published in a book titled, *A New Breed, Satlellite Terrorism in America* (Strategic Book Publishing, 2009).

"Unabomber" Ted Kaczynski was involved in mind control experiments in the sixties, *The New York Times* reported. The Aurora shooter, James Holmes, had a connection to a military psychologist. Holmes was seeing Airforce psychiatrist, Dr. Lynne Fenton at the University of Colorado. Fenton was known for dispensing dangerous pharmaceutical drugs, according to *The Washington Post*. Several other examples like this could be given. Many of the perpetrators of high profile shootings are found to have had connections with government psychologists, and almost always with SSRI pharmaceuticals. These connections beg the question of whether MK Ultra type programing was involved.

But mind control is more commonly carried out by much more subtle techniques. Movies like *National Treasure* portray the Masons as a positive group. Movies like *Angels and Demons* portray the Illuminati not as a satanic cult bent on world domination, but as a benevolent, persecuted group of intellectuals, trying to maintain pure doctrine. Indeed scores of movies have embedded occult images like the Masonic compass and the all seeing eye of Horus into the minds of people, making them 'cool'. What is probably even more persuasive than that though, is the way that the Illuminati is promoted in popular music. I am amazed at how successful this is, as I talk to people who think they are actually going be part of the Illuminati, just because their favorite artist promotes it in his or her music. These people have no idea that they are being brainwashed into being pawns and slaves, by a rich elite that actually hates them and wants to subjugate and kill them. The New World Order is not just trumpeted by politicians, but embedded in popular culture through movies, video games, cartoons, TV shows, big-time wrestling, you name it. Politicians play their part as well, of course. In his 1970 book, *Between Two Ages*, elite New World Order architect Zbigniew Brzezinski described a future "Technotronic Era" where populations would be controlled by advanced methods:

> The technotronic era involves the gradual appearance of a more controlled society. **Such a society would be dominated by an elite,** unrestrained by traditional values. Soon it will be possible to assert almost **continuous surveillance over every citizen** and maintain up-to-date complete files containing even the most personal information about the citizen. These files will be subject to instantaneous retrieval by the authorities,
> . . . In the technotronic society the trend would seem to be towards the aggregation of the individual support of millions of uncoordinated citizens, **easily within the reach of magnetic and attractive personalities exploiting the latest communications techniques to manipulate emotions and control reason.** [Emphasis added.]

— Zbigniew Brzezinski, 1970

A very effective mind-control technique is the idea that only the lunatic fringe buys into the beliefs of the liberty movement. There is in fact, however, a very long list of 'establishment' people who doubt the government's version of what happened on September 11th in 2001.[4] For example, Major General Albert Stubblebine, General Wesley Clark, and a litany of other colonels, captains and commanders, in addition to 1700 architects and engineers,[5] not to mention all the pilots,[6] actors, and artists.[7] I challenge anyone

---

[4] *patriotsquestion911.com*
[5] *ae911truth.org*
[6] *pilotsfor911truth.org*
[7] *aaa911truth.org*

to show me a list of 1700 architects and engineers who publicly state that they believe the government's version of the events on September 11th of 2001. Even Geraldo Rivera has admitted that the official story does not add up, yet for the most part, the MSM still persist with their theatrics, positing that only kooky conspiracy people believe in the laws of physics. Other than finding the truth behind disinformation campaigns, something that is as American as baseball and apple pie, the basic ideals that the liberty movement stands for are all things that are really just simple American ideals as well: freedom, defending the Constitution and its Bill of Rights, staying healthy and eating right, being self reliant, etc. Basically, the things that the baby-boomers considered to be American without question.

The trauma to the communities — and to the nation — when staged false-flag events take place, is an important component of the trauma-based mind control, as it is applied on a large scale at the national level. Referring to the WTC attack as 9/11 instead of September 11th, or WTC, instills fear. 911 was already in the minds of the public as the emergency number. The images of the towers falling were played over and over to shock the public. *The pharmaceuticals that the public voluntarily medicates themselves with*, together with trauma from September 11th and other events, are all part of the carefully constructed mind control program, using the well-refined techniques that were learned by the elite in the Nazi MK Ultra program. How well has it worked? I recently debated a friend from church about the believability of the September 11, WTC attack, according to the official version of events. When I asked him how he could explain Satam al Suqami's passport being found in the rubble unharmed, after the plane exploded and everything else in the tower had turned to dust, he said he believed it was a "miracle." That is what I call perfect mind control, ie when anything the government says that does not make sense must be the result of divine intervention.

Much of MK Ultra's and Mocking Bird's activities were discovered in 1975 through the Church investigations, chaired by Senator Frank Church (D-ID), which uncovered among other things, that

"The CIA currently maintains a network of several hundred foreign individuals around the world who provide intelligence for the CIA and at times attempt to influence opinion through the use of covert propaganda. These individuals provide the CIA with direct access to a large number of newspapers and periodicals, scores of press services and news agencies, radio and television stations, commercial book publishers, and other foreign media outlets." The next time you are watching the news, you may want to ask yourself, just what am I watching and what is it trying to influence me to believe? Recently CNN has been caught creating fake 'on the scene' stories with blue screens. Known CIA operative Anderson Cooper, pretended to conduct an interview at a Sandy Hook memorial, but sloppy CG work made it clear it was shot using green screen, as Cooper's nose was cut off as he moved his head. This was cached online before CNN took it down from their website, and can still be seen on YouTube: http://www.youtube.com/watch?v=rxAWy_bUuio

They have been caught using blue screen fake correspondence from embedded reporters as far back as the early nineties in Operation Desert Storm. And not only have they been using blue screen, they have been caught using crisis actors, posing as eye witnesses, or hurt family members of victims, after tragic events. Like ghouls, they seize on tragic events, and exploit them to further their political agenda. Aurora, Colorado; Sandy Hook, Connecticut; the Boston Marathon bombing; each of these tragic events bore the hallmark signs of staged events. In each case they were immediately seized on to promote a political agenda. In the case of the Boston bombing they were conducting drills at the same time for the same scenario (as was the case with 9/11). It gives them plausible deniability if they get caught.

The late great American republic has come a long way. We have passed child labor laws, enacted suffrage, and ended slavery. Indeed, we elected a black president by a landslide. However, as modern America was taking shape, behind the scenes, a political, economic and technocratic superstructure was quietly being constructed, below the radar of mainstream America. It is very powerful in its ability to form public opinion. So powerful in fact, that although America cheered as she elected her first black president, a man with virtually no public record, many Americans had never even heard of Alan Keys, his 2008 opponent who was also black, yet had a strong history as a public servant in politics. The reason Americans had not heard of Keys is because he stands for the Constitution and the rule of law.

As G. Edward Griffin said in *A Fearful Master*, "One case history is worth a thousand theoretical arguments." A case history that clearly demonstrates the blatant manipulation of the public by the mainstream media is the Eric Zimmerman – Trayvon Martin case. Americans were shown a seven-year-old picture of Martin after he was shot, that made the public believe him to be a cute twelve-year-old. But other pictures posted by Martin to his social media account showed him to be a thuggish 6'2" nineteen-year-old giving the camera the finger with both hands. The media then edited the 911 call, to make Zimmerman appear to be a racist. Zimmerman, conducting his routine neighborhood watch, told 911 dispatch that he was surveilling a suspicious looking teenager, and that there had been a lot of break-ins in the neighborhood. The dispatcher asked Zimmerman what the person looked like. Zimmerman gave a description that included the statement, "He's black." *But the media carefully edited out the request from the dispatcher to describe Martin's appearance.* This was purposely done to make it sound like Zimmerman was a racist who was only following Martin because he was black. Zimmerman was attacked by Martin, and suffered a broken nose and cuts to the back of his head as he was getting pummeled on the pavement by Martin, before drawing his gun and defending himself. There were several 911 calls from people who reported the disturbance, and Zimmerman can be heard screaming in the background as he was being beaten. However, the police photos that showed a bloody and beaten Zimmerman were not released for several weeks, until after initial reports that Zimmerman had shot a cute young boy who looked twelve years old, with a pack of Skittles in his pocket, because he was black. And I might also add, after the president had told the public, that if he had a son he would have looked like Trayvon Martin. All of this false reporting whipped up racial tensions, manipulating a mob mentality among many. Black on white violence skyrocketed. The lengths that the media went to, to spin the false narrative went even deeper though. Zimmerman is Latino. He thinks of himself as a Latino. But the press invented a new term, and insisted on calling him a "White Latino." Zimmerman was not a racist by all accounts from those who knew him and had even had a black girlfriend. The media kept repeating that Martin had a pack of Skittles in his pocket, to add to the seven-year-old boyish image they kept showing. But it was later revealed that Skittles, when mixed with Arizona Iced Tea (which he was also carrying), along with cough syrup, makes a concoction called 'Lean' which causes aggressive violent behavior. Autopsy reports confirmed that Martin was a 'Lean' user.

But why did the media go to such great lengths to distort the facts? To divide us, and to further the gun control agenda. Why did we not hear that during the 20-day Zimmerman trial, 4 minors — 3 teens and a five-year-old — were gunned down in Chicago?[8] You see, those kids do not concern the media because they already have gun control in Chicago, which is *exactly why they have such a high murder rate there*. The Bible says that God *hath made of one blood all nations of men for to dwell on all the face of the earth*. There was never any reason for race to be an issue in the Zimmerman story, because there is only one race, the human race. But those who forget God, neither are thankful, but become vain in their imaginations, having their foolish hearts darkened, insist on creating divisions. *And remember*, Zimmerman is not even white. *Thus, the race issue is a powerful tool used to control people's opinions, create civil unrest on demand, and spin the narrative of current events*. The enemy wants to divide and conquer, but Jesus said, *Blessed are the peacemakers*.

I have a dream today. . . . little black boys and black

---

8 "Four Children Gunned Down in Chicago During Zimmerman Trial", *CNSNEWS* July 15, 2013, http://cnsnews.com/news/article/four-children-gunned-down-chicago-during-zimmerman-trial

girls will be able to join hands with little white boys and white girls as sisters and brothers. I have a dream today.

— Dr. Martin Luther King, Jr.

Another technique that they use to control the narrative is planting operatives inside protests. People were filmed at Tea Party protests holding signs that said things such as "Racist And Proud Of It." When the bearer of the sign was questioned she admitted she was not part of the protest, but felt that it was 'her duty' to show people what the Tea Party stands for (in her sick and twisted opinion). The WWII veterans who protested and removed the "barrycades" to their own open-air memorial during the government shutdown were mocked by MSNBC and Rachel Maddow. On Oct 14, 2013, Maddow showed a young man with a confederate flag, standing in front of the White House and tried to equate him with the WWII veterans. Was he really a planted operative, like the lady posing as a Tea Party member with her 'racist and proud of it' sign? When they went off to war, the WWII vets were just scrawny kids who had survived the great depression. Yet they answered their call to duty, defeated Hitler, and saved the world. Yet Maddow agreed with Obama that they should not be allowed to visit their own memorial, and she wants us to believe that too. She defended the "poor, unpaid police officers" who were 'yelled at' by the mean vets. "Unpaid, because of the shutdown, that these folks made happen," Maddow said. *The vets made the shutdown happen?* It cost more money to put up the barrycades on the open air memorials than to just leave them open the way they were. Maddow is what is called a shill. She works for the New World Order. Everybody has to work I suppose, but to attack WWII veterans and lie about them has got to be the lowest, most Westboro Baptist kind of reporting imaginable. Yet she is not part of a small twenty-member cult; she is on national TV, and telling us what to think! While the mainstream media pushes its divide and conquer strategy, real reporters like Gary Webb,[9] Andrew Breitbart[10] and Michael Hastings[11] are dropping like flies.

Mass Hypnosis, using the term loosely, has been done to America. In the intelligence community it's called PSY-OPS, which is short for psychological operations. After the 2013 Boston bombing, they declared martial law in Boston to find one teenager who was later found unarmed. Militarized police conducting house to house searches, marched Americans out of their homes at gunpoint. It is clearer than ever now that the powers that be have crossed the Rubicon. The Posse Comitatus Act makes it illegal for the government to use federal military personnel to enforce the law. According to the press, the troops employed were not from the U.S. Armed Forces, which the Posse Comitatus Act specifically refers to. But, when military-style SWAT teams, FBI and other federal agents in riot gear, armored vehicles and Blackhawk helicopters descend on a city; when people are told to stay in their homes, only to then be marched out at gun point while their homes are raided, to search for one unarmed teenager, who is supposed to be innocent until proven guilty; when the American people willingly submit to this sort of hard core-tyranny without a protest, it was clear that the carefully crafted psy-op is complete. Americans by and large will accept anything now. Why is that?

I would say it is in large part because they have manipulated the American people into thinking that they need to be scared of terrorism. (Did you know that you are 3X more likely to be killed

---

9 Gary Webb was the reporter who almost single-handedly broke the story about the cocaine trafficking involved with the CIA-Contra rebels in Nicaragua. Webb's reporting prompted an internal investigation by the CIA's Inspector General, Frederick Hitz, who in 1998 finally admitted that the CIA withheld evidence of Contra drug-smuggling crimes from the Justice Department, Congress, and even the analytical division of the CIA. When Webb turned up dead in 2004 from two gunshot wounds to the head, the official cause of death was ruled, you guessed it, suicide.

10 Andrew Breitbart (who broke the ACORN child trafficking scandal) died the day before the date he publicly announced he would release new information that would "vet" Obama for the 2012 election. (Then LA medical examiner Michael Cormier died of arsenic poisoning the same day the official cause of death in the Breitbart case was made public. The LA County Coroner's office claims Cormier did not work on the Breitbart case.)

11 Michael Hastings died under equally suspicious circumstances shortly after he "declared war" on the establishment, and proclaimed he would no longer be following orders from them and asking permission to report what he wanted to.

by a bee sting, and 25X more likely to be killed by a lightning strike, than by a terrorist?) They do this by creating terrorists for the American people to be scared of. An act of terrorism happens, and the American people believe the talking heads on the TV that tell us what happened, or why it happened. When the Christmas Underwear Bomber was caught with a firecracker in his briefs in 2009, the naked-body scanners at the airports were immediately rolled out, as if there was an airport-scanner warehouse that had next-day delivery just waiting to come to our rescue. Obviously, this had all been well planned. An attorney who was on the flight, Kurt Haskell, testified he saw what appeared to be a federal agent force Delta airlines to allow Umar Farouk Abdulmutallab (AKA the Underwear Bomber) to board Delta flight 253 even though he did not have a passport. The FBI was later forced to admit that Haskell's testimony was true. In fact, after 9/11/2001, the FBI started cooking up multiple terrorist plots, in a fashion that can not be called anything other than entrapment by any reasonable person. So the public continues to see several stories about foiled terrorist plots, but what they are rarely told, is that the perpetrators are recruited, coached, and paid by the FBI, sometimes up to $250,000,[12] to commit these acts of terror. The FBI then foils the crime that they themselves engineered. And so we have a public that is scared to death of an imaginary threat. (Or a manufactured threat, that is blamed on the wrong people. For example, the FBI has yet to show the public the video that supposedly shows the Tsarnaev brothers planting their bomb along the Boston Marathon route.)[13] [14] Only through a knowledge of the Scriptures and the Spirit of God can somebody be completely free of mind control.

---

[12] Terror Plots Hatched by the FBI, *New York Times*, April 28, 2012.
http://www.nytimes.com/2012/04/29/opinion/sunday/terrorist-plots-helped-along-by-the-fbi.html?pagewanted=all&_r=1&
[13] One precedent is Operation Gladio. Between 1960 and 1980, NATO engaged in terror attacks in Europe. The truth of the operation has been proven in European courts and documented in *NATO's Secret Armies*, By Swiss historian Daniele Ganser.
[14] https://wikispooks.com/wiki/Operation_Gladio

The powers that be have always engaged in mind control. The first example of this was when the serpent convinced Eve that if she doubted God and his word, and ate from the tree of wisdom, that she would not die. He controlled her mind into believing him instead of believing God, with catastrophic results.

Pastor Erwin Lutzer of Moody Bible Church has written a book called *When a Nation Forgets God, 7 Lessons We Must Learn from Nazi Germany*. I find the premise of this book so compelling that I've decided to include the publisher's description of the book:

According to Dr. Lutzer, the German people's progression from civility to barbarity was not extraordinary, and more than a few benchmarks from their transition can be observed in present day American society (Do any of these sound familiar?):

- The Church is silenced
- The economy is king
- The lawmakers determine behaviors
- The media controls beliefs
- The Gospel and nationalism become inextricably tied to each other
- And yet, heroes still have power

We must take note of these lessons from history. The parallels are real, but the conclusion is not a foregone one. [End publisher's description.]

After the Allies liberated the Buchenwald concentration camp on April 11, 1945, General George S. Patton opened the camp as an exhibit to the public, and somewhere between 1500 - 2000 German civilians toured the camp. The phrase that could be heard over and over from the German public was "we didn't know." Why didn't they know? How could they have let their country fall so far and become so evil? Could it be because they didn't *want* to know? Or was it a result of careful planning?

Just as the Jews who were too trusting to believe anything bad would happen to them if they stayed in Germany, marched willingly to their demise without any resistance, the American people are likewise marching down the broad path that leads to destruction. Matthew 7:13,14 says, *Enter ye in at the strait gate: for wide is the gate, and broad is the way, that leadeth to destruction, and many there be which go in thereat: Because strait is the gate, and narrow is the way, which leadeth unto life, and few there be that find it.*

The media is assaulting us with a heavy onslaught of programing focusing on aliens and UFOs. Movies, TV shows and music are all conditioning us to buy into the mother of all mind-control hoaxes — when we are presented with an alternate reality and UFOs are rolled out for the public. This will be necessary to explain the rapture, convince people to forsake God and reject the Bible, and accept the mark of the beast. This is why the discovery of Noah's Ark has been dismissed.[15] This is why the discovery of Pharaoh's army's chariots at the bottom of the Red Sea has been dismissed.[16] This is why the discovery of the real Mt Sinai has been denied or dismissed.[17] According to Revelation 13, the day is coming when the entire world will worship the devil. The only way to keep yourself from being deceived is to know your Bible. Once you know the truth, the truth will set you free. I am not just talking about memorizing a few verses. I am talking about having good reasons to be sure in your beliefs. I am talking about the ability to defend your faith to the most agile evolution professor, or the most nimble Muslim apologist. It is not as hard as it may sound. When you have the truth on your side, the word is not that hard to defend. Here are some resources that serve as a good place to begin:

The Collapse of Evolution — Scott M. Huse
Evidence That Demands a Verdict — Josh McDowell
The Case for Christ — Lee Strobel
Halley's Bible Handbook — Henry H. Halley

---

[15] http://www.sunnyskyz.com/good-news/470/Noah-s-Ark-Has-Been-Found-Why-Are-They-Keeping-Us-In-The-Dark-
https://www.youtube.com/watch?v=i7iycpe16V0
[16] https://www.youtube.com/watch?v=t8USn3KlekM
[17] https://www.youtube.com/watch?v=-mB5Aw14e4M

Using the apparatus of the mainstream media, they have carefully conditioned unsuspecting Americans to believe that it is the 'conspiracy theory' believing libertarians who are the weirdos, not the establishment. Thus, the public feels they are informed when they watch the mainstream news. When Obama tells them not to question their government,[18] they are confident they can trust him. The president would not lie. When Bush says that conspiracy theories will not be tolerated,[19] they are sure he has good reasons for saying so. Listen to Kennedy's 1961 National Press Club Speech on YouTube, and compare it to what the politicians are telling us today. Then ask yourself, who is really the naive one? The one who doubts the intentions of the government or the one who believes their empty promises? Although both Christians and libertarians are often characterized as being detached from reality, consider this: NSA chief, General Keith Alexander, hired a Hollywood set designer to style his office to look like the flight deck of the Starship Enterprise, complete with a 22' wide viewing screen on the forward wall, and a captain's command chair. They even made sure the doors employ authentic Star Trek sound effects when they open and close. (All at the public's expense of course.)

So what if you are one of them? What if you are part of the system, but you are starting to come out of your trance and you want out? What do you do now? Pray about it, and do not be afraid to switch jobs if God tells you to. Whoever you are, or whatever you do, start controlling your media consumption. Read a good book instead watching TV to relax. Why do you think they call them programs? (Because they are programing you how to think?) The reality shows, comedies, the cop and crime thrillers — they are all carefully written to condition you to think the way the establishment wants you to think. The political talk shows are scripted. They pretend they are sitting around the round table and having a free-flowing exchange of ideas, but sometime try an experiment: TiVo all of the Sunday morning talk shows during the next election cycle, and you will find

18 Commencement Speech, Ohio State University, May 5, 2013.
19 Addressing the United Nations, November 10, 2001.

that they are all saying exactly the same thing. They are going by the script. They attack who they are supposed to attack, and they puff who they are supposed to puff. After you have watched them you are left with the impression that now you are informed, when nothing could be further from the truth. You have been programed to believe what they want you to believe. The Bible says,

> *Wisdom is before him that hath understanding; but the eyes of a fool are in the ends of the earth.*
>
> *Proverbs 17:27*

If you often respond to comments about current or past events by talking about a movie you saw, that may be an indication that you need to 'come out of the matrix', so to speak. Reality is a lot more interesting. Start filling your mind with wisdom. A good place to begin is the book of Proverbs. Then read the New Testament. Memorize Scripture. Strengthen your mind, and you will find you will be much more successful in your endeavors. Jesus said, *If ye continue in my word, then ye are my disciples indeed; And you shall know the truth, and **the truth shall make you free**.* When the Son sets you free, you are free indeed.

Therefore, only a God-sent revival will save our Republic. Furthermore, every revival there has ever been throughout history, beginning with Acts 2, began with prayer. When the Christians of America turn off their TVs, form prayer meetings, and pray for our country, we can and will see a revival that can reverse the trend towards bondage and oppression in America. Instead of watching TV, why not form a book club to discuss *Dragon Slayer Jesus Christ* with your friends from church? Why voluntarily submit yourself to the establishment's programing? Especially when one considers just how satanic the entertainment industry is. Corey Feldman and Corrie Haynes have both candidly admitted on their reality show that they were each molested by top Hollywood moguls. Corey Feldman went on to say in an interview that pedophilia is rampant in Hollywood. That took courage and may God protect them, in Jesus' name. Amen.

The media tells the truth in some ways, and at certain times, but they never come clean on the really important issues. For example, the Jews are looking for their Messiah today. The identity of the Messiah was discovered by Israel's most senior and beloved Rabbi, Yitzhak Kaduri. He placed his finding in a sealed envelope to be opened posthumously. Although 250,000 people marched in his funeral procession, and although the media loved to quote him while he was alive, and although he was the most respected Rabbi in Israel when he died at the ripe old age of 108 in 2006, his bombshell that Yeshua is the Messiah was virtually ignored by the world. Even the Israeli press barely mentioned it at all. That dear reader, is media mind control.

There are two main issues to be considered here. There is the issue of being a free and autonomous individual who is not deceived by the government, who will have the courage to resist tyranny and engage in civil disobedience, rather than carry out unlawful orders. Rosa Parks in the fifties, Michael New in the nineties, and Dietrich Bonhoeffer in the forties in Germany are a few examples of people who understood this principle. What do these three all have in common? They are all Christians. This brings me to the other issue that must be considered.

Being willing to stand for freedom is not enough. If you know all about the secret dealings of the illuminati, and you purpose in your heart to resist their tyranny, yet you miss the most important fundamental truth there is, that Jesus Christ died for your sins and rose again in fulfilment of the Scriptures, it will all be for nought. At the end of this life there is one central question that will matter above all else: What did you do with the person of Jesus Christ? The heart of the gospel is expressed in John 3:16:

> *For God so loved the world, that he gave his only begotten Son, that whosoever believeth in him should not perish, but have everlasting life.*

> — Dragon Slayer Jesus Christ

The gospel is not complicated. When Jesus called the disciples he just said, *Come and follow me.* He is saying the same thing to all of us. *Just come, and follow me.*

I cannot tell you what to do next, but I can tell you this; God does not like hypocrites. If you mean business, God will tell you what to do next. His grace is sufficient to cover all your sins, but the danger is to become so hardened through hypocrisy, that you stop caring about your sins and confessing them. The word hypocrite comes from the Greek word *hypokritēs*, which literally means 'actor'.

This is where mind control becomes very real for all of us. The mind is where the real battle takes place. Ninety-nine percent of spiritual warfare takes place in your mind. If you have still not accepted Jesus Christ as your personal Savior, you are under a powerful form of mind control (II Cor 4:4), which is keeping you from receiving the free gift of eternal life. There are many things that keep people from receiving the free gift, and they are all lies. Whatever else you get out of reading this book, above all else make sure you receive the free gift of everlasting life through Jesus Christ our Lord. If you have not already made that decision, **rebuke Satan in Jesus' name** (Jude 9) and say this prayer:

Father, I receive your Son as my personal Saviour; Lord Jesus, please come into my heart. Take control of my life. Thank you for the precious blood you shed for me on Calvary. I pray this in your holy and precious name. Amen.

P aul awoke the same way he did everyday, with thanks to God on his lips, and that before the sun arose. He crawled from off his straw mat and knelt beside it, rendering the calves of his lips unto his God. Paul was not the man he used to be. Pus ran from his eyes. His joints creaked and snapped when he moved. His arthritis did not begin to be anything close to manageable until the sixth hour. He had received many visitors in his home since he had come to Rome, mostly fellow Christians who sought instruction in righteousness, but now that Nero had begun to persecute the church his days were usually long and lonely, spent in prayer and meditation in his cell. Although he could scarcely read a parchment with his own eyes any longer, he had nevertheless committed all thirty-nine books of the Hebrew Scriptures to memory. He had written many epistles which had been sent out to various places in the Roman Empire. He felt now that his departure was soon at hand. He still had one faithful companion who attended him when all others had forsaken him, a beloved brother and Christian doctor named Luke. Now even Luke had to go into hiding, but there were times when some of the guards who had accepted Christ would sneak Luke in to visit Paul.

Paul's cell was dark but a beam of light from the portal overhead provided some illumination. It smelled of dung. There were flies. Paul could hear the blood-thirsty crowds roar outside in the arena. He did not fear death, far from it. Paul actually looked forward to it. He had finished his course. He had kept the faith. He longed for home. Paul knelt and prayed. "Father, allow me to use these last moments of my life for thy glory. I pray thee to use me to add to your church, yet one more soul. In the name of Yeshua Ha'Mashiach." Just as Paul was saying Amen, a rope was lowered from above, and a fellow prisoner descended into the cell. Gaius quickly climbed down, but not so quickly as to burn himself on the rope. Paul thanked the Lord under his breath for his new visitor and silently prayed for God to give him the words to reach the new inmate for Yeshua. He wasted no time. "I'm Paul," he said.

"Save it," Gaius replied curtly. "I'm not here to make friends. I'm here to kill you tomorrow in the arena."

"I see," Paul replied. "And you believe this will win you your freedom?"

"It's going to be you or me tomorrow, old man. Let's not hassle it."

Paul prayed again silently for wisdom. "It's not a hassle to me. I'm going to receive my reward after you kill me. It is you I am concerned about."

"Save your concerns for yourself old man," Gaius said. He was silent for a long moment, but then he took the bait. "Just what kind of rewards does your god give you anyway?" Gaius asked. Gaius was a talker and he did not like silence. Talking to someone he knew he was going to have to kill made him feel a little guilty but at least it would get his mind off the smell.

Paul silently thanked Yeshua and began, "Well there is the part I can tell you about, and then there are the things I cannot tell you about."

"What do you mean you can't tell me?" Gaius asked. "Is this one of those secret mystery religions?"

"Oh not at all," Paul replied. "My God does nothing in secret. I cannot tell you because there are not words to describe the things my God has prepared for me."

"You seem pretty sure he is going to be pleased with you," Gaius said.

"Oh I am more than sure about my reward," Paul said. "And believe me when I say, there are no words in your Latin language to describe it."

There was something different about this old man. He spoke Latin very well for a foreigner. He had an honest face. But it was not just his face per se, but his countenance, the expression on his face. He had a peace about him. It emanated from him. Gaius could feel it, and it was starting to make him uncomfortable. But strangely, not in a bad way. He was feeling unsure of himself, which was unusual for Gaius. He suddenly felt weak, like his confidence had drained out of him. But this old man seemed so confident and sure of himself. He did not even seem to mind being in prison, or the fact that he was going to die. Gaius felt an urge to surrender and befriend the old man. He decided to let his guard down. "Sounds interesting," Gaius said. "I know a little Greek. Would that help you explain it?"

"Oh I am afraid not," Paul said. "I cannot explain it in Hebrew either, or any language for that matter."

"You seem pretty sure of yourself. How do you know this secret treasure is really there waiting for you?"

"I've seen it already." Paul said.

Now that was something that rendered Gaius speechless, which was no mean feat. Gaius had looked into many men's eyes before he killed them, and he had never seen eyes like this man had. He felt like he had found the honest man Diogenese used to look for with his lantern. He asked himself how he could know for sure this man was for real. How did he know he was not being deceived? He realized he did not know it, per se. He *felt* it. He literally felt deep down in his guts that he could trust this man.

"What do you mean by that?" Gaius asked. His voice was no longer rough and curt. Now he spoke more softly. He actually wanted to show respect to Paul, for some reason he still had not quite figured out.

"I have seen the afterlife," Paul said. "I stopped breathing once in Asia. Lystra, to be precise. I healed a man there. He could not walk before I prayed for him. Well, they tried to deify me for it and make sacrifices to me, but that would have been blasphemy. There is only one true God. I worship Iesus, the King of the Jews."

It was starting to make sense to Gaius. The reason they killed Artellies. The reason Artellies had forsaken the Roman way and went Judean. The reason they wanted Paul dead. His emotions were taking over. He was losing control of himself and he knew it. He was scared. That definitely was not normal for Gaius. He was being challenged, in his soul. He was wondering now what Mars would do if he stopped worshipping him. He had never felt such of flood of different emotions before.

"So the people of Lycaonia were not a little offended when we restrained them. Then some of my fellow countrymen from Judah came down from Iconium and stirred the Lycaonians up against me.

They dragged me out of the city and stoned me to death."

Gaius stared intently at Paul.

"I was caught up into the third heaven. I saw unspeakable things there, which it is not lawful for a man to utter. There are riches beyond your wildest dreams if you accept Iesus as your Lord and Saviour."

"I've heard this before," Gaius said. "I've heard you have to repent and follow the Jewish laws. Not sure I'd do so well at that."

"That is not true," Paul said. "The Jewish law requires that you attend ceremonies and make sacrifices in Jerusalem. Iesus made one sacrifice to end all sacrifices, when he was crucified for the sins of all mankind. It is true that you will have to stop carousing and fornicating, and of course you have to stop worshipping idols. Iesus will put new desires in your heart. You will find that the things you used to find satisfying will not appeal to you anymore."

"Do I have to get circumcised?" Gaius asked, with a smirk on his face.

"No," Paul said. "That is all part of the Jewish law, which Iesus sets us free from."

"What about the women?" Gaius said, without smirking.

"God does not want you to be a eunuch, Gaius. His plan is for one man and one woman to love one another, and to live together in a covenant relationship." Although Gaius did not admit it, that sounded pretty good to him, almost too good to be true. Paul's words were piercing him. They stabbed his heart, and dug deep down into his soul.

"If you do not mind my asking," Paul said, "what did you do to get yourself in trouble?"

Gaius just stared blankly back at Paul.

"You must be in trouble or they would not have put you in here with me," Paul said.

"My commanding officer thought as you do," Gaius said. "I saw him crucified for it. After that I went on a drinking binge. After I got drunk I got into trouble of some sort, must have irritated the legate. I don't remember much of it." Gaius was getting tired and irritable now. "Well that's enough chatter for now," Gaius said. "We've got a big day today you and I." Paul was just waking up but Gaius was tired and he had a headache to sleep off. As Gaius was settling down and preparing to drift off, a rope was lowered down into the cell as the jailer called out to Gaius.

"Up now you," the jailer said. "Looks like you are going to receive a new assignment."

Seems to me that if you're afraid or living with some big fear, you're not really living. You're only half alive. I don't care if it's the boss you're scared of or a lot of people in a room or diving off of a dinky little board, you gotta get rid of it. You owe it to yourself. Makes sort of a zombie out of you being afraid. I mean you want to be free, don't you? And how can you if you are scared? That's prison. Fear's a jailer. Mind now, I'm not a professor on the subject. I just found it out for myself. But that's what I think.

— Audie Murphy

Fight the good fight of faith . . .

— The apostle Paul, I Timothy 6:12*a*

XVI

THE AMERICAN SOLDIER

I wrote this book because I believe there are still women and men in this country who want to stand for something, who want to believe in something, and who want to be something more than just slaves to the system. I believe there are men who want what is best for their families and are willing to fight for it. I believe there are men who will refuse to bow to the cowards that have worked in the shadows to steal our freedom from us. I believe there are men who will fight to protect their women instead of letting them be sterilized by Gardasil or letting them get breast cancer because nobody told them how to avoid it. I believe that there are still men who would rather fight for freedom than cower in fear and live like domesticated animals who lick their owners hands, and heel on command.

So what does that mean exactly. What do I want for America? It's a fair question. I want clean food and water back. I want a civilian police force back. I want good cops to stand up to their superiors and refuse to obey unconstitutional orders. I want an informed public that thinks for themselves. I want our constitutional rights back. I want people to understand that their rights come from God and not the government. I want people to understand that WE THE PEOPLE *are* the government. I want people to put down their mobile devices and start talking to each other again. I want people to go outside and enjoy what God has created. I want people to stop getting cancer (which is very possible).[1] I want the Constitution to be followed before we go to war, which means that Congress — not the president — has to act to declare war. I want a return to real money, instead of the inflationary fiat currency we have been given. Inflation is a hidden tax that is stealing our wealth. I want people to actually own their property again, instead of leasing it from the government, which is what our high property taxes now amount to. I want the legalized robbery to stop — the massive bail-outs and 'quantitative easing' which depletes our wealth even more. I want people to start treating each other like human beings again, and stop regressing to 'race' divisions. I want people to come out of their trances and wake up to reality. I want people to wake up to the fact that GMO causes cancer, and that Monsanto does not even serve it in their own cafeterias. I want people to realize that eating healthy and organic, and getting the proper vitamins and minerals are the best guards there are against cancer. I want people to recapture the vision of our forefathers, which was rugged individualism, that we may be free and independent. World socialism is forcing people into a collective that steals our individuality. All this is antithetical to what God wants for us. Jesus would never endorse socialism. He created us as individuals; he left the ninety-nine sheep to find the one who was lost. Every individual soul is precious in his sight. I want people to realize that they are created by God in his own image, that we are all going to stand before him one day, and that we will all have to give an account of every idle word we have ever said. I want men to start acting like men again, to realize that we have a responsibility to do our civic duty, which means getting

---

[1] Juicing with organic vegetables and quitting junk food goes a long way towards this. The next step is to start doing some research. Watch this video: *Cancer, the Forbidden Cures*, http://www.youtube.com/watch?v=gWLrfNJICeM If Western doctors know so much, why is their average life expectancy 56?

out of the boxes that they have created for us and being salt and light, not playing Xbox and watching the idiot box. I am confident Jesus wants these things as well.

Dwight D Eisenhower said, "We should take nothing for granted. Only an alert and knowledgeable citizenry, can compel the proper meshing of the huge industrial and military machinery of defence with our peaceful methods and goals, so that security and liberty may prosper together." President Eisenhower saw that the military and its supporting infrastructure had become a powerful apparatus that could be misused if it was controlled by the wrong people. It is ultimately the military itself, that has to maintain integrity and honor. It would appear that there are those who understand this, and are therefore trying to stack the deck in their favor. The military is therefore being gutted to suit the agenda of the New World Order. Obama has sacked 200 officers since he took office, and an unprecedented number four-star generals. Allegedly, anyone who disagrees with him on key military issues like homosexuality, women in combat, etc., is purged. The Navy SEALs were ordered to take the 'Don't Tread On Me' flag off their uniforms — a flag that has been part of the Navy since the American Revolution.

It has been reported that there is a litmus test now for career advancement in the military. The question asked is, "Do you feel comfortable disarming American citizens?" The way this question is answered has had serious implications for the careers of many military personnel.

Historically, the American soldier represented freedom and justice. He defended our Republic and kept us free. He liberated those who suffered under tyranny, and gave his life for the cause of liberty. It was clear that he was one of the good guys. Something has gone very wrong. In 1935, Major General Smedley Butler published his exposé *War Is a Racket*, showing the underlying reason for war in most cases, which is profiteering. Profiteering at the expense of the victims of war who die for it, and the saps who pay for it. Not to mention those who are permanently disfigured. A quick startpage/images search for "deformities caused by agent orange" or "deformities caused by depleted uranium" reveals the horrific damage that has been done by our country's use of chemical weapons.

Soldiers need to be informed about the reasons for the recent wars the U.S. has engaged in. They have been lied to. This is what Major General Butler learned after working his way up from the enlisted ranks to become the most decorated war hero in the history of the Marine Corps. I believe many in the military are waking up to the ugly truth. They have recently had their pay and benefits cut. They are demonized in the media. They are now listed as a threat in Homeland Security documents. Things like these are hard to ignore.

The American soldier is still a man with a conscience, who has the power to stand against evil. The New World Order knows this, and has flipped the script, so it is not the Muslims we need to worry about any longer, they say, but the returning veterans. This is who Homeland Security says is the real terrorist threat. The American soldier is one of the biggest threats to the New World Order. Therefore the New World Order has gone into a Orwellian frenzy over the handling of American soldiers. Soldiers are now heavily medicated with psychotropic drugs. As recently as the 90s this would have actually disqualified them from combat duty. Now they are not only issued these dangerous and addictive meds, but actually *forced* to take them.[2] Soldiers are subjected to Nazi style brainwashing techniques, as they are told that Christian ministries are now 'domestic hate groups'. Soldiers are shown slides of Westboro Baptist members holding their infamous hate signs, as they are warned that the American Family Association, a wholesome Christian group who teaches the love of Jesus Christ is a hate group. Equating the AFA to the Westboro Baptists is like equating the people of London to Jack the Ripper. The Westboro Baptist cult only has **20 members**, but there are **millions** of Christians in the United States, so why is the military trying to equate the Westboro Baptist cult with the mainline American Family Association? Why

---

[2] Drugging of US Troops an Underreported Scandal, *Infowars, August 19, 2013*
http://www.infowars.com/mass-drugging-of-us-troops-an-underreported-scandal/

are the soldiers being taught that the founding fathers would not be welcome in today's military?[3]

Why is the federal government, in coordinated operations with local police, now routinely detaining returning veterans, over 20,000 in Virginia alone in 2011? Because these are the guys that love America and are willing to fight for her. These are the guys that are still men, who have a backbone, and the New World Order is scared to death of them. It was veterans who tore down the 'barrycades' during the government shutdown of 2013 and dumped them on the lawn of the White House. It is veterans who come from families that have a long history of patriotism and are knowledgeable about our nation's history. *That's why* according to Homeland Security documents, the real terror threat is not the Muslim extremists, but the returning veterans. They have declared war on the American people, beginning with the veterans. Soldiers are now sent back to fight with injuries. They are deployed for four tours overseas, an unprecedented amount of combat. Because of the heavy strain on them, they are committing suicide in record numbers. Once the New World Order has used you it casts you aside. The best way we can support our troops is by educating them about how they are being used by the New World Order, who hates them and wants to destroy them. The military is waking up, thanks be to God. If we lose our military, the NWO can go after the rest of us, once the trained soldiers are out of the way.

Charlie Strange, the father of fallen Navy SEAL hero Michael Strange, has been speaking out. He is represented by stalwart freedom defender Larry Klayman of Judical Watch and *Freedomwatchusa.org*. This story dramatically illustrates just how grave our situation is. Charlie's son, Michael, warned him before his death that it was only a matter of time. The last time they spoke he told his dad he had prepared a will and his whole

---

[3] DOD Trainging Manual: 'Extremist' Founding Fathers 'Would Not Be Welcome In Today's Military', *Infowars*, August 24, 2013.
http://www.infowars.com/dod-training-manual-suggests-extremist-founding-fathers-would-not-be-welcome-in-todays-military/

demeanor was different than usual, after eight years as a SEAL. He told his dad that somebody had been leaking things and he was not going to be around much longer.

On August 6, 2011, 22 members of Navy SEAL Team VI, were loaded onto a CH-47 Chinook, along with 16 other men as part of a special-ops mission to hit a high-value target. According to the official version of events, the helicopter was shot down, and all thirty-eight men died. This was the biggest loss of life in a single day since the beginning of the war in Afghanistan. After the incident, the military claimed they could not recover the black box. They claimed it was washed away by a flash flood. (In a desert mind you.) Black boxes are virtually indestructible, and have tracking devices which make them easy to locate. Not only that, but CH-47 helicopters have 2 black boxes in them. But adding to the outright abomination of the story the families were handed, is the fact that 22 Navy SEALs would never be loaded onto a dinosaur CH-47 unless there was something terribly wrong. The SEALs work exclusively with state of the art MH-47 Night Stalkers, and they are always divided into small groups of 4 or 5 on multiple different aircraft.

The SEALs and everyone else on board were all cremated after the incident. The families were told that this was necessary because the bodies were burned badly in the crash. Documentation given to the families on disk revealed that Michael was not in fact burned. There was a picture of him lying on the ground fully intact, without so much as his hair singed. After printing out all of the information on the disk, which was no easy task according to Charles Strange, it was abundantly clear that the cremating of the bodies was to cover up what had happened. The families were asked to give the disks back, but Charles had already figured out how to use the disk and had printed out 1300 pages of information it contained.

Eight Afghan commandos were onboard the Chinook. At the last minute, they were replaced without changing the manifest. The official story is that the Chinook was hit by a "lucky shot" by an RPG from between 600 and 700 meters away, that the Chinook exploded two times in mid-air, then exploded a third time after it crashed. Normal protocol would have been to clear the area with drone strikes prior to the mission. The families of the fallen SEALs were told that this was not done because there were "friendlies" among the Taliban militants, and that they were attempting to "win the hearts and minds" of the Afghan militants. But what happened after the crash, at the first memorial is where the story gets even more twisted.

The Afghan Muslims who were onboard the Chinook were flown to Kabul along with the SEALs and the eight other U.S. soldiers who were onboard. The initial memorial service was given by a Muslim cleric who cursed the SEALs and damned them to hell in Arabic. His sermon has been translated by at least eight different people and they all came to the same conclusion.

The families are being bullied and told to stay quiet, but many of them realize what I have written this book to tell you; that we are at war with pure evil, that criminal elements have infiltrated our government and our military, and they are not above murdering our best and bravest soldiers, to cover up what only they knew about the raid on the bin Laden compound in Pakistan.

After the deaths of 22 of the military's best and most elite soldiers, along with eight other Americans, those involved at the highest levels were promoted, moved to different posts, or resigned. On August 8, Admiral William H. McRaven became the new Commander, U.S. Special Operations Command. General David Petraeus left Afghanistan ten days after the incident and was promoted to CIA Director in September. Admiral Eric T. Olson resigned two days after the tragedy, after 38 years of service. The investigation (with the conclusion about the lucky RPG) was conducted by Brig. Gen Jeffrey Colt, who was promoted to Major General in February of 2013.

The names of the eight Muslim Afghans who were placed on the helicopter at the last minute are still unknown. It is believed by many that they were suicide bombers.

There were also mysterious deaths on the ship that carried out the bin Laden mission. The military court-martialed 30 people involved with the operation who were speaking out. There are no witnesses to the 'burial at sea' of the deceased Osama bin Laden; internal emails between military officers indicate no sailors were present. In fact, it has been reported by high level sources inside the military that it was a body double look-alike that was in the bin Laden compound, and not the real Osama bin Laden.

Wanting to seize on the opportunity for political advantage, the Obama-Biden ticket released the information that "SEAL Team VI" had killed Osama bin Laden during the 2012 election cycle. This was the first tragic leak that led to the deaths of SEAL Team VI. There were fake photos released of the president and his team watching the raid in the situation room. (Leon Panetta admitted there was no live feed of the raid on the compound. The famous situation room photo, that we were led to believe showed the president and his team watching the raid was either posed for, or else they were all watching something entirely different than we were led to believe.) The evidence is mounting to make it evermore clear that 22 SEAL Team VI members were murdered to cover up what they knew about the bin Laden raid.

If the Christians of the twenty-first century can not find the courage to stand against the tyranny of the New World Order, then God help us. If we are not willing to tell our friends, pastors and co-workers the truth about what is happening in America and world-wide, then God help us. If we can not find the courage to wrench ourselves free of the false narrative of what has been transpiring since the beginning of the twenty-first century, then God help us. In the Revolutionary War, the Christians, led by Rev Jonas Clark, were the first to answer the call to arms. If the church does not answer their call of duty and join the liberty movement, we will be held accountable by a holy God. God commands us to speak out. Circumstances demand we speak out. God help us if we do not speak out. The greatest military leader of all commands us,

> [W]*hat ye hear in the ear, that preach ye upon the housetops.*

And again,

And I say unto you my friends, Be not afraid of them that kill the body, and after that have no more that they can do.

But I will forewarn you whom ye shall fear: Fear him, which after he hath killed hath power to cast into hell; yea, I say unto you, Fear him.

— Dragon Slayer Jesus Christ

The American soldier is committing suicide at the rate of 22 fallen soldiers per day. Seven of the 22 soldiers in that statistic are active duty. It is now more likely that a soldier will commit suicide than be killed in combat. Until recently, I supposed that this was mainly due to the increased tour duty and forced medicating with cocktails of pharmaceuticals. However, the truth is much uglier than that. In the 90s Bill Clinton opened a Pandora's box when he rolled out the 'don't ask don't tell' policy. Then Obama removed all restraints and ended 'don't ask don't tell'. What has been the fruit of this? According to a report released by the Department of Defense, more than half of the sexual assaults in the military — and there are a lot of them, 26,000 in 2012 — are male on male. This even though males are much less likely to report being assaulted than women. What is even worse perhaps, is that when males do report being raped, the attackers are much less likely to be disciplined. That should make it abundantly clear what the cause of the high suicide rate is. If you are a soldier and you are struggling with depression, I want to pray for you:

Father, I pray for this brave soldier who has been wounded and desperately needs your help. I ask you to strengthen him and breathe power into his soul. I pray you will fight for him, and give him the faith to believe in the future you have prepared for him. I pray you will give him the courage to fight and not give up. I pray you will pour your Spirit into him, that he will know that he is not alone, but that your Son, the greatest Warrior of all is with him, and will never leave him or forsake him. I pray this in Jesus' name. Ämen.

There is a great warrior in the Bible named David who wrote several songs when he was being hunted down by his enemies. These songs are prayers to God and they are in the middle of the Bible in the Book of Psalms. The Psalms also show the mind of Jesus in his times of suffering. They are a tremendous resource in hard times of despair. Read the New Testament too. Talk to your chaplain. Hang on and pray to God for strength in Jesus' name. He can and will get you through. His name is I AM. When you are not strong enough to go on, he says I AM. His strength and guidance are freely yours and you do not have to earn his favor. The Bible says that salvation through Jesus Christ is a free gift, available to all who ask for it. Anyone — that includes you. If you have sinned then he will forgive you. That is the whole reason Jesus came, to save sinners and call them to repentance. *For by **grace** are ye saved through faith; and that not of yourselves: it is the **gift of God: Not of works**, lest any man should boast* (Eph 2:8,9). Grace means unmerited favor, ie it's free. If we could earn favor by being good, Jesus would not have had to go to the cross (Matt 26:39). The whole reason he came was so we could be forgiven for our sins. Jesus wants to come into your heart and make all things new for you. He will show you the way, if you just trust him (John 14:6).

Satan knows full well the power of the American soldier, and he is doing everything he can to attack the soldiers and destroy the power of the American military. Not only are returning veterans being targeted by Homeland Security as possible terrorist threats, but the active military has become a battleground for religious freedom as soldiers are watching their basic religious freedoms being taken from them. The military has blocked *Infowars.com* from their servers and servicemen are being told they are forbidden to view it, even when they are at home and off duty. This is chillingly similar to the Soviet Union, where it was illegal to listen to an American radio broadcast.

America was founded on the principle that we would not need a standing army, because the citizens would by themselves be able to defend the borders. Citizens would be well armed and well equipped to defend America from all enemies, whether foreign or domestic. This was the reason for the 2nd Amendment to the

Constitution. However, just as Satan hates the U.S. military, he hates the citizens of the U.S. to be armed too. Why? Study after study has proven that more guns means less violent crime. While gun ownership has been consistently increasing for the last twenty years in the U.S., homicides and other crimes with firearms has been predictably and consistently decreasing. Gun control advocate Pierce Morgan loves to point out that there are more gun homicides in the U.S. than there are in Great Britain, but has disarming the people of England really made them safer? Here are a few of the points made by Michael Snyder in a recent article posted at *The American Dream*:

#10 Despite the very strict ban on guns in the UK, the overall rate of violent crime in the UK is about 4 times higher than it is in the United States. In one recent year, there were 2,034 violent crimes per 100,000 people in the UK. In the United States, there were only 466 violent crimes per 100,000 people during that same year. Do we really want to be more like the UK?

#11 The UK has approximately 125 percent more rape victims per 100,000 people each year than the United States does.

#12 The UK has approximately 133 percent more assault victims per 100,000 people each year than the United States does.

#13 The UK has the fourth highest burglary rate in the EU.

#14 The UK has the second highest overall crime rate in the EU.[4]

A major part of the mind control that we touched on in the last chapter, is geared towards the gun-control agenda. This is an actual quote from the attorney general of the United States, from when he was a U.S. attorney working for the Clinton

[4] 18 Little-Known Gun Facts That Prove That Guns Make Us Safer, Michael Snyder, *The American Dream*. August 11th, 2013. http://endoftheamericandream.com/archives/18-little-known-gun-facts-that-prove-that-guns-make-us-safer

Administration in 1995:

> We need to . . . brainwash people into thinking about guns in a vastly different way.
>
> — Eric Holder

In the same article by Michael Snyder cited above on page 251, Snyder went on to say,

> "Democratic strategists have drafted a how-to manual on manipulating the public's emotions toward gun control in the aftermath of a major shooting.
>
> "A high-profile gun-violence incident temporarily draws more people into the conversation about gun violence," asserts the guide. "We should rely on emotionally powerful language, feelings and images to bring home the terrible impact of gun violence."
>
> "The 80-page document titled "Preventing Gun Violence Through Effective Messaging," also urges gun-control advocates use images of frightening-looking guns and shooting scenes to make their point.
>
> "The most powerful time to communicate is when concern and emotions are running at their peak," the guide insists. "The debate over gun violence in America is periodically punctuated by high-profile gun violence incidents including Columbine, Virginia Tech, Tucson, the Trayvon Martin killing, Aurora and Oak Creek. When an incident such as these attracts sustained media attention, it creates a unique climate for our communications efforts." [5]

It was the American soldier that won the War of Independence against Great Britain. It was the American soldier that defeated the Kaiser Wilhelm II in WWI and Hitler in WWII, not to mention countless other battles around the world most of us never hear

[5] Michael Snyder, *The American Dream.* August 11th, 2013.
http://endoftheamericandream.com/archives/18-little-known-gun-facts-that-prove-that-guns-make-us-safer

about. If you are a soldier, then it is essential you recognize how important you are, and that you take steps to protect yourself from the attacks of the enemy, Satan, who wants to destroy you. You need to be strong. You need to stand for righteousness when you are ordered to disarm American citizens, contrary to oath you took to support and defend the Constitution against all enemies, foreign and domestic. You need to stand for righteousness when you are told to take orders from foreign commanders in blue helmets. Michael New stood up to his CO when he was ordered to wear a U.N. patch on his uniform. God was with him and gave him the strength to stand for the truth. You need to stand for righteousness when you are given unlawful orders of any kind. Stewart Rhodes and the members of Oath Keepers are committed to disobeying unlawful orders, especially if they involve disarming Americans. If you are too then you are the resistance. You are not alone. Jesus is with you. As Luther used to say, "One with God is a majority."

Whether you are in the military or not, if you are a Christian you are a soldier. May we stand in this evil day, having done all to stand, that we may finish our course, and keep the faith.

It is clearer now than ever that the second coming of our Lord is nigh. The blood moons of 2014 and 2015 indicate that something huge is on the horizon. Whether or not this will be the rapture that I wrote about in *Where Did All the People GO?* I do not know, but it is definitely worth considering. When a lunar eclipse occurs, it is referred to as a 'blood moon' because of the way the light of the sun refracting through the earth's atmosphere can cause the moon to appear red. The term 'blood moon' is an old one and has been used from ancient times. When four of these lunar eclipses occur consecutively over two years, it is called a tetrad. When they correspond with four Jewish feast days it has a prophetic significance. This is a rare occurrence, and appears to be one that is divinely designed to mark occasions that are significant in the history of Israel. For example this happened in 1492- 1493, which marked the Spanish Inquisition, when the Jewish people were persecuted in Spain. There was a prophetic tetrad in

1949-1950, when the first government offices were set up in the new nation of Israel, immediately following the Israeli War of Independence. There was a prophetic tetrad in 1967-1968 to mark the Six Day War, when Israel regained Jerusalem. What the current tetrad of 2014-2015 will mark remains yet to be seen, but there will not be another prophetic tetrad for at least 100 years. Could this phenomenon possibly mark the beginning of the seventieth week of Daniel? The current prophetic tetrad is unique in that it also corresponds with two solar eclipses:

> *The **sun shall be turned into darkness**, and the **moon into blood**, before the great and the terrible day of the LORD come.*
>
> *Joel 2:31*

> *And there shall be signs in the **sun, and in the moon, and in the stars**; and upon the earth distress of nations, with perplexity; the sea and the waves roaring . . .*
>
> — Dragon Slayer Jesus Christ

There are all sorts of ways to engage the battle in these last days. Share the information in this book with your friends and family. Some have the gift of administration and can get involved in their local government. Some people can form prayer meetings. Prayer is a desperately needed ministry in these last days. Along with the rise of the New World Order, we also have a unique opportunity for evangelism. The doors are open to an English speaking world. Could God be calling you into the foreign mission field? Whatever it is that you are called to do, find out and do it (James 4:14).

Father, bless all who read this and give them the wisdom to make good decisions. Increase their faith, and keep their souls against the day of your coming. I pray this in Jesus' name. Amen.

Mike

EPILOGUE

And the great dragon was cast out, that old serpent, called the Devil, and Satan, which deceiveth the whole world: he was cast out into the earth, and his angels were cast out with him.

The Revelation 12:9

The love of Jesus Christ is something that we will probably never fully comprehend. Our Western minds are so confused about the true nature of love. We think of it as an emotion. Yet according to Scripture, love is not something you feel, it is something you do. (John 15:13; I John 3:16, 5:2,3)

The love of Jesus Christ is demonstrated most visibly at the cross, where he suffered and died for us; yet his love is so much deeper than that. He is not only our kinsman Redeemer (Lev 25:25; Ruth 3:9); he is also our Avenger of blood (Num 35:19; Josh 20:5).

Hence, when people point to the evil in the world, and question God's goodness, it only shows the human condition, not the nature of God. *God is love*, and since he loves us, he has not only made a way for us to be free from this wicked world, but he is also guiding and governing in the affairs of men — and he is allowing us to be part of the story. If we were to write the story ourselves, we may remove the bad guys, or make them be 'good', but that would only show that we are despots who deny people their free will, which is the most fundamental human right there is. All good stories have a villain and a hero. The best stories involve people who triumph over adversity. If God removed the pain, he would be denying us the dignity of overcoming our adversity. If he handed everything to us without any effort on our part, we would be spoiled brats. *[T]ribulation works patience; And patience, experience; and experience, hope. . .* This life is our training period. He *hath made us kings and priests unto God and his Father;* Jesus is allowing us to play a part in the war that has been waged against all who dwell on the earth. He calls us soldiers. He calls us friends. He has written the story as it pleased him. We are granted the privilege of co-authoring the story together with him. As far as the evil in the world goes, the worst part is still yet to come. If you have been paying attention it should be plain to see that it is all leading to this final tragic event:

> *And they worshipped the dragon which gave power unto the beast: and they worshipped the beast, saying, Who is like unto the beast? who is able to make war with him?*

> *The Revelation 13:4*

He made a way of escaping this terrible time of God's wrath. Yet in his mercy, he will give those who were not ready another chance to receive him, and encourage them in their tribulation:

> *He that leadeth into captivity shall go into captivity: he that killeth with the sword must be killed with the sword. Here is the patience and the faith of the saints.*

> *The Revelation 13:10*

When you think about it, who is more loving? A lover who enables you in your bad habits, makes excuses for you, and cleans up all your messes as you grow more and more dependent on him? Or a lover who patiently corrects you, that you may reach your true potential; one who gives his life for you, and rescues you from a fire breathing dragon (Job 41:19–21)? You see, *you* are what all the fuss is over. In the final analysis, all the war and destruction on planet earth comes down to a war between God and Satan, and you are what they are fighting over. Satan wants your soul, and so does Jesus. Ultimately, Jesus wins.

> *And he laid hold on the dragon, that old serpent, which is the Devil, and Satan . . . And the devil that deceived them was cast into the lake of fire and brimstone, where the beast and the false prophet are, and shall be tormented day and night for ever and ever.*
>
> *The Revelation, Chapter XX*

Jesus is coming back in glory. He will rule from the throne of David in Jerusalem. His kingdom will have no end. He loved us enough to make us part of it. It is the will of God that we be *rooted and grounded in love*, and that we may comprehend *the breadth, and length, and depth, and height; And . . . know the love of Christ, which passeth knowledge.* His love is something that cannot be explained. There are countless illustrations and anecdotes that describe the love of Christ, but after walking with him for twenty years I am convinced that I have yet to even begin to understand his love for us. I know this, all our love and sacrifice in this world, compared to Jesus' love, is like a thimble of water, compared to the Pacific Ocean.

> *Omnia vincit amor; et nos cedamus Amori.*
> Love conquers all; let us, too, yield to Love!
>
> — Virgil, Roman poet, *Eclogue X,* 37 BC

So what ever became of our first century Christians? According to Fox, Paul traveled to Hispania after his first imprisonment. He returned to Rome only to be imprisoned again in 66 AD. After Paul was saved from the mouth of the lion (II Tim 4:17), he was beheaded under Nero in 68 AD.

Rufus was crucified. Antonina was purchased from her master

by a fellow Christian who paid four times what she was worth on the open market. She later had an opportunity to talk to Sexta, and she led her to Christ. However Antonina and her new master were later found out, and they were both beheaded for illegal religious activity. Rufus's father was a Stoic who was set in his ways. He never accepted Christ and died in his sins. Lucius went on to become a 'priest', a covert sect of quasi-Christians who gathered intelligence for the empire. These would continue to gain power and influence, and later be the administrators of the state-run religion under Emperor Constantine, when he enacted his Edict of Toleration (Edict of Milan). Sexta led her family to Christ, and they kept a covert fellowship in their house through the persecutions. She never married. Africanus and Anna, as well as the other servants became Christians too. Cadmus was given a writ of emancipation by Rufus, in haste before he surrendered to the Praetorian Guard. Cadmus used his freedom to travel to Tarshish (Great Britain), where he started a new life with a Celtic bride, and kept the faith by raising his family to honor Christ, sharing his testimony and teaching in the community. Marcus, having been evangelized by Antonina and Cadmus, eventually married and moved up into the Alps of Northern Italy. There he encountered a team of scouts that the king of Germania had sent out to recover his prized dagger. He shared the gospel with them, which they received and took back to Germania. Marcus kept the faith, preserving the word of God. Gaius was assigned to a special unit to track and persecute Christians, all the while striving against the witness of the Holy Spirit. His exploits eventually led him to a community of Christians who were hiding out just north of the Rubicon. When he captured the outlaws, he attempted to force them to recant. The Romans had various methods they used. Sometimes they forced the Christian to make a sacrifice to a pagan god. Sometimes they would force a young maiden into a house of prostitution. Sometimes it was something as simple as saying "Cæsar is Lord." Gaius brought his 40 prisoners, each bound at the wrists, to his commanding officer.

"What are your orders sir?" Gaius asked.

"We have made base camp by the lake just beyond that ridge," the commander answered. "Bring the prisoners and meet me there." It was midwinter, and cold. The lake was frozen over. The cold wind bit at Gaius' neck and ears as he led his shivering prisoners to the camp. The glow of a bonfire in the distance marked the location of the camp. When Gaius arrived, he saluted his fellow soldiers and joined them around the fire. He commanded the prisoners to stand at a distance. When his commanding officer arrived, he returned the salute from the men and addressed Gaius.

"Bring the prisoners here," he said.

"Come over here! Come now, over here, pronto!" Gaius shouted, choosing not to leave the warmth of the fire. The prisoners eagerly came forward, hoping to receive some warmth.

"Come, come close," The commander said. "Warm yourself by the fire. It feels good does it not? There you go, warm your bones. Look friends, we are all Romans here. There is no need for this. If you renounce your allegiance to this ... Messiah of yours, you can sup with us, get warm. We can put this all behind us. After you are warmed up, you can go about your business. In the morning you can go home, with full bellies, and warm feet. We have hot stew here. All you have to do is confess that Cæsar is Lord. What say you?"

In unison the Christians all responded, "Christus is Lord."

The commander drew his sword, and proceeded to carve the clothing off of the prisoners. He looked at Gaius and the other soldiers. "Are you going to just stand there??!!" he barked. Gaius and the others drew their swords and assisted their commander until the prisoners stood naked, shivering in the cold night air.

"Take the prisoners out on the ice, and make them sit down," he barked at Gaius. "When you get some sense in your head, when you are ready to recant, you can come back to the fire and get your clothes back!!"

Gaius obeyed, and led the prisoners out on the ice, frozen solid and covered with a thin layer of snow. After about fifty cubits, he forced them to sit down. Then one of them looked up at Gaius. He said, "I want you to know that we forgive you. Iesus forgives you. I was worse than you. Iesus forgave me and he will forgive you too."

As Gaius walked back to the fire a war was taking place in his soul. The words of the prisoner were piercing his heart like daggers. He had seen enough to know who was in the right. He could feel a peace emanating from those prisoners that was more powerful than the cold wind that was whipping across the lake. When he arrived back at the fire, he beheld the grotesque visage of his commander in the orange glow of the fire, his twisted smile, and the cackling of the men as they laughed and joked about the Christians out on the ice. He felt an evil aura around the fire. The sparks flew upward into the cold night air. His fellow soldiers spat. They laughed. They glutted their mouths with meat that was roasting over the fire on a spit, and stew that ran down their scarred faces as they gorged themselves. Gaius never liked his commander. He did not care much for his fellow soldiers now either. The daggers were digging deeply now. He did not want to be a soldier anymore. A noise started to arise across the ice. It started faintly, then grew louder. "Forty brave soldiers for Christus! Forty brave soldiers for Christus!"

This new noise silenced the laughter around the campfire. Gaius's fellow soldiers looked at each other with open mouths, smiling with sick satisfaction at this unexpected development, before they all broke out in laughter.

One of the soldiers shouted, "You are going to be forty dead soldiers for Christus before long," provoking more laughter from his fellow soldiers. After they were done laughing they broke out a couple of wineskins; one with strong drink, and one with wine to use for a chaser. They passed them around as they each took turns. The glow of the fire exposing the demonic looks on the faces of the men, the sick and twisted banter back and forth between them, the bodily sounds they made — it was a sharp contrast to what Gaius heard coming from across the ice.

"Forty brave soldiers for Christus. Forty brave soldiers for Christus."

When the wineskins came to Gaius, he already knew what he was going to do. Instead of taking them he began to disrobe. The others looked at him with bewilderment.

"What are you doing Mate?" one of his cohorts asked him.

"I am not your mate anymore," Gaius answered. "I am a

Christian now." Gaius made his way out to his new brothers. By the time he reached them he had shed every bit of clothing. As he sat down with them, a strange new peace, a warmth, came over him. It was not as bad as he thought it would be. The cold wind bit at his flesh but he was going to be okay. It was bearable. He felt a peace he had never felt before. He had come home.

The other soldiers back on the shore shook their heads and went on with their wine and their strong drink. They were not laughing any longer. They drank in silence. Except for the wind and the crackle of the fire, nothing could be heard except for the chanting that rang out across the ice. "Forty-one brave soldiers for Christus. Forty-one brave soldiers for Christus."

Within a short time the pain was over for Gaius and his brothers. They were in the presence of Christ.

Their fellow soldiers who went before them were there to greet them. Artellies was there to welcome Gaius. They now knew the full meaning of Psalm 16:11; *Thou wilt shew me the path of life: in thy presence is fulness of joy; at thy right hand there are pleasures for evermore.*

We began with how it all started. Now it is up to us to decide how it is going to end. The people of the early church made their decisions and chose their battles. They lived and died, and passed the baton to the next generation. We would live in a very different world today if it were not for Christians who were willing get involved in the battle. It was the Christian culture of the West that gave us (*a*) widespread education, (*b*) medical care that was effective and widely available, (*c*) an economic system that brought financial freedom to those who are willing to work hard and invest wisely, and (*d*) a legal system that provides protection from persecution and government overreach.

First of all, free public education was a uniquely Christian concept, created by Martin Luther. All of our early colleges and universities were originally founded as Christian colleges and seminaries. Noah Webster, the father of public education in America said, "Education is useless without the Bible," and "The

Bible is America's basic textbook in all fields." Secondly, public health care also grew out of Christianity. Modern hospitals were originally founded by churches, as a ministry to provide medical care for those who need it. Third of all, it was the Christian,[1] Adam Smith, who wrote *The Wealth of Nations*. Smith is considered the father of free market capitalism (not to be confused with corporatism). This system brings economic growth and prosperity wherever it is implemented — eg America, England, Chile, India, Hong Kong, etc. (Even communist nations such as China, that have turned to capitalism as their economic model have experienced a tremendous amount of market growth.) By contrast, communism is an economic philosophy that plainly asserts that there is no God. Example after example have proven that wherever this economic model has been implemented, poverty has followed — eg Cuba, Venezuela, North Korea, pre-capitalist China, etc. Lastly, it was Christianity that gave us common law. The man most responsible for our form of common law today is William Blackstone. His *Commentaries* were deeply rooted in his Christian faith and based on the Mosaic Law of the Bible. In common-law countries an accused individual is innocent until proven guilty. He has a lawyer who vigorously defends him and attempts to prove his innocence. This is a heritage that is enjoyed in the U.S., the U.K., and some of the commonwealth nations, such as India for example. By contrast, in countries where civil law and canon law[2] are practiced (not to mention sharia), an accused individual is most likely not innocent until proven guilty. His fate is typically decided not by a jury, but by one judge. Law is not developed by courts based on precedent, but by the powers that be, based on their own dictates, edicts or bulls.

Now it is our turn. The book of Acts is one of the few books in the New Testament that does not end with *Amen*. It is still being written. It is our privilege to have a part in how this New Testament book ends, and it will not end until the last *tekiah gedolah* sounds (Lev 23:24; I Cor 15:52). The Bible tells us over and over again to not be afraid. It tells us to be courageous. In times like these we need women and men who will not fear what men can do to the body, but fear God. Each of the four institutions mentioned above are being systematically dismantled by people who have no faith whatsoever in the God of our forefathers. We are at war with pure evil. There is far more than our precious freedom at stake in this conflict. If we lose, the consequences will be unthinkable. We have been called for a time such as this. The baton has been passed to us.

What will you do with your legacy?

What's past is prologue.

— William Shakespeare, *The Tempest*

---

[1] I am always amazed at how certain atheists and agnostics suddenly become theologians whenever the faith of some historic figure is brought up, and will vigorously debate whether their faith would have met the biblical criteria for a born again Christian. Adam Smith attended church his entire life, and made clear confessions of faith in Christ. It was very common in that day for Christians to use terms like 'nature's God' or the 'Architect of the universe' when referring to the God of the Bible. To suggest that Adam Smith was not really a Christian because he used such terms for God, or because he was friends with David Hume, is like suggesting that Gandhi was not really a Hindu, because he expressed admiration for Jesus Christ, and was friends with Charles Andrews.

[2] Even today, countries that have concordats with the Vatican are bound in many ways by canon law. For more information go to: http://www.concordatwatch.eu/

APPENDIX A

My Country Tis of Thee

My country tis of thee,
Sweet land of Liberty,
Of thee I sing
Land where my fathers died
Land of the Pilgrim's pride
From every mountain side
Let freedom ring

Our fathers' God to thee
Author of Liberty
To thee we sing
Long may our land be bright
With freedom's holy light
Protect us by thy might
Great God our King

America the Beautiful

Oh beautiful for spacious skies, for amber waves of grain
For purple mountains' majesty, across the fruited plane
America, America, God shed his grace on thee
And crown the good with brotherhood, from sea to shining sea

Oh beautiful for patriot's dream that shines throughout the years
Thine alabaster cities gleam, undimmed by human tears
America, America, God shed his grace on thee
And crown the good with brotherhood, from sea to shining sea

The Battle Hymn of the Republic

Mine eyes have seen the glory
Of the coming of the Lord;
He is trampling out the vintage
Where the grapes of wrath are stored;
He hath loosed the fateful lightning
Of His terrible swift sword;
His truth is marching on.

Chorus
Glory! Glory! Hallelujah!
Glory! Glory! Hallelujah!
Glory! Glory! Hallelujah!
His truth is marching on.

I have seen Him in the watchfires
Of a hundred circling camps
They have builded Him an altar
In the evening dews and damps;
I can read His righteous sentence
By the dim and flaring lamps;
His day is marching on.

Chorus

I have read a fiery gospel writ
In burnished rows of steel:
"As ye deal with my contemners,   [Ie, *With what measure you mete, it*
So with you my grace shall deal":   *will be measured back to you.*]
Let the Hero born of woman
Crush the serpent with His heel,
Since God is marching on.

Chorus

He has sounded forth the trumpet
That shall never call retreat;
He is sifting out the hearts of men
Before His judgement seat;
Oh, be swift, my soul, to answer Him;
Be jubilant, my feet;
Our God is marching on.

Chorus

In the beauty of the lilies
Christ was born across the sea,
With a glory in His bosom
That transfigures you and me;
As He died to make men holy,
Let us fight to make men free;
While God is marching on.

Chorus

He is coming like the glory of the morning on the wave,
He is Wisdom to the mighty, He is Succour [helper] to the brave,
So the world shall be His footstool, and the soul of wrong His slave,
Our God is marching on.

APPENDIX B

The quotes and commentary in this section were collated and written by Pastor Chuck Baldwin, and can be seen online at *Chuck Baldwin Live*.

Abigail Adams

"The race is not to the swift, nor the battle to the strong; but the God of Israel is He that giveth strength and power unto His people. Trust in Him at all times, ye people, pour out your hearts before him; God is a refuge for us.

"Charleston is laid in ashes. The battle began upon our entrenchments upon Bunker's Hill, Saturday morning about 3 o'clock, and has not ceased yet, and it is now three o'clock Sabbath afternoon. It is expected they will come out over the Neck tonight, and a dreadful battle must ensue. Almighty God, cover the heads of our countrymen, and be a shield to our dear friends..."

"A patriot without religion in my estimation is as great a paradox as an honest Man without the fear of God. Is it possible that he whom no moral obligations bind, can have any real Good Will towards Men? Can he be a patriot who, by an openly vicious conduct, is undermining the very bonds of Society?....The Scriptures tell us "righteousness exalteth a Nation.""

John Adams

"[America's] glory is not dominion, but liberty. Her march is in the march of the mind. She has a spear and a shield: but the motto upon her shield is, FREEDOM, INDEPENDENCE, PEACE. This has been her Declaration: this has been, as far as her necessary intercourse with the rest of mankind would permit, her practice."

"[America] has . . . respected the independence of other nations while asserting and maintaining her own. She has abstained from interference in the concerns of others, even when conflict has been for principles to which she clings . . . Whenever the standard of freedom and independence has been or shall be unfurled, there will her heart, her benedictions and her prayers be. But she goes not abroad, in search of monsters to destroy. She is well-wisher to the freedom and independence of all. She is the champion and vindicator only of her own . . . She well knows that by once enlisting under other banners than her own, were they even the banners of foreign independence, she would involve herself beyond the power of extrication, in all the wars of interest and intrigue, of individual avarice, envy, and ambition, which assume the colors and usurp the standard of freedom. The fundamental maxims of her policy would insensibly change from liberty to force . . . She might become the dictatress of the world . . . "

July 4, 1774
"We went to meeting at Wells and had the pleasure of hearing my friend upon "Be not partakers in other men's sins. Keep yourselves pure.

"We...took our horses to the meeting in the afternoon and heard the minister again upon "Seek first the kingdom of God and his righteousness, and all these things shall be added unto you." There is great pleasure in hearing sermons so serious, so clear, so sensible and instructive as these ...."

October 9, 1774

"This day I went to Dr. Allison's meeting in the afternoon, and heard the Dr. Francis Allison . . . give a good discourse upon the Lord's Supper .... I had rather go to Church. We have better sermons, better prayers, better speakers, softer, sweeter music, and genteeler company. And I must confess that the Episcopal church is quite as agreeable to my taste as the Presbyterian.... I like the Congregational way best, next to that the Independent...."

1754

"It is the duty of the clergy to accommodate their discourses to the times, to preach against such sins as are most prevalent, and recommend such virtues as are most wanted. For example, if exorbitant ambition and venality are predominant, ought they not to warn their hearers against those vices? If public spirit is much wanted, should they not inculcate this great virtue? If the rights and duties of Christian magistrates and subjects are disputed, should they not explain them, show their nature, ends, limitations, and restrictions, how muchsoever it may move the gall of Massachusetts."

June 21, 1776

"Statesmen, my dear Sir, may plan and speculate for liberty, but it is Religion and Morality alone, which can establish the Principles upon which Freedom can securely stand.

"The only foundation of a free Constitution is pure Virtue, and if this cannot be inspired into our People in a greater Measure, than they have it now, they may change their Rulers and the forms of Government, but they will not obtain a lasting liberty."

July 1, 1776

"Before God, I believe the hour has come. My judgement approves this measure, and my whole heart is in it. All that I have, and all that I am, and all that I hope in this life, I am now ready here to stake upon it. And I leave off as I began, that live or die, survive or perish, I am for the Declaration. It is my living sentiment, and by the blessing of God it shall be my dying sentiment. Independence now, and Independence for ever!"

In a July 1, 1776 letter to Archibald Bullock, former member of the Continental Congress from Georgia, Adams wrote:
"The object is great which We have in View, and We must expect a great expense of blood to obtain it. But We should always remember that a free Constitution of civil Government cannot be purchased at too dear a rate as there is nothing, on this side (of) the New Jerusalem, of equal importance to Mankind."

July 3, 1776
"The second day of July, 1776, will be the most memorable epoch in the history of America. I am apt to believe that it will be celebrated by succeeding generations as the great anniversary Festival. It ought to be commemorated, as the Day of Deliverance, by solemn acts of devotion to God Almighty. It ought to be solemnized with pomp and parade, with shows, games, sports, guns, bells, bonfires and illuminations, from one end of this continent to the other, from this time forward forever.

"You will think me transported with enthusiasm, but I am not. I am well aware of the toil and blood and treasure that it will cost to maintain this Declaration, and support and defend these States. Yet through all the gloom I can see the rays of ravishing light and glory I can see that the end is worth more than all the means; that posterity will triumph in that day's transaction, even though we [may regret] it, which I trust in God we shall not."

In concern for his sons, John Adams advised his wife Abigail to:

"Let them revere nothing but Religion, Morality and Liberty."

Oct. 11, 1798 (Address to the military)
"We have no government armed with power capable of contending

with human passions unbridled by morality and religion. Avarice, ambition, revenge, or gallantry, would break the strongest cords of our Constitution as a whale goes through a net. Our Constitution was made only for a moral and religious people. It is wholly inadequate to the government of any other."

On March 6, 1799, President John Adams called for a National Fast Day.

"As no truth is more clearly taught in the Volume of Inspiration, nor any more fully demonstrated by the experience of all ages, than that a deep sense and a due acknowledgement of the growing providence of a Supreme Being and of the accountableness of men to Him as the searcher of hearts and righteous distributer of rewards and punishments are conducive equally to the happiness of individuals and to the well-being of communities....

"I have thought proper to recommend, and I hereby recommend accordingly, that Thursday, the twenty-fifth day of April next, be observed throughout the United States of America as a day of solemn humiliation, fasting and prayer; that the citizens on that day abstain, as far as may be, from their secular occupation, and devote the time to the sacred duties of religion, in public and in private; that they call to mind our numerous offenses against the most high God, confess them before Him with the sincerest penitence, implore his pardoning mercy, through the Great Mediator and Redeemer, for our past transgressions, and that through the grace of His Holy Spirit, we may be disposed and enabled to yield a more suitable obedience to his righteous requisitions in time to come; that He would interpose to arrest the progress of that impiety and licentiousness in principle and practice so offensive to Himself and so ruinous to mankind; that He would make us deeply sensible that "righteousness exalteth a nation but sin is a reproach to any people" (Pr 14:34)"

On November 2, 1800, John Adams became the first president to move into the White House. As he was writing a letter to his wife, he composed a beautiful prayer, which was later engraved upon the mantel in the State dining room:

"I pray Heaven to bestow THE BEST OF BLESSINGS ON THIS HOUSE and All that shall hereafter Inhabit it, May none but Honest and Wise Men ever rule under This Roof."

August 28, 1811
"Religion and virtue are the only foundations, not only of all free government, but of social felicity under all governments and in all the combinations of human society."

June 28, 1813
"Now I will avow, that I then believe, and now believe, that those general Principles of Christianity, are as eternal and immutable, as the Existence and Attributes of God; and that those Principles of liberty, are as unalterable as human Nature and our terrestrial, mundane System."

In a letter to Thomas Jefferson, John Adams wrote:

"Have you ever found in history, one single example of a Nation thoroughly corrupted that was afterwards restored to virtue?... And without virtue, there can be no political liberty....Will you tell me how to prevent riches from becoming the effects of temperance and industry? Will you tell me how to prevent luxury from producing effeminacy, intoxication, extravagance, vice and folly? ... I believe no effort in favor is lost..."

In a letter dated November 4, 1816, John Adams wrote to Thomas Jefferson:

"The Ten Commandments and the Sermon on the Mount contain my religion..."

December 27, 1816
"As I understand the Christian religion, it was, and is, a revelation."

"Liberty cannot be preserved without a general knowledge among the people, who have...a right, an indisputable, unalienable, indefeasible, divine right to that most dreaded and envied kind of knowledge, I mean the character and conduct of their rulers."

John Quincy Adams

"Duty is ours; results are God's."

September, 1811, in a letter to his son:

"I have myself, for many years, made it a practice to read through the Bible once ever year.... My custom is, to read four to five chapters every morning immediately after rising from my bed. I employs about an hour of my time...."

July 4, 1821
"The highest glory of the American Revolution was this; it connected in one indissoluble bond the principles of civil government with the principles of Christianity.

"From the day of the Declaration ... they (the American people) were bound by the laws of God, which they all, and by the laws of The Gospel, which they nearly all, acknowledge as the rules of their conduct."

July 4, 1837
"Why is it that, next to the birthday of the Savior of the World, your most joyous and most venerated festival returns on this day. Is it not that, in the chain of human events, the birthday of the nation is indissolubly linked with the birthday of the Savior? That it forms a leading event in the Progress of the Gospel dispensation? Is it

not that the Declaration of Independence first organized the social compact on the foundation of the Redeemer's mission upon earth? That it laid the cornerstone of human government upon the first precepts of Christianity and gave to the world the first irrevocable pledge of the fulfillment of the prophecies announced directly from Heaven at the birth of the Saviour and predicted by the greatest of the Hebrew prophets 600 years before."

"I speak as a man of the world to men of the world; and I say to you, Search the Scriptures! The Bible is the book of all others, to be read at all ages, and in all conditions of human life; not to be read in small portions of one or two chapters every day, and never to be intermitted, unless by some overruling necessity."

"Posterity--you will never know how much it has cost my generation to preserve your freedom. I hope you will make good use of it."

February 27, 1844
"The Bible carries with it the history of the creation, the fall and redemption of man, and discloses to him, in the infant born at Bethlehem, the Legislator and Savior of the world."

Samuel Adams

"If ye love wealth better than liberty, the tranquility of servitude than the animated contest of freedom -- go home from us in peace. We ask not your counsels or arms. Crouch down and lick the hands which feed you. May your chains sit lightly upon you, and may posterity forget that you were our countrymen!"

"Among the natural rights of the colonists are these: first, a right to life; second, to liberty; third, to property; together with the right to support and defend them in the best manner they can. These are evident branches of ... the duty of self-preservation, commonly called the first law of nature. All men have a right to remain in a state of nature as long as they please; and in case of intolerable oppression, civil or religious, to leave the society they belong to, and enter into another... Now what liberty can there be where property is taken away without consent?" (Nov 20, 1772)

"The rights of the colonists as Christians ... may be best understood by reading and carefully studying the institution of The Great Law Giver and Head of the Christian Church, which are to be found clearly written and promulgated in the New Testament." (From The Rights of Colonists, 1772)

As the Declaration of Independence was being signed, 1776, Samuel Adams declared:

"We have this day restored the Sovereign to Whom all men ought to be obedient. He reigns in heaven and from the rising to the setting of the sun, let His kingdom come."

"He therefore is the truest friend to the liberty of this country who tries most to promote its virtue, and who, so far as his power and influence extend, will not suffer a man to be chosen into any office of power and trust who is not a wise and virtuous man ... The sum of all is, if we would most truly enjoy this gift of Heaven, let us become a virtuous people."

"He who is void of virtuous attachments in private life is, or very soon will be, void of all regard for his country. There is seldom an instance of a man guilty of betraying his country, who had not before lost the feeling of moral obligations in his private connections." --in a letter to James Warren, Nov. 4, 1775--

"The said Constitution shall never be construed to authorize congress to prevent the people of the United States who are peaceable citizens from keeping their own arms."

Samuel Adams wrote in his Will:

"Principally, and first of all, I resign my soul to the Almighty Being who gave it, and my body I commit to the dust, relying on the merits of Jesus Christ for the pardon of my sins."

Fisher Ames
(Author of the First Amendment)

"Should not the Bible regain the place it once held as a school-book? Its morals are pure, its examples are captivating and noble... In no Book is there so good English, so pure and so elegant, and by teaching all the same they will speak alike, and the Bible will justly remain the standard of language as well as of faith."

Abraham Baldwin
(Founder of the University of Georgia)

"It should therefore be among the first objects of those who wish well to the national prosperity to encourage and support the principles of religion and morality, and early to place the youth under the forming hand of society, that by instruction they may be molded to the love of virtue and good order."

Sir William Blackstone

(Blackstone's Commentaries on the Law was the recognized authority on the law for well over a century after 1776)

"Man, considered as a creature, must necessarily be subject to the laws of his Creator, for he is entirely a dependent being .... And, consequently, as man depends absolutely upon his Maker for everything, it is necessary that he should in all points conform to his Maker's will ... this will of his Maker is called the law of nature. These laws laid down by God are the eternal immutable laws of good and evil ...This law of nature dictated by God himself, is of course superior in obligation to any other. It is binding over all the globe, in all countries, and at all times: no human laws are of any validity if contrary to this...

"The doctrines thus delivered we call the revealed or divine law, and they are to be found only in the holy scriptures ... [and] are found upon comparison to be really part of the original law of nature. Upon these two foundations, the law of nature and the law of revelation, depend all human laws; that is to say, no human laws should be suffered to contradict these.

"Blasphemy against the Almighty is denying his being or providence, or uttering contumelious reproaches on our Savior Christ. It is punished, at common law by fine and imprisonment, for Christianity is part of the laws of the land.

"If [the legislature] will positively enact a thing to be done, the judges are not at liberty to reject it, for that were to set the judicial power above that of the legislature, which should be subversive of all government."

"The preservation of Christianity as a national religion is abstracted from its own intrinsic truth, of the utmost consequence to the civil state, which a single instance will sufficiently demonstrate.

"The belief of a future state of rewards and punishments, the entertaining just ideas of the main attributes of the Supreme Being, and a firm persuasion that He superintends and will finally compensate every action in human life (all which are revealed in the doctrines of our Savior, Christ), these are the grand foundations of all judicial oaths, which call God to witness the truth of those facts which perhaps may be only known to Him and the party attesting; all moral evidences, therefore, all confidence in human veracity, must be weakened by apostasy, and overthrown by total infidelity.

"Wherefore, all affronts to Christianity, or endeavors to depreciate its efficacy, in those who have once professed it, are highly deserving of censure."

Samuel Chase

"By our form of government, the Christian religion is the established religion; and all sects and denominations of Christians are placed upon the same equal footing, and are equally entitled to protection in their religious liberty."

Ben Franklin

"They that would give up essential liberty for a little temporary safety deserve neither liberty nor safety."

Congressional Congress, 1787
"I have lived, Sir, a long time, and the longer I live, the more convincing proofs I see of this truth--that God Governs the affairs of men. And if a sparrow cannot fall to the ground without His notice, is it probable that an empire can rise without His aid?

"We have been assured, Sir, in the Sacred Writings, that "except the Lord build the House, they labor in vain that build it." I firmly believe this; and I also believe that without his concurring aid we shall succeed in this political building no better than the Builders of Babel: We shall be divided by our partial local interests; our projects will be confounded, and we ourselves shall become a reproach and bye word down to future ages. And what is worse, mankind may hereafter from this unfortunate instance, despair of establishing Governments by Human wisdom and leave it to chance, war and conquest.

"I therefore beg leave to move--that henceforth prayers imploring the assistance of Heaven, and its blessing on our deliberations, be held in this Assembly every morning before we proceed to business, and that one or more of the clergy of this city be requested to officiate in that service."

In 1748, as Pennsylvania's Governor, Benjamin Franklin proposed Pennsylvania's first Fast Day:
"It is the duty of mankind on all suitable occasions to acknowledge their dependence on the Divine Being... [that] Almighty God would mercifully interpose and still the rage of war among the nations ... [and that] He would take this province under his protection, confound the designs and defeat the attempts of its enemies, and unite our hearts and strengthen our hands in every undertaking that may be for the public good, and for our defense and security in this time of danger."

"I never doubted, for instance, the existence of the Deity; that he made the world, and governed it by his Providence; that the most acceptable service of God was the doing good to man; that our souls are immortal; and that all crime will be punished, and virtue rewarded either here or hereafter.

"Freedom is not a gift bestowed upon us by other men, but a right that belongs to us by the laws of God and nature.

"The pleasures of this world are rather from God's goodness than our own merit."

Benjamin Franklin, in July of 1776, was appointed part of a committee to draft a seal for the newly united states which would characterize the spirit of this new nation. He proposed:

"Moses lifting up his wand, and dividing the Red Sea, and Pharaoh in his chariot overwhelmed with the waters. This motto:

'Rebellion to tyrants is obedience to God."

"A Bible and a newspaper in every house, a good school in every district--all studied and appreciated as they merit--are the principal support of virtue, morality, and civil liberty."

Ben Franklin wrote a pamphlet called, "Information to Those who would Remove to America." It was intended to be a guide for Europeans who were thinking of relocating in America. In it he said:

"Hence bad examples to youth are more rare in America, which must be comfortable consideration to parents. To this may be truly added, that serious religion, under its various denominations, is not only tolerated, but respected and practiced.

"Atheism is unknown there; Infidelity rare and secret; so that persons may live to a great age in that country without having their piety shocked by meeting with either an Atheist or an Infidel.

"And the Divine Being seems to have manifested his approbation of the mutual forbearance and kindness with which the different sects treat each other; by the remarkable prosperity with which he has been pleased to favor the whole country."

"Here is my Creed. I believe in one God, the Creator of the Universe. That He governs it by His Providence. That he ought to be worshipped."

As a young man in 1728, Franklin had composed his own mock epitaph which read:

The Body of B. Franklin
Printer;
Like the Cover of an old Book,
Its Contents torn out,
And stript of its Lettering and Gilding,

Lies here, Food for Worms.
But the Work shall not be wholly lost:
For it will, as he believ'd, appear once more,
In a new & more perfect Edition,
Corrected and Amended
By the Author.
He was born on January 6, 1706.
Died 17

His gravestone would simply read:
BENJAMIN And DEBORAH FRANKLIN 1790

Alexander Hamilton
(Co-Author of the Federalist Papers)

It was desirable that the sense of the people should operate in the choice of the person to whom so important a trust (the office of President) was to be confided.... Nothing was more to be desired than that every practicable obstacle should be opposed to cabal, intrigue, and corruption.... The process of election affords a moral certainty that the office of President will never fall to the lot of any man who is not in an eminent degree endowed with the requisite qualifications.... It will not be too strong to say that there be constant probability of seeing the station filled by characters preeminent for ability and virtue...." (In Federalist No. 68)

"I now offer you the outline of the plan they have suggested. Let an association be formed to be denominated 'The Christian Constitutional Society,' its object to be first: The support of the Christian religion. second: The support of the United States.

"I have carefully examined the evidences of the Christian religion, and if I was sitting as a juror upon its authenticity I would unhesitatingly give my verdict in its favor. I can prove its truth as clearly as any proposition ever submitted to the mind of man.

"A ... virtuous citizen will regard his own country as a wife, to whom he is bound to be exclusively faithful and affectionate; and he will watch ... every propensity of his heart to wander towards a foreign country, which he will regard as a mistress that may pervert his fidelity."

John Hancock

April 15, 1775
"In circumstances dark as these, it becomes us, as Men and Christians, to reflect that, whilst every prudent Measure should be taken to ward off the impending Judgements ... All confidence must be withheld from the Means we use; and reposed only on that GOD who rules in the Armies of Heaven, and without whose Blessing the best human Counsels are but Foolishness--and all created Power Vanity;

"It is the Happiness of his Church that, when the Powers of Earth and Hell combine against it ... that the Throne of Grace is of the easiest access--and its Appeal thither is graciously invited by the Father of Mercies, who has assured it, that when his Children ask Bread he will not give them a Stone....

"RESOLVED, That it be, and hereby is recommended to the good People of this Colony of all Denominations, that THURSDAY the Eleventh Day of May next be set apart as a Day of Public Humiliation, Fasting and Prayer...to confess the sins...to implore the Forgiveness of all our Transgression...and a blessing on the Husbandry, Manufactures, and other lawful Employments of this People; and especially that the union of the American Colonies in Defense of their Rights (for hitherto we desire to thank Almighty GOD) may be preserved and confirmed....And that AMERICA may soon behold a gracious Interposition of Heaven."
By Order of the [Massachusetts] Provincial
Congress, John Hancock, President.

Patrick Henry

March 23, 1775

"Is life so dear, or peace so sweet, as to be purchased at the price of chains and slavery? Forbid it, Almighty God! I know not what course others may take; but as for me, give me liberty or give me death!"

"It cannot be emphasized too strongly or too often that this great nation was founded, not by religionists, but by Christians; not on religions, but on the Gospel of Jesus Christ. For this very reason peoples of other faiths have been afforded asylum, prosperity, and freedom of worship here."

"The Bible is worth all other books which have ever been printed."

"Bad men cannot make good citizens. A vitiated state of morals, a corrupted public conscience are incompatible with freedom."

"It is when people forget God that tyrants forge their chains."

"The great object is that every man be armed. Everyone who is able may have a gun."

On November 20, 1798, in his Last Will and Testament, Patrick Henry wrote:

"This is all the inheritance I give to my dear family. The religion of Christ will give them one which will make them rich indeed."

John Jay
(America's first Supreme Court Chief Justice and Co-Author of the Federalist Papers)

October 12, 1816
"Providence has given to our people the choice of their rulers, and it is the duty, as well as the privilege and interest of our Christian nation to select and prefer Christians for their rulers.

In his Last Will and Testament, John Jay wrote:

"Unto Him who is the author and giver of all good, I render sincere and humble thanks for His merciful and unmerited blessings, and especially for our redemption and salvation by his beloved Son."

Thomas Jefferson

"I think this is the most extraordinary collection of talent, of human knowledge, that has ever been gathered together at the White House, with the possible exception of when Thomas Jefferson dined alone."
John F. Kennedy to Nobel Prize winners of the Western Hemisphere, at a White House function, April 29, 1962

"And I sincerely believe, with you, that banking establishments are more dangerous than standing armies; and that the principle of spending money to be paid by posterity, under the name of funding, is but swindling futurity on a large scale."
Thomas Jefferson to John Taylor, Monticello, 28 May 1816.

"I think our governments will remain virtuous for many centuries; as long as they are chiefly agricultural; and this will be as long as there shall be vacant lands in any part of America. When they get piled upon one another in large cities, as in Europe, they will become corrupt as in Europe."
Thomas Jefferson to James Madison, December 20, 1787

"Self-love ... is the sole antagonist of virtue, leading us constantly by our propensities to self-gratification in violation of our moral duties to others."

"(If a) people (are) so demoralized and depraved as to be incapable of exercising a wholesome control, their reformation must be taken up ab incunablis (from the beginning). Their minds (must) be informed by education what is right and what wrong, (must) be encouraged in habits of virtue and deterred from those of vice by the dread of punishments, proportioned indeed, but irremissible. In all cases, (they must) follow truth as the only safe guide and eschew error which bewilders us in one false consequence after another in endless succession. These are the inculcations necessary to render the people a sure basis for the structure of order and good government."
In a letter to John Adams in 1819

"He who permits himself to tell a lie once, finds it much easier to do it a second and third time, till at length it becomes habitual; he tells lies without attending to it, and truths without the world's believing him. This falsehood of the tongue leads to that of the heart, and in time depraves all its good dispositions." (1785)

"I never ... believed there was one code of morality for a public and another for a private man."
In a letter to Don Valentine de Feronda, 1809

"It is incumbent on every generation to pay its own debts as it goes. A principle which if acted on would save one-half the wars of the world."
Thomas Jefferson to A. L. C. Destutt de Tracy, 1820.

"I predict future happiness for Americans if they can prevent the government from wasting the labors of the people under the pretense of taking care of them."

"My reading of history convinces me that most bad government has grown out of too much government."
Senator John Sharp Williams, Thomas Jefferson: His Permanent Influence on American Institutions, p.49 (1913). Lecture delivered at Columbia University, New York City, 1912.

"To compel a man to subsidize with his taxes the propagation of ideas which he disbelieves and abhors is sinful and tyrannical."

"The only foundation for useful education in a republic is to be laid in religion."

"God who gave us life gave us liberty. And can the liberties of a nation be thought secure when we have removed their only firm basis, a conviction in the minds of the people that these liberties are of the Gift of God? That they are not to be violated but with His wrath? Indeed, I tremble for my country when I reflect that God is just, that His justice cannot sleep forever."

"To the corruptions of Christianity I am, indeed, opposed; but not to the genuine precepts of Jesus himself. I am a Christian in the only sense in which he wished any one to be; sincerely attached to his doctrines in preference to all others..."

"I consider the doctrines of Jesus as delivered by himself to contain the outlines of the sublimest system of morality that has ever been taught but I hold in the most profound detestation and execration the corruptions of it which have been invented..."

As President, Thomas Jefferson not only signed bills which appropriated financial support for chaplains in Congress and in the armed services, but he also signed the Articles of War, April 10, 1806, in which he:

"Earnestly recommended to all officers and soldiers, diligently to attend divine services."

"A more beautiful or precious morsel of ethics I have never seen; it is a document in proof that I am a real Christian; that is to say, a disciple of the doctrines of Jesus."

Jefferson declared that religion is: "Deemed in other countries incompatible with good government and yet proved by our experience to be its best support."

"If a nation expects to be ignorant and free, in a state of civilization, it expects what never was and never will be."

"No freeman shall ever be debarred the use of arms."
Thomas Jefferson, while writing the 1st draft of the Virginia State Constitution.

"The tree of liberty must be refreshed from time to time with the blood of patriots and tyrants."

"In questions of power, then, let no more be heard of confidence in man, but bind him down from mischief by the chains of the Constitution."

Jefferson's "separation of church & state letter written to the Baptists in Danbury, Connecticut on January 1, 1802

"Gentlemen:

The affectionate sentiments of esteem and approbation which are so good to express towards me, on behalf of the Danbury Association, give me the highest satisfaction. My duties dictate a faithful and zealous pursuit of the interests of my constituents, and in proportion as they are persuaded of my fidelity to those duties, the discharge of them becomes more and more pleasing. Believing with you that religion is a matter which lies solely between man and his God; that he owes account to none other for his faith or his worship; that the legislative powers of the government reach actions only, and not opinions, I contemplate with sovereign reverence that act of the whole American people which declared that their legislature should 'make no law respecting an establishment of religion, of prohibiting the free excercise thereof,' thus building a wall of separation between church and state. Adhering to this expression of the supreme will of the nation in behalf of the rights of conscience, I shall see with sincere satisfaction the progress of those sentiments which tend to restore man to all of his natural rights, convinced he has no natural right in opposition to his social duties.

I reciprocate your kind prayers for the protection and blessings of the common Father and Creator of man, and tender you and your religious association, assurances of my high respect and esteem."

Francis Scott Key
(Author of the Star Spangled Banner)

February 22, 1812
"The patriot who feels himself in the service of God, who acknowledges Him in all his ways, has the promise of Almighty direction, and will find His Word in his greatest darkness, a lantern to his feet and a lamp unto his paths.' He will therefore seek to establish for his country in the eyes of the world, such a character as shall make her not unworthy of the name of a Christian nation...."

James Madison
(Architect of the U.S. Constitution & Co-Author of the Federalist Papers)

"History records that the money changers have used every form of abuse, intrigue, deceit, and violent means possible to maintain their control over governments by controlling the money and its issuance."

"There are more instances of the abridgement of the freedom of the of the people by the gradual and silent encroachment of those in power, than by violent an sudden usurpation."

"[It] is indispensable that some provision should be made for defending the Community agst [against] the incapicity, negligence or perfidy of the chief Magistrate."

From his notes
Note: Perfidy is defined as "The quality or state of being faithless or disloyal."

"Cursed be all that learning that is contrary to the cross of Christ."

"Religion [is] the basis and Foundation of Government."

"It is the duty of every man to render to the Creator such homage.... Before any man can be considered as a member of Civil Society, he must be considered as a subject of the Governor of the Universe."

"We have staked the whole future of American civilization, not upon the power of government, far from it. We have staked the future of all of our political institutions upon the capacity of each and all of us to govern ourselves, to control ourselves, to sustain ourselves according to the Ten Commandments of God."

George Mason

"No point is of more importance than that the right of impeachment should be continued. Shall any man be above Justice?

Gouverneur Morris

"... If the people should elect, they will never fail to prefer some man of distinguished character, or services; some man, if he might so speak of continental reputation... a notoriety and eminence of character... to merit this high trust ... an Executive Magistrate of distinguished character... an object of general attention and esteem..." (1787)

"Religion is the only solid basis of good morals; therefore education should teach the precepts of religion, and the duties of man toward God."

"Americans need never fear their government because of the advantage of being armed, which the Americans possess over the people of almost every other nation."

Dr. Jedidah Morse

"To the kindly influence of Christianity, we owe that degree of civil freedom, and political and social happiness which mankind now enjoy. In proportion, as the genuine effects of Christianity are diminished in any nation, either through unbelief, or the corruption of its doctrines, or the neglect of its institutions; in the same proportion will the people of the nation recede from the blessings of genuine freedom and approximate the miseries of complete despotism." (1799)

John Peter Muhlenberg

(He was elected as a member of the Virginia House of Burgesses in 1774, and was a 30-year-old pastor who preached on the Christian's responsibility to be involved in securing freedom for America. He was the son of Henry Muhlenberg, one of the founders of the Lutheran Church in America.)

In 1775, after preaching a message on Ecclesiastes 3:1, "For everything there is a season, and a time for every matter under heaven," John Peter Muhlenberg closed his message by saying:

"In the language of the Holy Writ, there is a time for all things. There is a time to preach and a time to fight."

He then threw off his robes to reveal the uniform of a soldier in the Revolutionary Army. That afternoon, at the head of 300 men, he marched off to join General Washington's troops, becoming Colonel of the 8th Virginia Regiment. He served until the end of the war being promoted to the rank of Major-general. In 1785 he became the Vice-President of Pennsylvania and in 1790 was a member of the Pennsylvania Constitutional Convention. He then served as a U.S. Congressman from Pennsylvania and in 1801 was elected to the U. S. Senate.

Thomas Paine

"THESE are the times that try men's souls. The summer soldier and the sunshine patriot will, in this crisis, shrink from the service of their country; but he that stands by it now, deserves the love and thanks of man and woman. Tyranny, like hell, is not easily conquered; yet we have this consolation with us, that the harder the conflict, the more glorious the triumph. What we obtain too cheap, we esteem too lightly: it is dearness only that gives every thing its value. Heaven knows how to put a proper price upon its goods; and it would be strange indeed if so celestial an article as FREEDOM should not be highly rated. Britain, with an army to enforce her tyranny, has declared that she has a right (not only to TAX) but "to BIND us in ALL CASES WHATSOEVER" and if being bound in that manner, is not slavery, then is there not such a thing as slavery upon earth. Even the expression is impious; for so unlimited a power can belong only to God." "Those who expect to reap the blessings of freedom must, like men, undergo the fatigue of supporting it."

"The cause of America is in a great measure the cause of all mankind. Where, some say, is the king of America? I'll tell you, friend, He reigns above.

"Yet that we may not appear to be defective even in earthly honors, let a day be solemnly set apart for proclaiming the charter; let it be placed on the divine law, the Word of God; let a crown be placed thereon.
"The Almighty implanted in us these inextinguishable feelings for good and wise purposes. They are the guardians of His image in our heart. They distinguish us from the herd of common animals."

"I would give worlds, if I had them, if The Age of Reason had never been published. O Lord, help! Stay with me! It is hell to be left alone."

"I die in perfect composure and resignation to the will of my Creator, God."

William Penn
(Founder of Pennsylvania)

"If thou wouldst rule well, thou must rule for God, and to do that, thou must be ruled by him....Those who will not be governed by God will be ruled by tyrants."

Josiah Quincy

"Blandishments will not fascinate us, nor will threats of a "halter" intimidate. For, under God, we are determined that wheresoever, whensoever, or howsoever we shall be called to make our exit, we will die free men."

Benjamin Rush

"By removing the Bible from schools we would be wasting so much time and money in punishing criminals and so little pains to prevent crime. Take the Bible out of our schools and there would be an explosion in crime."

"I have alternately been called an Aristocrat and a Democrat. I am neither. I am a Christocrat."

Jonathan Trumbull

(He was the British Governor of Connecticut who had been appointed by King George III. He was also the father of the famous Revolutionary artist of the same name. Jonathan Trumbull became sympathetic to the American cause in 1773.)

"If you ask an American, who is his master? He will tell you he has none, nor any governor but Jesus Christ."

George Washington

George Washington And Free Masonry

"... So far as I am acquainted with the principles and Doctrines of Free Masonry, I conceive them to be founded on benevolence and to be exercised for the good of mankind. If it has been a Cloak to promote improper or nefarious objects, it is a melancholly proof that in unworthy hands, the best institutions may be made use of to promote the worst designs."

Rev. G.W. Snyder, who said he was with the Reformed Church of Fredericktown, Maryland, sent Washington a letter on August 22, 1798, saying, "a Society of Free Masons, that distinguished itself by the name of 'Illuminati,' whose Plan is to over throw all Government and all Religion ... it might be within your power to prevent the Horrid plan from corrupting the brethren of the English Lodges over which you preside."

September 25, 1798, Washington wrote a letter to Snyder, including the following language, referring to Masonic lodges:

"... to correct an error ..., of my presiding over English Lodges in this country. The fact is I preside over none, nor have I been in one more than once or twice within the last thirty years...."

October 24, 1798

Washington wrote another letter to Rev. Snyder, after Snyder responded to Washington's previous letter. Washington included the following language in this letter:

"... [referring to] the doctrines of the Illuminati, and principles of Jacobism ... in the United States ... I did not believe that the Lodges of Freemasons in this Country had, as Societies, endeavored to propagate the diabolical tenets of the first, or the pernicious principles of the latter... That individuals of them may have done it ... is too evident to be questioned..."

George Washington may have attended, at most, 9 Lodge meetings in his entire life after he became a Master Mason, plus a few other Masonic Lodge events (not Lodge meetings) as listed. There is no proof that he attended several of the events in this list, just claims by Masons who may have been basing their claims on rumors.

Conclusions

Washington admired the principles and goals of Freemasonry, but he was not very familiar with them and did not attempt to learn more about Freemasonry.

Washington wrote letters indicating that he was happy to be a Mason; presided in a major Masonic ceremony laying the cornerstone of the U.S. Capitol in Masonic regalia, and possibly in some other Masonic ceremonies; never sought to resign or repudiate his Masonic membership; and did not say or do anything negative toward Freemasonry, other than that some Masons promoted the radicalism of the French Revolution (as did others).

However, there is little or no evidence that Washington attended many Masonic lodge meetings in his whole life after becoming a Mason 1753.

Washington attended at most 3 meetings, possibly fewer or none (he may have attended dinners but not the preceding meetings), of the lodge that today is called Alexandria-Washington Lodge #22, and of which he was the first Master under its Virginia Charter. While he was Master of that lodge, he did not do anything to assist the work of the lodge, and he attended, at most, one meeting (if he attended that one), when officers were reelected. There is no indication that he actually presided as Master on that occasion and it is unlikely that he did so. Paintings and sculpture showing Washington presiding as a Master of that or any other Masonic lodge are probably based only on wishful thinking.

Some Masons may have gotten carried away with their delight that the most eminent citizen of the United States, George Washington, joined the Freemasons when we was very young and continued to be a member throughout his life and wrote letters supporting Freemasonry, and they may have attempted to portray him as an active and enthusiastic member of the Craft even though the evidence indicates that he was not.

George Washington was apparently a Mason who was not very interested in attending lodge meetings, although there is considerable evidence that he was happy to be a member and publicly supported Freemasonry.

"It is not my intention to doubt that the doctrine of the Illuminati and the principles of Jacobinism had not spread in the United States. On the contrary, no one is more satisfied of this fact than I am.

The idea that I meant to convey, was, that I did not believe that the Lodges of Free Masons in this Country had, as Societies, endeavoured to propagate the diabolical tenets of the first, or pernicious principles of the latter (if they are susceptible of separation). That Individuals of them may have done it, or that the founder, or instrument employed to found, the Democratic Societies in the United States, may have had these objects; and actually had a separation of the People from their Government in view, is too evident to be questioned."

"My ardent desire is, and my aim has been ... to comply strictly with all our engagements foreign and domestic; but to keep the United States free from political connections with every other Country. To see that they may be independent of all, and under the influence of none. In a word, I want an American character, that the powers of Europe may be convinced we act for ourselves and not for others; this, in my judgment, is the only way to be respected abroad and happy at home."

"Government is not reason; it is not eloquence; it is force! Like fire, it is a dangerous servant and a fearful master."

"The thing that separates the American Christian from every other person on earth is the fact that he would rather die on his feet, than live on his knees!"

From Washington's First Inaugural address, "I hope that the foundation of our national policy will be laid in the pure and immutable principles of private morality. The preeminence of free government exemplifies by all the attributes which can win the affections of its citizens and command the respect of the world."

"The General orders this day to be religiously observed by the forces under his Command, exactly in manner directed by the Continental Congress. It is therefore strictly enjoined on all officers and soldiers to attend Divine service, And it is expected that all those who go to worship do take their arms, ammunition and accoutrements, and are prepared for immediate action, if called upon."

"The time is now near at hand which must probably determine whether Americans are to be freemen or slaves; whether they are to have any property they can call their own; whether their houses and farms are to be pillaged and destroyed, and themselves consigned to a state of wretchedness from which no human efforts will deliver them.

The fate of unborn millions will now depend, under God, on the courage of this army. Our cruel and unrelenting enemy leaves us only the choice of brave resistance, or the most abject submission. We have, therefore to resolve to conquer or die."

"While we are zealously performing the duties of good citizens and soldiers, we certainly ought not to be inattentive to the higher duties of religion.

To the distinguished character of Patriot, it should be our highest Glory to laud the more distinguished Character of Christian."

In his Inaugural Speech, April 30, 1789,

"...it would be peculiarly improper to omit, in this first official act, my fervent supplications to that Almighty Being who rules over the universe, who presides in the councils of nations and whose providential aids can supply every human defect, that His benediction may consecrate to the liberties and happiness of the people of the United States a Government instituted by themselves for these essential purposes...."

"No people can be bound to acknowledge and adore the Invisible Hand which conducts the affairs of men more than the people of the United States."

October 3, 1789, National Day of Thanksgiving

"Whereas it is the duty of all nations to acknowledge the providence of Almighty God, to obey His will, to be grateful for his benefits, and humbly to implore His protection and favor....

"Now, therefore, I do recommend and assign Thursday, the twenty-sixth day of November next, to be devoted by the people of these United States...

"that we then may all unite unto him our sincere and humble thanks for His kind care and protection of the people of this country previous to their becoming a nation; for the signal and manifold mercies and the favorable interpositions of His providence in the course and conclusion of the late war;
"for the great degree of tranquility, union, and plenty which we have since enjoyed; for the peaceable and rational manner in which we have been enabled to establish constitutions of government for our safety and happiness, and particularly the national one now lately instituted; for the civil and religious liberty with which we are blessed...

"And also that we may then unite in most humbly offering our prayers and supplications to the great Lord and Ruler of Nations, and beseech him to pardon our national and other transgressions ...

to promote the knowledge and practice of the true religion and virtue...

Given under my hand, at the city of New York, the 3rd of October, AD 1789"

George Washington's personal prayer book, consisting of 24 pages in his field notebook, written in his own handwriting, reveal the depth of his character:

"SUNDAY MORNING....Almighty God, and most merciful Father, who didst command the children of Israel to offer a daily sacrifice to Thee, that thereby they might glorify and praise Thee for Thy protection both night and day, receive O Lord, my morning sacrifice which I now offer up to thee;

"I yield Thee humble and hearty thanks, that Thou hast preserved me from the dangers of the night past and brought me to the Light of this day, and the comfort thereof, a day which is consecrated to Thine own service and for Thine own honour.

"Let my heart therefore gracious God be so affected with the glory and majesty of it, that I may not do mine own works but wait on Thee, and discharge those weighty duties Thou required of me: and since Thou art a God of pure eyes, and will be sanctified in all who draw nearer to Thee, who dost not regard the sacrifice of fools, nor hear sinners who tread in Thy courts, pardon I beseech Thee, my sins, remove them from Thy presence, as far as the east is from the west, and accept of me for the merits of Thy son Jesus Christ, that when I come into Thy temple and compass Thine altar, my prayer may come before Thee as incense, and as I desire Thou wouldst hear me calling upon Thee in my prayers, so give me peace to hear the calling on me in Thy word, that it may be wisdom, righteousness, reconciliation and peace to the saving of my soul in the day of the Lord Jesus.

"Grant that I may hear it with reverence, receive it with meekness, mingle it with faith, and that it may accomplish in me gracious God, the good work for which Thou hast sent it.
"Bless my family, kindred, friends and country, be our God and guide this day and forever for His sake, who lay down in the grave and arose again for us, Jesus Christ our Lord. Amen."

"It is impossible to rightly govern the world without God and the Bible."
"It is impossible to account for the creation of the universe, without the agency of a Supreme Being. It is impossible to govern the universe without the aid of a Supreme Being. It is impossible to reason without arriving at a Supreme Being."

"Of all the dispositions and habits which lead to political prosperity, Religion and morality are indispensable supports. In vain would that man claim the tribute of Patriotism, who should labor to subvert these great Pillars of human happiness, these firmest props of the duties of Men and Citizens."

Washington proclaimed firearms to be "the people's liberty teeth."

Daniel Webster

"There is no nation on earth powerful enough to accomplish our overthrow. Our destruction, should it come at all, will be from another quarter. From the inattention of the people to the concerns of their government, from their carelessness and negligence. I must confess that I do apprehend some danger. I fear that they may place too implicit a confidence in their public servants and fail properly to scrutinize their conduct; that in this way they may be made the dupes of designing men and become the instruments of their own undoing."

"Hold on, my friends, to the Constitution and to the Republic for which it stands. Miracles do not cluster, and what has happened once in 6000 years, may not happen again. Hold on to the Constitution, for if the American Constitution should fail, there will be anarchy throughout the world."

"If we abide by the principles taught in the Bible, our country will go on prospering and to prosper; but if we and our posterity neglect its instruction and authority, no man can tell how sudden a catastrophe may ovenvhelm us and bury all our glory in profound obscurity."

"Finally, let us not forget the religious character of our origin. Our fathers were brought hither by their high veneration for the Christian religion. They journeyed by its light, and labored in its hope. They sought to incorporate its principles with the elements of their society, and to diffuse its influence through all their institutions, civil, political, or literary.

"Let us cherish these sentiments, and extend this influence still more widely; in full conviction that that is the happiest society which partakes in the highest degree of the mild and peaceful spirit of Christianity."

"God grants liberty only to those who love it, and are always ready to guard and defend it."
"The hand that destroys the Constitution rends our Union asunder forever."

"Thank God! I--I also--am an American!"

"If religious books are not widely circulated among the masses in this country, I do not know what is going to become of us as a nation. If truth be not diffused, error will be; If God and His Word are not known and received, the devil and his works will gain the ascendancy, If the evangelical volume does not reach every hamlet, the pages of a corrupt and licentious literature will; If the power of the Gospel is not felt throughout the length and breadth of the land, anarchy and misrule, degradation and misery, corruption and darkness will reign without mitigation or end."

"I shall stand by the Union, and by all who stand by it. I shall do justice to the whole country ... in all I say, and act for the good of the whole country in all I do. I mean to stand upon the Constitution. I need no other platform. I shall know but one country. The ends I aim at shall be my country's, my God's, and Truth's. I was born an American; I live an American; I shall die an American; and I intend to perform the duties incumbent upon me in that character to the end of my career. I mean to do this with absolute disregard of personal consequences. What are the personal consequences? What is the individual man, with all the good or evil that may betide him, in comparison with the good or evil which may befall a great country, and in the midst of great transactions which concern that country's fate? Let the consequences be what they will, I am careless. No man can suffer too much, and no man can fall too soon, if he suffer, or if he fall, in the defense of the liberties and constitution of his country."

"This is the Book. I have read the Bible through many times, and now make it a practice to read it through once every year. It is a book of all others for lawyers, as well as divines; and I pity the man who cannot find in it a rich supply of thought and of rules for conduct. It fits man for life--it prepares him for death."

When asked the question, "What is the greatest thought that ever passed through your mind?" Daniel Webster responded: "My accountability to God."

Noah Webster
(The father of public education in America)

He declared government was responsible to:

"Discipline our youth in early life in sound maxims of moral, political, and religious duties."

"Education is useless without the Bible."

"The Bible was America's basic text book in all fields."

"God's Word, contained in the Bible, has furnished all necessary rules to direct our conduct."

"In my view, the Christian religion is the most important and one of the first things in which all children, under a free government ought to be instructed....No truth is more evident to my mind than that the Christian religion must be the basis of any government intended to secure the rights and privileges of a free people."

In 1832, Noah Webster published his History of the United States, in which he wrote:

"The brief exposition of the constitution of the United States, will unfold to young persons the principles of republican government; and it is the sincere desire of the writer that our citizens should early understand that the genuine source of correct republican principles is the Bible, particularly the New Testament or the Christian religion.

"The religion which has introduced civil liberty is the religion of Christ and His apostles, which enjoins humility, piety, and benevolence; which acknowledges in every person a brother, or a sister, and a citizen with equal rights. This is genuine Christianity, and to this we owe our free Constitutions of Government.

"The moral principles and precepts contained in the Scriptures ought to form the basis of all of our civil constitutions and laws ... All the miseries and evils which men suffer from vice, crime, ambition, injustice, oppression, slavery and war, proceed from their despising or neglecting the precepts contained in the Bible. "When you become entitled to exercise the right of voting for public officers, let it be impressed on your mind that God commands you to choose for rulers just men who will rule in the fear of God. The preservation of a republican government depends on the faithful discharge of this duty;

"If the citizens neglect their duty and place unprincipled men in office, the government will soon be corrupted; laws will be made not for the public good so much as for the selfish or local purposes;

"Corrupt or incompetent men will be appointed to execute the laws; the public revenues will be squandered on unworthy men; and the rights of the citizens will be violated or disregarded.

"If a republican government fails to secure public prosperity and happiness, it must be because the citizens neglect the divine commands, and elect bad men to make and administer the laws."

"Corruption of morals is rapid enough in any country without a bounty from government. And ... the Chief Magistrate of the United States should be the last man to accelerate its progress."

APPENDIX C

NBRA ARTICLES OF IMPEACHMENT

The National Black Republican Association (NBRA) based in Sarasota, FL, headed by Chairman Frances Rice, filed Articles of Impeachment against President Barack Obama with the following language:

We, black American citizens, in order to free ourselves and our fellow citizens from governmental tyranny, do herewith submit these Articles of Impeachment to Congress for the removal of President Barack H. Obama, aka, Barry Soetoro, from office for his attack on liberty and commission of egregious acts of despotism that constitute high crimes and misdemeanors.

On July 4, 1776, the founders of our nation declared their independence from governmental tyranny and reaffirmed their faith in independence with the ratification of the Bill of Rights in 1791. Asserting their right to break free from the tyranny of a nation that denied them the civil liberties that are our birthright, the founders declared:

"When a long train of abuses and usurpations, pursuing

invariably the same Object evinces a design to reduce them under absolute Despotism, it is their right, it is their duty, to throw off such Government, and to provide new Guards for their future security."

— Declaration of Independence, July 4, 1776

THE IMPEACHMENT POWER

Article II, Section IV of the United States Constitution provides: "The President, Vice President and all civil Officers of the United States, shall be removed from Office on Impeachment for, and Conviction of, Treason, Bribery, or other high Crimes and Misdemeanors."

THE ARTICLES OF IMPEACHMENT

In his conduct of the office of President of the United States, Barack H. Obama, aka Barry Soetoro, personally and through his subordinates and agents, in violation or disregard of the constitutional rights of citizens and in violation of his constitutional duty to take care that the laws be faithfully executed, has prevented, obstructed, and impeded the administration of justice, in that:

ARTICLE 1

He has covered up, delayed, impeded and obstructed the investigation of the Benghazi Battle. Specific conduct includes: (1) failing to adequately secure the US Consulate and the CIA annex in Benghazi; (2) failing to send a response team to rescue embattled US citizens in Benghazi; (3) lying to the American people about why the US Consulate and the CIA annex were attacked in Benghazi; and (4) hiding from the media and congressional investigators the Central Intelligence Agency personnel and other wounded US citizens who were on the ground in Benghazi by scattering them throughout the United States, forcing them to adopt new identities and subjecting them to monthly polygraph tests. Benghazi Battle elements that are under investigation: On September 11, 2012, the anniversary of the September 11, 2001, the US Consulate and the CIA annex in Benghazi, Libya was targeted in a premeditated, preplanned attack launched without warning by Islamist militants. Footage of the attack broadcast in real time showed armed men attacking the consulate with rocket-propelled grenades, hand grenades, assault rifles, 14.5 mm anti-aircraft machine guns, truck mounted artillery, diesel canisters, and mortars. It was not an act of savage mob violence, nor a spontaneous protest in response to an anti-Islamic video on YouTube. In that attack, four American citizens were killed: US Ambassador J. Christopher Stevens; Information Officer Sean Smith; and two embassy security personnel, Glen Doherty and Tyrone Woods, both former Navy SEALs. Ambassador Stevens is the first U.S. ambassador killed in an attack since Adolph Dubs was killed in 1979.

ARTICLE 2
He has disclosed secret grand jury material by exposing the existence of a sealed indictment of one of the Benghazi attackers in violation of Rule 6(e) of the Federal Rules of Criminal Procedure that clearly states: "... no person may disclose the indictment's existence except as necessary to issue or execute a warrant or summons."

ARTICLE 3
He has authorized and permitted the Bureau of Alcohol, Tobacco, Firearms and Explosives, a division of the Justice Department, to conduct Operation Fast and Furious, wherein guns were sold to Mexican drug trafficking organizations that were used to kill innocent Mexican civilians and two rifles sold to a smuggler in January 2010 ended up at the scene of the murder of U.S. Border Patrol Agent Brian Terry in December 2010.

ARTICLE 4
He has authorized and permitted confidential income tax returns information from the Internal Revenue Service to be provided to unauthorized individuals, organizations and agencies.

ARTICLE 5

He has caused investigations and audits to be initiated or conducted by the Internal Revenue Service in a discriminatory manner, including harassment and intimidation of conservative, evangelical and Tea Party groups applying for non-profit status between 2010 and 2012. Elements of this illegal conduct include the facts that: (1) the head of the Internal Revenue Service tax-exempt organization division, Lois Lerner, admitted during a telephonic press event that illegal targeting occurred, then invoked her Fifth Amendment right and refused to answer questions before Congress about the targeting out of fear of self-incrimination; (2) two other career Internal Revenue Service employees stated that they acted at the behest of superiors in Washington — Carter Hull, a retired Internal Revenue Service Attorney and Elizabeth Hofacre, an employee of the Cincinnati IRS office which oversaw tax-exempt applications; and (3) Carter Hull stated that he was directed to forward the targeted applications to, among others, one of only two political appointees in the Internal Revenue Service Chief Counsel William Wilkins.

ARTICLE 6

He has (1) authorized and permitted the National Security Agency to conduct or continue electronic surveillance of over 300 million average Americans; (2) given access to National Security Agency surveillance data to other intelligence units within the Drug Enforcement Administration, the Secret Service, the Department of Defense and the Department of Homeland Security in violation of the law; and (3) conducted the surveillance of average Americans unconstrained by Congress, the United States Supreme Court or the US Foreign Intelligence Surveillance Court which has, to this date, functioned as a rubber stamp, having approved every request made of it in 2012 and rejecting only two of the 8,591 requests submitted between 2008 and 2012.

ARTICLE 7

He has authorized and permitted the Department of Justice to wiretap and secretly obtain two months of telephone and e-mail records of Fox News Reporter James Rosen and over one hundred Associated Press journalists.

ARTICLE 8
He has thwarted Congress by (1) failing to enforce all or parts of laws duly enacted by Congress, including the Defense of Marriage Act, the No Child Left Behind Act, and the Affordable Care Act; and (2) after Congress refused to pass his Dream Act, unilaterally issuing an executive order directing immigration officers to no longer deport an entire class of illegal immigrants who came here as children, regardless of individual circumstances, and to give them work-authorization permits.

ARTICLE 9
He has violated the Constitution when, on January 4, 2012, (1) he bypassed the U.S. Senate to appoint three members of the National Labor Relations Board, actions that were ruled unconstitutional by the United States Court of Appeals for the Fourth Circuit which affirmed previous decisions by the Court of Appeal for the D.C. Circuit and the Third Circuit; and (2) he bypassed the U. S. Senate to appoint Richard Cordray to head the Consumer Financial Protection Bureau.

ARTICLE 10
He has intimidated whistleblowers and brought twice as many prosecutions against whistleblowers as all prior presidents combined. Egregiously, while refusing to prosecute anyone for actual torture, he prosecuted former Central Intelligence Agency employee John Kiriakou for disclosing the torture program. Wherefore Barack H. Obama, aka Barry Soetoro, by such conduct, warrants impeachment and trial, and removal from office. The Articles of Impeachment have been sent to President Obama, Senate Majority Leader Harry Reid, Senate Minority Leader Mitch McConnell, House Speaker Boehner, House Minority Leader Pelosi and the full Judiciary Committee of the US House

of Representatives for action.

Frances Rice, Esquire, Lieutenant Colonel, US Army (Retired)
President NBRA.

Frances Rice joined the Army in 1964 as a Private and
retired as a Lieutenant Colonel after 20 years of active service.
She received a Bachelor of Science degree from Drury College
in 1973, a Master of Business Administration from Golden
Gate University in 1976, and a Juris Doctorate degree from the
University of California, Hastings College of Law in 1977—all
while serving in the US Army. During twenty years of active
duty in the US Army, Frances served in a variety of positions,
including commander of a WAC company, adjutant of a basic
combat training brigade, a prosecuting attorney, and chief of the
administrative law division. She also served as a special assistant
to the Army Judge Advocate General and an adviser to the Deputy
Assistant Secretary of Defense for Equal Opportunity. Subsequent
to her military career, Frances worked for the McDonnell Douglas
corporation, serving first as a member of that company's "think
tank," and then as a government contract advisor. She later taught
Business Law for the European Division of the University of
Maryland in Brussels, Belgium. Frances became politically active
in 1982 and served as a member of President Ronald Reagan's
Private Sector Initiatives Task Force. She worked as a volunteer in
the campaigns of Presidents Ronald Reagan, George H. W. Bush,
and George W. Bush, as well as Governors Jeb Bush, Charlie Crist
and Rick Scott. Frances is active in the Executive Committee of
the Republican Party of Sarasota County. In 2005, she became
a co-founder and Chairman of the National Black Republican
Association, an organization that is committed to returning
African Americans to their Republican Party roots. Recently she
was honored as the Volunteer of the Year by the Republican Party
of Sarasota County. Governor Rick Scott appointed Frances to
the Government Efficiency Task Force in July 2011 for the task
force's one-year duration. Among the awards she received during

her military career is the Legion of Merit, the second highest honor that can be bestowed upon a non-combatant. In 1987, she was accorded the distinction of being one of America's top 100 Black Business and Professional Women by the editorial board of Dollars and Sense magazine.

APPENDIX D

In CONGRESS, July 4, 1776.

THE UNANIMOUS DECLARATION
OF THE THIRTEEN UNITED STATES OF AMERICA,

When in the Course of human events, it becomes necessary for one people to dissolve the political bands which have connected them with another, and to assume among the powers of the earth, the separate and equal station to which the Laws of Nature and of Nature's God entitle them, a decent respect to the opinions of mankind requires that they should declare the causes which impel them to the separation.

We hold these truths to be self-evident, that all men are created equal, that they are endowed by their Creator with certain unalienable Rights, that among these are Life, Liberty and the pursuit of Happiness.– That to secure these rights, Governments are instituted among Men, deriving their just powers from the consent of the governed, –That whenever any Form of Government becomes destructive of these ends, it is the Right of the People to alter or to abolish it, and to institute new Government, laying its foundation on such principles and organizing its powers in such form, as to them shall seem most likely to effect their Safety and Happiness.

Prudence, indeed, will dictate that Governments long established should not be changed for light and transient causes; and accordingly all experience hath shewn, that mankind are more disposed to suffer, while evils are sufferable, than to right themselves by abolishing the forms to which they are accustomed. But when a long train of abuses and usurpations, pursuing invariably the same Object evinces a design to reduce them under absolute Despotism, it is their right, it is their duty, to throw off such Government, and to provide new Guards for their future security.–Such has been the patient sufferance of these Colonies; and such is now the necessity which constrains them to alter their former Systems of Government. The history of the present King of Great Britain is a history of repeated injuries and usurpations, all having in direct object the establishment of an absolute Tyranny over these States. To prove this, let Facts be submitted to a candid world.

He has refused his Assent to Laws, the most wholesome and necessary for the public good.

He has forbidden his Governors to pass Laws of immediate and pressing importance, unless suspended in their operation till his Assent should be obtained; and when so suspended, he has utterly neglected to attend to them.

He has refused to pass other Laws for the accommodation of large districts of people, unless those people would relinquish the right of Representation in the Legislature, a right inestimable to them and formidable to tyrants only.

He has called together legislative bodies at places unusual, uncomfortable, and distant from the depository of their public Records, for the sole purpose of fatiguing them into compliance with his measures.

He has dissolved Representative Houses repeatedly, for opposing with manly firmness his invasions on the rights of the people.

He has refused for a long time, after such dissolutions, to cause others to be elected; whereby the Legislative powers, incapable of Annihilation, have returned to the People at large for their exercise; the State remaining in the mean time exposed to all the dangers of invasion from without, and convulsions within.

He has endeavoured to prevent the population of these States; for that purpose obstructing the Laws for Naturalization of Foreigners; refusing to pass others to encourage their migrations hither, and raising the conditions of new Appropriations of Lands.

He has obstructed the Administration of Justice, by refusing his Assent to Laws for establishing Judiciary powers.

He has made Judges dependent on his Will alone, for the tenure of their offices, and the amount and payment of their salaries.

He has erected a multitude of New Offices, and sent hither swarms of Officers to harrass our people, and eat out their substance.

He has kept among us, in times of peace, Standing Armies without the Consent of our legislatures.

He has affected to render the Military independent of and superior to the Civil power.

He has combined with others to subject us to a jurisdiction foreign to our constitution, and unacknowledged by our laws; giving his Assent to their Acts of pretended Legislation:

For Quartering large bodies of armed troops among us:

For protecting them, by a mock Trial, from punishment for any Murders which they should commit on the Inhabitants of these States:

For cutting off our Trade with all parts of the world:

For imposing Taxes on us without our Consent:

For depriving us in many cases, of the benefits of Trial by Jury:

For transporting us beyond Seas to be tried for pretended offences

For abolishing the free System of English Laws in a neighbouring Province, establishing therein an Arbitrary government, and enlarging its Boundaries so as to render it at once an example and fit instrument for introducing the same absolute rule into these Colonies:

For taking away our Charters, abolishing our most valuable Laws, and altering fundamentally the Forms of our Governments:

For suspending our own Legislatures, and declaring themselves invested with power to legislate for us in all cases whatsoever.

He has abdicated Government here, by declaring us out of his Protection and waging War against us.

He has plundered our seas, ravaged our Coasts, burnt our towns, and destroyed the lives of our people.

He is at this time transporting large Armies of foreign Mercenaries to compleat the works of death, desolation and tyranny, already begun with circumstances of Cruelty & perfidy scarcely paralleled in the most barbarous ages, and totally unworthy the Head of a civilized nation.

He has constrained our fellow Citizens taken Captive on the high Seas to bear Arms against their Country, to become the executioners of their friends and Brethren, or to fall themselves by their Hands.

He has excited domestic insurrections amongst us, and has endeavoured to bring on the inhabitants of our frontiers, the merciless Indian Savages, whose known rule of warfare, is an undistinguished destruction of all ages, sexes and conditions.

In every stage of these Oppressions We have Petitioned for Redress in the most humble terms: Our repeated Petitions have been answered only by repeated injury. A Prince whose character is thus marked by every act which may define a Tyrant, is unfit to be the ruler of a free people.

Nor have We been wanting in attentions to our Brittish brethren. We have warned them from time to time of attempts by their legislature to extend an unwarrantable jurisdiction over us. We have reminded them of the circumstances of our emigration and settlement here. We have appealed to their native justice and magnanimity, and we have conjured them by the ties of our common kindred to disavow these usurpations, which, would inevitably interrupt our connections and correspondence. They too have been deaf to the voice of justice and of consanguinity. We must, therefore, acquiesce in the necessity, which denounces our Separation, and hold them, as we hold the rest of mankind, Enemies in War, in Peace Friends.

We, therefore, the Representatives of the united States of America, in General Congress, Assembled, appealing to the Supreme Judge of the world for the rectitude of our intentions, do, in the Name, and by Authority of the good People of these Colonies, solemnly publish and declare, That these United Colonies are, and of Right ought to be Free and Independent States; that they are Absolved from all Allegiance to the British Crown, and that all political connection between them and the State of Great Britain, is and ought to be totally dissolved; and that as Free and Independent States, they have full Power to levy War, conclude Peace, contract Alliances, establish Commerce, and to do all other Acts and Things which Independent States may of right do. And for the support of this Declaration, with a firm reliance on the protection of divine Providence, we mutually pledge to each other our Lives, our Fortunes and our sacred Honor.

APPENDIX E

We the People of the United States, in Order to form a more perfect Union, establish Justice, insure domestic Tranquility, provide for the common defence, promote the general Welfare, and secure the Blessings of Liberty to ourselves and our Posterity, do ordain and establish this Constitution for the United States of America.

ARTICLE I

SECTION. 1. All legislative Powers herein granted shall be vested in a Congress of the United States, which shall consist of a Senate and House of Representatives.

SECTION. 2. The House of Representatives shall be composed of Members chosen every second Year by the People of the several States, and the Electors in each State shall have the Qualifications requisite for Electors of the most numerous Branch of the State Legislature.

No Person shall be a Representative who shall not have attained to the Age of twenty five Years, and been seven Years a Citizen of the United States, and who shall not, when elected, be an Inhabitant of that State in which he shall be chosen.

Representatives and direct Taxes shall be apportioned among the several States which may be included within this Union, according to their respective

Numbers, which shall be determined by adding to the whole Number of free Persons, including those bound to Service for a Term of Years, and excluding Indians not taxed, three fifths of all other Persons. The actual Enumeration shall be made within three Years after the first Meeting of the Congress of the United States, and within every subsequent Term of ten Years, in such Manner as they shall by Law direct. The number of Representatives shall not exceed one for every thirty Thousand, but each State shall have at Least one Representative; and until such enumeration shall be made, the State of New Hampshire shall be entitled to chuse three, Massachusetts eight, Rhode-Island and Providence Plantations one, Connecticut five, New-York six, New Jersey four, Pennsylvania eight, Delaware one, Maryland six, Virginia ten, North Carolina five, South Carolina five, and Georgia three.

When vacancies happen in the Representation from any State, the Executive Authority thereof shall issue Writs of Election to fill such Vacancies.

The House of Representatives shall chuse their Speaker and other Officers; and shall have the sole Power of Impeachment.

SECTION. 3. The Senate of the United States shall be composed of two Senators from each State, chosen by the Legislature thereof, for six Years; and each Senator shall have one Vote.

Immediately after they shall be assembled in Consequence of the first Election, they shall be divided as equally as may be into three Classes. The Seats of the Senators of the first Class shall be vacated at the Expiration of the second Year, of the second Class at the Expiration of the fourth Year, and of the third Class at the Expiration of the sixth Year, so that one third may be chosen every second Year; and if Vacancies happen by Resignation, or otherwise, during the Recess of the Legislature of any State, the Executive thereof may make temporary Appointments until the next Meeting of the Legislature, which shall then fill such Vacancies.

No Person shall be a Senator who shall not have attained to the Age of thirty Years, and been nine Years a Citizen of the United States, and who shall not, when elected, be an Inhabitant of that State for which he shall be chosen.

The Vice President of the United States shall be President of the Senate, but shall have no Vote, unless they be equally divided.

The Senate shall chuse their other Officers, and also a President pro tempore, in the Absence of the Vice President, or when he shall exercise the Office of President of the United States.

The Senate shall have the sole Power to try all Impeachments. When sitting for that Purpose, they shall be on Oath or Affirmation. When the President of the United States is tried, the Chief Justice shall preside: And no Person shall be convicted without the Concurrence of two thirds of the Members present.

Judgment in Cases of Impeachment shall not extend further than to removal from Office, and disqualification to hold and enjoy any Office of honor, Trust or Profit under the United States: but the Party convicted shall nevertheless be liable and subject to Indictment, Trial, Judgment and Punishment, according to Law.

SECTION. 4. The Times, Places and Manner of holding Elections for Senators and Representatives, shall be prescribed in each State by the Legislature thereof; but the Congress may at any time by Law make or alter such Regulations, except as to the Places of chusing Senators.

The Congress shall assemble at least once in every Year, and such Meeting shall be on the first Monday in December, unless they shall by Law appoint a different Day.

SECTION. 5. Each House shall be the Judge of the Elections, Returns and Qualifications of its own Members, and a Majority of each shall constitute a Quorum to do Business; but a smaller Number may adjourn from day to day, and may be authorized to compel the Attendance of absent Members, in such Manner, and under such Penalties as each House may provide.

Each House may determine the Rules of its Proceedings, punish its Members for disorderly Behaviour, and, with the Concurrence of two thirds, expel a Member.

Each House shall keep a Journal of its Proceedings, and from time to time publish the same, excepting such Parts as may in their Judgment require Secrecy; and the Yeas and Nays of the Members of either House on any question shall, at the Desire of one fifth of those Present, be entered on the Journal.

Neither House, during the Session of Congress, shall, without the Consent of the other, adjourn for more than three days, nor to any other Place than that in which the two Houses shall be sitting.

SECTION. 6. The Senators and Representatives shall receive a Compensation for their Services, to be ascertained by Law, and paid out of the Treasury of the United States. They shall in all Cases, except Treason, Felony and Breach of the Peace, be privileged from Arrest during their Attendance at the Session of their respective Houses, and in going to and returning from the same; and for any Speech or Debate in either House, they shall not be questioned in any other Place.

No Senator or Representative shall, during the Time for which he was elected, be appointed to any civil Office under the Authority of the United States, which shall have been created, or the Emoluments whereof shall have been encreased during such time; and no Person holding any Office under the United States, shall be a Member of either House during his Continuance in Office.

SECTION. 7. All Bills for raising Revenue shall originate in the House of Representatives; but the Senate may propose or concur with Amendments as on other Bills.

Every Bill which shall have passed the House of Representatives and the Senate, shall, before it become a Law, be presented to the President of the United States; If he approve he shall sign it, but if not he shall return it, with his Objections to that House in which it shall have originated, who shall enter the Objections at large on their Journal, and proceed to reconsider it. If after such Reconsideration two thirds of that House shall agree to pass the Bill, it shall be sent, together with the Objections, to the other House, by which it shall likewise be reconsidered, and if approved by two thirds of that House, it shall become a Law. But in all such Cases the Votes of both Houses shall be determined by Yeas and Nays, and the Names of the Persons voting for and against the Bill shall be entered on the Journal of each House respectively. If any Bill shall not be returned by the President within ten Days (Sundays excepted) after it shall have been presented to him, the Same shall be a Law, in like Manner as if he had signed it, unless the Congress by their Adjournment prevent its Return, in which Case it shall not be a Law.

Every Order, Resolution, or Vote to which the Concurrence of the Senate and House of Representatives may be necessary (except on a question of Adjournment) shall be presented to the President of the United States; and before the Same shall take Effect, shall be approved by him, or being disapproved by him, shall be repassed by two thirds of the Senate and House of Representatives, according to the Rules and Limitations prescribed in the Case of a Bill.

SECTION. 8. The Congress shall have Power To lay and collect Taxes, Duties, Imposts and Excises, to pay the Debts and provide for the common Defence and general Welfare of the United States; but all Duties, Imposts and Excises shall be uniform throughout the United States;

To borrow Money on the credit of the United States;

To regulate Commerce with foreign Nations, and among the several States, and with the Indian Tribes;

To establish an uniform Rule of Naturalization, and uniform Laws on the subject of Bankruptcies throughout the United States;

To coin Money, regulate the Value thereof, and of foreign Coin, and fix the Standard of Weights and Measures;

To provide for the Punishment of counterfeiting the Securities and current Coin of the United States;

To establish Post Offices and post Roads;

To promote the Progress of Science and useful Arts, by securing for limited Times to Authors and Inventors the exclusive Right to their respective Writings and Discoveries;

To constitute Tribunals inferior to the supreme Court;

To define and punish Piracies and Felonies committed on the high Seas, and Offenses against the Law of Nations;

To declare War, grant Letters of Marque and Reprisal, and make Rules concerning Captures on Land and Water;

To raise and support Armies, but no Appropriation of Money to that Use shall be for a longer Term than two Years;

To provide and maintain a Navy; To make Rules for the Government and Regulation of the land and naval Forces;

To provide for calling forth the Militia to execute the Laws of the Union, suppress Insurrections and repel Invasions;

To provide for organizing, arming, and disciplining, the Militia, and for governing such Part of them as may be employed in the Service of the United States, reserving to the States respectively, the Appointment of the Officers, and the Authority of training the Militia according to the discipline prescribed by Congress; To exercise exclusive Legislation in all Cases whatsoever, over such District (not exceeding ten Miles square) as may, by Cession of particular

States, and the Acceptance of Congress, become the Seat of the Government of the United States, and to exercise like Authority over all Places purchased by the Consent of the Legislature of the State in which the Same shall be, for the Erection of Forts, Magazines, Arsenals, dock-Yards and other needful Buildings; -And

To make all Laws which shall be necessary and proper for carrying into Execution the foregoing Powers, and all other Powers vested by this Constitution in the Government of the United States, or in any Department or Officer thereof.

SECTION. 9. The Migration or Importation of such Persons as any of the States now existing shall think proper to admit, shall not be prohibited by the Congress prior to the Year one thousand eight hundred and eight, but a Tax or duty may be imposed on such Importation, not exceeding ten dollars for each Person.

The Privilege of the Writ of Habeas Corpus shall not be suspended, unless when in Cases of Rebellion or Invasion the public Safety may require it.

No Bill of Attainder or ex post facto Law shall be passed.

No Capitation, or other direct, Tax shall be laid, unless in Proportion to the Census or Enumeration herein before directed to be taken.

No Tax or Duty shall be laid on Articles exported from any State.

No Preference shall be given by any Regulation of Commerce or Revenue to the Ports of one State over those of another: nor shall Vessels bound to, or from, one State, be obliged to enter, clear, or pay Duties in another.

No Money shall be drawn from the Treasury, but in Consequence of Appropriations made by Law; and a regular Statement and Account of the Receipts and Expenditures of all public Money shall be published from time to time.

No Title of Nobility shall be granted by the United States: And no Person holding any Office of Profit or Trust under them, shall, without the Consent of the Congress, accept of any present, Emolument, Office, or Title, of any kind whatever, from any King, Prince, or foreign State.

SECTION. 10. No State shall enter into any Treaty, Alliance, or Confederation; grant Letters of Marque and Reprisal; coin Money; emit Bills of Credit; make any Thing but gold and silver Coin a Tender in Payment of Debts; pass any Bill of Attainder, ex post facto Law, or Law impairing the Obligation of Contracts, or grant any Title of Nobility.

No State shall, without the Consent of the Congress, lay any Imposts or Duties on Imports or Exports, except what may be absolutely necessary for executing it's inspection Laws: and the net Produce of all Duties and Imposts, laid by any State on Imports or Exports, shall be for the Use of the Treasury of the United States; and all such Laws shall be subject to the Revision and Controul of the Congress.

No State shall, without the Consent of Congress, lay any Duty of Tonnage, keep Troops, or Ships of War in time of Peace, enter into any Agreement or Compact with another State, or with a foreign Power, or engage in War, unless actually invaded, or in such imminent Danger as will not admit of delay.

ARTICLE II

SECTION. 1. The executive Power shall be vested in a President of the United States of America. He shall hold his Office during the Term of four Years, and, together with the Vice President, chosen for the same Term, be elected, as follows:

Each State shall appoint, in such Manner as the Legislature thereof may direct, a Number of Electors, equal to the whole Number of Senators and Representatives to which the State may be entitled in the Congress: but no Senator or Representative, or Person holding an Office of Trust or Profit under the United States, shall be appointed an Elector.

The Electors shall meet in their respective States, and vote by Ballot for two Persons, of whom one at least shall not be an Inhabitant of the same State with themselves. And they shall make a List of all the Persons voted for, and of the Number of Votes for each; which List they shall sign and certify, and transmit sealed to the Seat of the Government of the United States, directed to the President of the Senate. The President of the Senate shall, in the Presence of the Senate and House of Representatives, open all the Certificates, and the Votes shall then be counted. The Person having the greatest Number of Votes shall be the President, if such Number be a Majority of the whole Number of Electors appointed; and if there be more than one who have such Majority, and have an equal Number of Votes, then the House of Representatives shall immediately chuse by Ballot one of them for President; and if no Person have a Majority, then from the five highest on the List the said House shall in like Manner chuse the President. But in chusing the President, the Votes shall be taken by States, the Representation from each State having one Vote; A quorum for this Purpose shall consist of a Member or Members from two thirds of the States, and a Majority of all the States shall be necessary to a Choice. In every Case, after the Choice of the President, the Person having the greatest Number of Votes of the Electors shall be the Vice President. But if there should remain two or more who have equal Votes, the Senate shall chuse from them by Ballot the Vice President.

The Congress may determine the Time of chusing the Electors, and the Day on which they shall give their Votes; which Day shall be the same throughout the United States.

No Person except a natural born Citizen, or a Citizen of the United States, at the time of the Adoption of this Constitution, shall be eligible to the Office of President; neither shall any person be eligible to that Office who shall not have attained to the Age of thirty five Years, and been fourteen Years a Resident within the United States.

In Case of the Removal of the President from Office, or of his Death, Resignation, or Inability to discharge the Powers and Duties of the said Office, the Same shall devolve on the Vice President, and the Congress may by Law provide for the Case of Removal, Death, Resignation or Inability, both of the President and Vice President, declaring what Officer shall then act as President, and such Officer shall act accordingly, until the Disability be removed, or a President shall be elected.

The President shall, at stated Times, receive for his Services, a Compensation, which shall neither be increased nor diminished during the Period for which he shall have been elected, and he shall not receive within that Period any other Emolument from the United States, or any of them.

Before he enter on the Execution of his Office, he shall take the following Oath or Affirmation:--"I do solemnly swear (or affirm) that I will faithfully execute the Office of President of the United States, and will to the best of my Ability, preserve, protect and defend the Constitution of the United States."

SECTION. 2. The President shall be Commander in Chief of the Army and Navy of the United States, and of the Militia of the several States, when called into the actual Service of the United States; he may require the Opinion, in writing, of the principal Officer in each of the executive Departments, upon any Subject relating to the Duties of their respective Offices, and he shall have Power to grant Reprieves and Pardons for Offenses against the United States, except in Cases of Impeachment. He shall have Power, by and with the Advice and Consent of the Senate, to make Treaties, provided two thirds of the Senators present concur; and he shall nominate, and by and with the Advice and Consent of the Senate, shall appoint Ambassadors, other public Ministers and Consuls, Judges of the supreme Court, and all other Officers of the United States, whose Appointments are not herein otherwise provided for, and which shall be established by Law: but the Congress may by Law vest the Appointment of such inferior Officers, as they think proper, in the President alone, in the Courts of Law, or in the Heads of Departments.

The President shall have Power to fill up all Vacancies that may happen during the Recess of the Senate, by granting Commissions which shall expire at the End of their next Session.

SECTION. 3. He shall from time to time give to the Congress Information of the State of the Union, and recommend to their Consideration such Measures as he shall judge necessary and expedient; he may, on extraordinary Occasions, convene both Houses, or either of them, and in Case of Disagreement between them, with Respect to the Time of Adjournment, he may adjourn them to such Time as he shall think proper; he shall receive Ambassadors and other public Ministers; he shall take Care that the Laws be faithfully executed, and shall Commission all the Officers of the United States.

SECTION. 4. The President, Vice President and all civil Officers of the United States, shall be removed from Office on Impeachment for, and Conviction of, Treason, Bribery, or other high Crimes and Misdemeanors.

ARTICLE III

SECTION. 1. The judicial Power of the United States, shall be vested in one supreme Court, and in such inferior Courts as the Congress may from time to time ordain and establish. The Judges, both of the supreme and inferior Courts, shall hold their Offices during good Behaviour, and shall, at stated Times, receive for their Services, a Compensation, which shall not be diminished during their Continuance in Office.

SECTION. 2. The judicial Power shall extend to all Cases, in Law and Equity, arising under this Constitution, the Laws of the United States, and Treaties made, or which shall be made, under their Authority;--to all Cases affecting Ambassadors, other public Ministers and Consuls;--to all Cases of admiralty and maritime Jurisdiction;--to Controversies to which the United States shall be a Party;--to Controversies between two or more States;--between a State and Citizens of another State;--between Citizens of different States;--between Citizens of the same State claiming Lands under Grants of different States, and between a State, or the Citizens thereof, and foreign States, Citizens or Subjects.

In all Cases affecting Ambassadors, other public Ministers and Consuls, and those in which a State shall be Party, the supreme Court shall have original Jurisdiction. In all the other Cases before mentioned, the supreme Court shall have appellate Jurisdiction, both as to Law and Fact, with such Exceptions, and under such Regulations as the Congress shall make.

The Trial of all Crimes, except in Cases of Impeachment; shall be by Jury; and such Trial shall be held in the State where the said Crimes shall have been committed; but when not committed within any State, the Trial shall be at such Place or Places as the Congress may by Law have directed.

SECTION. 3. Treason against the United States, shall consist only in levying War against them, or in adhering to their Enemies, giving them Aid and Comfort. No Person shall be convicted of Treason unless on the Testimony of two Witnesses to the same overt Act, or on Confession in open Court.

The Congress shall have Power to declare the Punishment of Treason, but no Attainder of Treason shall work Corruption of Blood, or Forfeiture except during the Life of the Person attainted.

ARTICLE IV

SECTION. 1. Full Faith and Credit shall be given in each State to the public Acts, Records, and judicial Proceedings of every other State. And the Congress may by general Laws prescribe the Manner in which such Acts, Records and Proceedings shall be proved, and the Effect thereof.

SECTION. 2. The Citizens of each State shall be entitled to all Privileges and Immunities of Citizens in the several States.

A Person charged in any State with Treason, Felony, or other Crime, who shall flee from Justice, and be found in another State, shall on Demand of the executive Authority of the State from which he fled, be delivered up, to be removed to the State having Jurisdiction of the Crime.

No Person held to Service or Labour in one State, under the Laws thereof, escaping into another, shall, in Consequence of any Law or Regulation therein, be discharged from such Service or Labour, but shall be delivered up on Claim of the Party to whom such Service or Labour may be due.

SECTION. 3. New States may be admitted by the Congress into this Union; but no new State shall be formed or erected within the Jurisdiction of any other State; nor any State be formed by the Junction of two or more States, or Parts of States, without the Consent of the Legislatures of the States concerned as well as of the Congress.

The Congress shall have Power to dispose of and make all needful Rules and Regulations respecting the Territory or other Property belonging to the United States; and nothing in this Constitution shall be so construed as to Prejudice any Claims of the United States, or of any particular State.

SECTION. 4. The United States shall guarantee to every State in this Union a Republican Form of Government, and shall protect each of them against Invasion; and on Application of the Legislature, or of the Executive (when the Legislature cannot be convened) against domestic Violence.

ARTICLE V

The Congress, whenever two thirds of both Houses shall deem it necessary, shall propose Amendments to this Constitution, or, on the Application of the Legislatures of two thirds of the several States, shall call a Convention for proposing Amendments, which, in either Case, shall be valid to all Intents and Purposes, as Part of this Constitution, when ratified by the Legislatures of three fourths of the several States, or by Conventions in three fourths thereof, as the one or the other Mode of Ratification may be proposed by the Congress; Provided that no Amendment which may be made prior to the Year One thousand eight hundred and eight shall in any Manner affect the first and fourth Clauses in the Ninth Section of the first Article; and that no State, without its Consent, shall be deprived of its equal Suffrage in the Senate.

ARTICLE VI

All Debts contracted and Engagements entered into, before the Adoption of this Constitution, shall be as valid against the United States under this Constitution, as under the Confederation.

This Constitution, and the Laws of the United States which shall be made in Pursuance thereof; and all Treaties made, or which shall be made, under the Authority of the United States, shall be the supreme Law of the Land; and the Judges in every State shall be bound thereby, any Thing in the Constitution or Laws of any State to the Contrary notwithstanding.

The Senators and Representatives before mentioned, and the Members of the several State Legislatures, and all executive and judicial Officers, both of the United States and of the several States, shall be bound by Oath or Affirmation, to support this Constitution; but no religious Test shall ever be required as a

Qualification to any Office or public Trust under the United States.

ARTICLE VII

The Ratification of the Conventions of nine States, shall be sufficient for the Establishment of this Constitution between the States so ratifying the Same.

done in Convention by the Unanimous Consent of the States present the Seventeenth Day of September in the Year of our Lord one thousand seven hundred and Eighty seven and of the Independence of the United States of America the Twelfth In witness whereof We have hereunto subscribed our Names,

Attest
William Jackson
Secretary

G^o: *Washington -Presid^t. and deputy from Virginia*

Delaware
Geo: Read
Gunning Bedford jun
John Dickinson
Richard Bassett
Jaco: Broom

Maryland
James McHenry
Dan of St Thos. Jenifer
Danl Carroll.

Virginia
John Blair--
James Madison Jr.

North Carolina
Wm Blount
Richd. Dobbs Spaight.
Hu Williamson

South Carolina
J. Rutledge
Charles Cotesworth Pinckney
Charles Pinckney
Pierce Butler.

Georgia
William Few
Abr Baldwin

New Hampshire
John Langdon
Nicholas Gilman

Massachusetts
Nathaniel Gorham
Rufus King

Connecticut
Wm. Saml. Johnson
Roger Sherman

New York
Alexander Hamilton

New Jersey
Wil. Livingston
David Brearley.
Wm. Paterson.
Jona: Dayton

Pennsylvania
B Franklin
Thomas Mifflin
Robt Morris
Geo. Clymer
Thos. FitzSimons
Jared Ingersoll
James Wilson.
Gouv Morris

AMENDMENT I

Congress shall make no law respecting an establishment of religion, or prohibiting the free exercise thereof; or abridging the freedom of speech, or of the press; or the right of the people peaceably to assemble, and to petition the Government for a redress of grievances.

AMENDMENT II

A well regulated Militia, being necessary to the security of a free State, the right of the people to keep and bear Arms, shall not be infringed.

AMENDMENT III

No Soldier shall, in time of peace be quartered in any house, without the consent of the Owner, nor in time of war, but in a manner to be prescribed by law.

AMENDMENT IV

The right of the people to be secure in their persons, houses, papers, and effects, against unreasonable searches and seizures, shall not be violated, and no Warrants shall issue, but upon probable cause, supported by Oath or affirmation, and particularly describing the place to be searched, and the persons or things to be seized.

AMENDMENT V

No person shall be held to answer for a capital, or otherwise infamous crime, unless on a presentment or indictment of a Grand Jury, except in cases arising in the land or naval forces, or in the Militia, when in actual service in time of War or public danger; nor shall any person be subject for the same offence to be twice put in jeopardy of life or limb; nor shall be compelled in any criminal case to be a witness against himself, nor be deprived of life, liberty, or property, without due process of law; nor shall private property be taken for public use, without just compensation.

AMENDMENT VI

In all criminal prosecutions, the accused shall enjoy the right to a speedy and public trial, by an impartial jury of the State and district wherein the crime shall have been committed, which district shall have been previously ascertained by law, and to be informed of the nature and cause of the accusation; to be confronted with the witnesses against him; to have compulsory process for obtaining witnesses in his favor, and to have the Assistance of Counsel for his defence.

AMENDMENT VII

In suits at common law, where the value in controversy shall exceed twenty dollars, the right of trial by jury shall be preserved, and no fact tried by a jury, shall be otherwise reexamined in any Court of the United States, than according to the rules of the common law.

AMENDMENT VIII

Excessive bail shall not be required, nor excessive fines imposed, nor cruel and unusual punishments inflicted.

AMENDMENT IX

The enumeration in the Constitution, of certain rights, shall not be construed to deny or disparage others retained by the people.

AMENDMENT X

The powers not delegated to the United States by the Constitution, nor prohibited by it to the States, are reserved to the States respectively, or to the people.

AMENDMENT XI

The Judicial power of the United States shall not be construed to extend to any suit in law or equity, commenced or prosecuted against one of the United States by Citizens of another State, or by Citizens or Subjects of any Foreign State.

AMENDMENT XII

The Electors shall meet in their respective states and vote by ballot for President and Vice-President, one of whom, at least, shall not be an inhabitant of the same state with themselves; they shall name in their ballots the person voted for as President, and in distinct ballots the person voted for as Vice-President, and they shall make distinct lists of all persons voted for as President, and of all persons voted for as Vice-President, and of the number of votes for each, which lists they shall sign and certify, and transmit sealed to the seat of the government of the United States, directed to the President of the Senate; -- The President of the Senate shall, in the presence of the Senate and House of Representatives, open all the certificates and the votes shall then be counted; -- The person having the greatest number of votes for President, shall be the President, if such number be a majority of the whole number of Electors appointed; and if no person have such majority, then from the persons having the highest numbers not exceeding three on the list of those voted for as President, the House of Representatives shall choose immediately, by ballot, the President. But in choosing the President, the votes shall be taken by states, the representation from each state having one vote; a quorum for this purpose shall consist of a member or members from two-thirds of the states, and a majority of all the states shall be necessary to a choice. And if the House of Representatives shall not choose a President whenever the right of choice shall devolve upon them, before the fourth day of March next following, then the Vice-President shall act as President, as in case of the death or other constitutional disability of the President.-- The person having the greatest number of votes as Vice-President, shall be the Vice-President, if such number be a majority of the whole number of Electors appointed, and if no person have a majority, then from the two highest numbers on the list, the Senate shall choose the Vice-President; a quorum for the purpose shall consist of two-thirds of the whole number of Senators, and a majority of the whole number shall be necessary to a choice. But no person constitutionally ineligible to the office of President shall be eligible to that of Vice-President of the United States.

AMENDMENT XIII

SECTION. 1. Neither slavery nor involuntary servitude, except as a punishment for crime whereof the party shall have been duly convicted, shall exist within the United States, or any place subject to their jurisdiction.

SECTION. 2. Congress shall have power to enforce this article by appropriate legislation.

AMENDMENT XIV

SECTION. 1. All persons born or naturalized in the United States, and subject to the jurisdiction thereof, are citizens of the United States and of the State wherein they reside. No State shall make or enforce any law which shall abridge the privileges or immunities of citizens of the United States; nor shall any State deprive any person of life, liberty, or property, without due process of law; nor deny to any person within its jurisdiction the equal protection of the laws.

SECTION. 2. Representatives shall be apportioned among the several States according to their respective numbers, counting the whole number of persons in each State, excluding Indians not taxed. But when the right to vote at any election for the choice of electors for President and Vice-President of the United States, Representatives in Congress, the Executive and Judicial officers of a State, or the members of the Legislature thereof, is denied to any of the male inhabitants of such State, being twenty-one years of age, and citizens of the United States, or in any way abridged, except for participation in rebellion, or other crime, the basis of representation therein shall be reduced in the proportion which the number of such male citizens shall bear to the whole number of male citizens twenty-one years of age in such State.

SECTION. 3. No person shall be a Senator or Representative in Congress, or elector of President and Vice-President, or hold any office, civil or military, under the United States, or under any State, who, having previously taken an oath, as a member of Congress, or as an officer of the United States, or as a member of any State legislature, or as an executive or judicial officer of any State, to support the Constitution of the United States, shall have engaged in insurrection or rebellion against the same, or given aid or comfort to the enemies thereof. But Congress may by a vote of two-thirds of each House, remove such disability.

SECTION. 4. The validity of the public debt of the United States, authorized by law, including debts incurred for payment of pensions and bounties for services in suppressing insurrection or rebellion, shall not be questioned. But neither the United States nor any State shall assume or pay any debt or obligation incurred in aid of insurrection or rebellion against the United States, or any claim for the loss or emancipation of any slave; but all such debts, obligations and claims shall be held illegal and void.

SECTION. 5. The Congress shall have the power to enforce, by appropriate legislation, the provisions of this article.

AMENDMENT XV

SECTION. 1. The right of citizens of the United States to vote shall not be denied or abridged by the United States or by any State on account of race, color, or previous condition of servitude.

SECTION. 2. The Congress shall have the power to enforce this article by appropriate legislation.

AMENDMENT XVI

The Congress shall have power to lay and collect taxes on incomes, from whatever source derived, without apportionment among the several States, and without regard to any census or enumeration.

AMENDMENT XVII

The Senate of the United States shall be composed of two Senators from each State, elected by the people thereof, for six years; and each Senator shall have one vote. The electors in each State shall have the qualifications requisite for electors of the most numerous branch of the State legislatures.

When vacancies happen in the representation of any State in the Senate, the executive authority of such State shall issue writs of election to fill such vacancies: Provided, That the legislature of any State may empower the executive thereof to make temporary appointments until the people fill the vacancies by election as the legislature may direct.

This amendment shall not be so construed as to affect the election or term of any Senator chosen before it becomes valid as part of the Constitution.

AMENDMENT XVIII

SECTION. 1. After one year from the ratification of this article the manufacture, sale, or transportation of intoxicating liquors within, the importation thereof into, or the exportation thereof from the United States and all territory subject to the jurisdiction thereof for beverage purposes is hereby prohibited.

SECTION. 2. The Congress and the several States shall have concurrent power to enforce this article by appropriate legislation.

SECTION. 3. This article shall be inoperative unless it shall have been ratified as an amendment to the Constitution by the legislatures of the several States, as provided in the Constitution, within seven years from the date of the submission hereof to the States by the Congress.

AMENDMENT XIX

The right of citizens of the United States to vote shall not be denied or abridged by the United States or by any State on account of sex.

Congress shall have power to enforce this article by appropriate legislation.

AMENDMENT XX

SECTION. 1. The terms of the President and the Vice President shall end at noon on the 20th day of January, and the terms of Senators and Representatives at noon on the 3d day of January, of the years in which such terms would have ended if this article had not been ratified; and the terms of their successors shall then begin.

SECTION. 2. The Congress shall assemble at least once in every year, and such meeting shall begin at noon on the 3d day of January, unless they shall by law appoint a different day.

SECTION. 3. If, at the time fixed for the beginning of the term of the President, the President elect shall have died, the Vice President elect shall become President. If a President shall not have been chosen before the time fixed for the beginning of his term, or if the President elect shall have failed to qualify, then the Vice President elect shall act as President until a President shall have qualified; and the Congress may by law provide for the case wherein neither a President elect nor a Vice President shall have qualified, declaring who shall then act as President, or the manner in which one who is to act shall be selected, and such person shall act accordingly until a President or Vice President shall have qualified.

SECTION. 4. The Congress may by law provide for the case of the death of any of the persons from whom the House of Representatives may choose a President whenever the right of choice shall have devolved upon them, and for the case of the death of any of the persons from whom the Senate may choose a Vice President whenever the right of choice shall have devolved upon them.

SECTION. 5. Sections 1 and 2 shall take effect on the 15th day of October following the ratification of this article.

SECTION. 6. This article shall be inoperative unless it shall have been ratified as an amendment to the Constitution by the legislatures of three-fourths of the several States within seven years from the date of its submission.

AMENDMENT XXI

SECTION. 1. The eighteenth article of amendment to the Constitution of the United States is hereby repealed.

SECTION. 2. The transportation or importation into any State, Territory, or Possession of the United States for delivery or use therein of intoxicating liquors, in violation of the laws thereof, is hereby prohibited.

SECTION. 3. This article shall be inoperative unless it shall have been ratified as an amendment to the Constitution by conventions in the several States, as provided in the Constitution, within seven years from the date of the submission hereof to the States by the Congress.

AMENDMENT XXII

SECTION. 1. No person shall be elected to the office of the President more than twice, and no person who has held the office of President, or acted as President, for more than two years of a term to which some other person was elected President shall be elected to the office of President more than once. But this Article shall not apply to any person holding the office of President when this Article was proposed by Congress, and shall not prevent any person who may be holding the office of President, or acting as President, during the term within which this Article becomes operative from holding the office of President or acting as President during the remainder of such term.

SECTION. 2. This article shall be inoperative unless it shall have been ratified as an amendment to the Constitution by the legislatures of three-fourths of the several States within seven years from the date of its submission to the States by the Congress.

AMENDMENT XXIII

SECTION. 1. The District constituting the seat of Government of the United States shall appoint in such manner as Congress may direct:

A number of electors of President and Vice President equal to the whole number of Senators and Representatives in Congress to which the District would be entitled if it were a State, but in no event more than the least populous State; they shall be in addition to those appointed by the States, but they shall be considered, for the purposes of the election of President and Vice President, to be electors appointed by a State; and they shall meet in the District and perform such duties as provided by the twelfth article of amendment.

SECTION. 2. The Congress shall have power to enforce this article by appropriate legislation.

AMENDMENT XXIV

SECTION. 1. The right of citizens of the United States to vote in any primary or other election for President or Vice President, for electors for President or Vice President, or for Senator or Representative in Congress, shall not be denied or abridged by the United States or any State by reason of failure to pay poll tax or other tax.

SECTION. 2. The Congress shall have power to enforce this article by appropriate legislation.

AMENDMENT XXV

SECTION. 1. In case of the removal of the President from office or of his death or resignation, the Vice President shall become President.

SECTION. 2. Whenever there is a vacancy in the office of the Vice President, the President shall nominate a Vice President who shall take office upon confirmation by a majority vote of both Houses of Congress.

SECTION. 3. Whenever the President transmits to the President pro tempore of the Senate and the Speaker of the House of Representatives his written declaration that he is unable to discharge the powers and duties of his office, and until he transmits to them a written declaration to the contrary, such powers and duties shall be discharged by the Vice President as Acting President.

SECTION. 4. Whenever the Vice President and a majority of either the principal officers of the executive departments or of such other body as Congress may by law provide, transmit to the President pro tempore of the Senate and the Speaker of the House of Representatives their written declaration that the President is unable to discharge the powers and duties of his office, the Vice President shall immediately assume the powers and duties of the office as Acting President.

Thereafter, when the President transmits to the President pro tempore of the Senate and the Speaker of the House of Representatives his written declaration that no inability exists, he shall resume the powers and duties of his office unless the Vice President and a majority of either the principal officers of the executive department or of such other body as Congress may by law provide, transmit within four days to the President pro tempore of the Senate and the Speaker of the House of Representatives their written declaration that the President is unable to discharge the powers and duties of his office. Thereupon Congress shall decide the issue, assembling within forty-eight hours for that purpose if not in session. If the Congress, within twenty-one days after receipt of the latter written declaration, or, if Congress is not in session, within twenty-one days after Congress is required to assemble, determines by two-thirds vote of both Houses that the President is unable to discharge the powers and duties of his office, the Vice President shall continue to discharge the same as Acting President; otherwise, the President shall resume the powers and duties of his office.

AMENDMENT XXVI

SECTION. 1. The right of citizens of the United States, who are eighteen years of age or older, to vote shall not be denied or abridged by the United States or by any State on account of age.

SECTION. 2. The Congress shall have power to enforce this article by appropriate legislation.

AMENDMENT XXVII

No law, varying the compensation for the services of the Senators and Representatives, shall take effect, until an election of representatives shall have intervened.

APPENDIX F

THE ONE ANOTHERS OF THE NEW TESTAMENT

1. ...*have peace one with another Mark 9:50*
2. ...*wash one another's feet John 13:14*
3. ...*love one another John 13:34*
4. ...*have love one to another John 13:35*
5. ...*love one another... John 15:12*
6. ...*love one another John 15:17*
7. *Be kindly affectioned one to another with brotherly love, in honor preferring one another Romans 12:10*
8. *Be of the same mind one toward another.... Romans 12:16*
9. ...*love one another, for he that loveth another hath fulfilled the law Romans 13:8*
10. *Let us not therefore judge one another... Romans 14:13*
11. ...*admonish one another Romans 15:14*
12. *Salute (greet) one another with a holy kiss Romans 16:16*
13. ...*when ye come together to eat, tarry (wait) one for another I Corinthians 11:33*
14. ...*have the same care one for another I Corinthians 12:25*
15. *Greet ye one another with a holy kiss I Corinthians 16:20*
16. *Greet one another with a holy kiss II Corinthians 13:12*
17. ...*by love serve one another Galatians 5:13*

18. *Let us not be desirous of vain glory, provoking one another, envying one another Galatians 5:26*
19. *Bear ye one another's burdens... Galatians 6:2*
20. *...walk worthy... With all lowliness and meekness, with longsuffering, forbearing one another in love Ephesians 4:1, 2*
21. *And be ye kind one to another, tenderhearted, forgiving one another Ephesians 4:32*
22. *Submitting yourselves one to another in the fear of God Ephesians 5:21*
23. *...in lowliness of mind let each esteem other better than themselves Philippians 2:3*
24. *Lie not one to another... Colossians 3:9*
25. *Let the word of Christ dwell in you... teaching and admonishing one another in psalms and spiritual hymns Col 3:16*
26. *...abound in love one toward another... 1 Thessalonians 3:12*
27. *...love one another I Thessalonians 4:9*
28. *...comfort one another... I Thessalonians 4:18*
29. *...comfort yourselves together, and edify (instruct and improve, build up) one another... I Thessalonians 5:11*
30. *...exhort (encourage, urge to good conduct) one another daily... Hebrews 3:13*
31. *...consider one another to provoke unto love and good works... Hebrews 10:24*
32. *Not forsaking the assembling of ourselves together... but exhorting one another... Hebrews 10:25*
33. *Speak not evil one of another... James 4:11*
34. *Confess your faults one to another, and pray one for another... James 5:16*
35. *...love one another with a pure heart fervently... I Peter 1:22*
36. *...be ye all of one mind, having compassion one of another, love as brethren, be pitiful, be courteous... I Peter 3:8*
37. *Above all things have fervent charity (love) among yourselves... I Peter 4:8*
38. *Use hospitality one to another without grudging I Peter 4:9*
39. *As every man hath received the gift, even so minister the same one to another... I Peter 4:10*

40. *...be subject one to another, and be clothed with humility...*
    I Peter 5:5
41. *...love one another I John 3:11*
42. *...love one another... I John 3:23*
43. *...love one another I John 4:11*
44. *...love one another... I John 4:12*
45. *...love one another II John 5*

To him that overcometh will I grant to sit with me in my throne, even as I also overcame, and am set down with my Father in his throne.

He that hath an ear, let him hear what the Spirit saith unto the churches.

— Dragon Slayer Jesus Christ

Letter to the church in Laodicea
The Revelation of St. John the Divine 3:21,22

ABOUT THE AUTHOR

As an expositional Bible teacher, Michael has taught through every book in the word of God chapter by chapter, verse by verse. In the mid-nineties he began tracking the rise of the New World Order because of his interest in the prophetic books of the Bible. After publishing *Dragon Slayer Jesus Christ*, he moved to India where he spent two years teaching and evangelizing. He currently lives in Southern California.